Woolf Studies Annual

Volume 26, 2020

PACE UNIVERSITY PRESS • NEW YORK

Copyright © 2020 by
Pace University Press
41 Park Row, 15th Floor, Rm. 1510
New York, NY 10038

All rights reserved
Printed in the United States of America

ISSN: 1080-9317
ISBN: 978-1-935625-46-9

Member

Council of Editors of Learned Journals

Paper used in this publication meets the minimum requirements of
American National Standard for Information
Sciences–Permanence of Paper for Printed Library Materials,
ANSI Z39.48–1984

Editor

Mark Hussey — Pace University

Associate Editor

Vara Neverow — Southern Connecticut State University

Book Review Editor

Amanda Golden — New York Institute of Technology

Editorial Advisory Board

Tuzyline Allan	Baruch College, CUNY
Judith Allen	Kelly Writers House, University of Pennsylvania
Morris Beja	Academy Professor Emeritus, Ohio State University
Pamela L. Caughie	Loyola University Chicago
Kimberly Engdahl Coates	Bowling Green State University
Sarah Cole	Columbia University
Kristin Czarnecki	Georgetown College
Emily Dalgarno	Boston University (Emeritus)
Beth Rigel Daugherty	Otterbein University
Claire Davison	Université Paris III–Sorbonne Nouvelle
Jane de Gay	Leeds Trinity University
Erica Gene Delsandro	Bucknell University
Madelyn Detloff	Miami University
Jeanne Dubino	Appalachian State University
Jane Goldman	University of Glasgow
Elizabeth Willson Gordon	King's University, Canada
Leslie Kathleen Hankins	Cornell College
Alice Keane	Queens College, CUNY
Emily Kopley	Concordia University
Karen V. Kukil	Special Collections, Smith College
Michael Lackey	Distinguished McKnight University Professor, University of Minnesota, Morris
Jane Lilienfeld	Curator's Distinguished Professor of English, Lincoln University of Missouri
Maren Linett	Purdue University
Gill Lowe	University of Suffolk
Celia Marshik	Stony Brook University
Ann Martin	University of Saskatchewan
Gabrielle McIntire	Queen's University, Canada
Toni A. H. McNaron	University of Minnesota (Emerita)
Eleanor McNees	University of Denver
Jeanette McVicker	SUNY Fredonia
Jean Mills	John Jay College, CUNY
Patricia Moran	London City University

Editorial Advisory Board (continued)

Steven Putzel	Penn State Wilkes-Barre
Beth C. Rosenberg	University of Nevada, Las Vegas
Victoria Rosner	Columbia University
Derek Ryan	University of Kent
Randi Saloman	Wake Forest University
Bonnie Kime Scott	University of San Diego (Emerita)
Urmila Seshagiri	University of Tennessee
Drew Shannon	Mount St. Joseph University
Anna Snaith	King's College London
Helen Southworth	University of Oregon
Elisa Sparks	Clemson University (Emerita)
Peter Stansky	Stanford University
Alice Staveley	Stanford University
Diana L. Swanson	Northern Illinois University (Emerita)
Janine Utell	Widener University
Julie Vandivere	Bloomsburg University
Susan Wegener	Purdue University
Michael Whitworth	University of Oxford
Alice Wood	De Montfort University
John Young	Marshall University

Many thanks to readers for Volume 26 (in addition to the Editorial Board): Ria Banerjee (Guttman Community C, CUNY); Emily Bloom (Columbia U); Rachel Crossland (U of Chichester); Benjamin Harvey (Mississippi SU); Holly Henry (California SU, San Bernardino); Maggie Humm (Emeritus, U of E London)

Woolf Studies Annual is indexed in *Humanities International Complete, ABELL,* and the *MLA Bibliography.*

Contents

Woolf Studies Annual

Volume 26, 2020

vii	Abbreviations

ARTICLES

Josh Phillips	1	Thoughts on Peace in a Wine Cellar: On Transcribing the 1917 Dinner Party in the Holograph *Years*
	13	Transcription of the 1917 Dinner Party in the Holograph *Years*
Catriona Livingstone	87	"Unacted Part[s]": Subjunctive Science-Fictional Identities in Virginia Woolf's Later Work
Sebastian Williams	105	Woolf's Bioethics: Animals and Dependency in "The Widow and the Parrot"

GUIDE

| | 121 | Guide to Library Special Collections |

REVIEWS

Elizabeth Outka	143	*Night and Day* by Virginia Woolf, Michael H. Whitworth, ed.
Lise Jaillant	146	*Modernist Lives: Biography and Autobiography at Leonard and Virginia Woolf's Hogarth Press* by Claire Battershill
		Virginia Woolf and the World of Books, Nicola Wilson and Claire Battershill, eds.

Celia Marshik	**150**	*Modernism à la Mode: Fashion and the Ends of Literature* by Elizabeth M. Sheehan
Peter Stansky	**152**	*The Politics of 1930s British Literature: Education, Class, Gender* by Natasha Periyan
Emma Sutton	**155**	*Virginia Woolf: Music, Sound, Language* by Elicia Clements
Emily Griesinger	**158**	*Religion Around Virginia Woolf* by Stephanie Paulsell
Wayne K. Chapman	**161**	*Leonard Woolf: Bloomsbury Socialist* by Fred Leventhal and Peter Stansky
Ria Banerjee	**164**	*Threshold Modernism: New Public Women and the Literary Spaces of Imperial London* by Elizabeth Evans
		Virginia Woolf's Rooms and the Spaces of Modernity by Suzana Zink
Claire Davison	**167**	*Virginia Woolf's Portraits of Russian Writers: Creating the Literary Other* by Darya Protopopova
	171	Notes on Contributors
	172	Submission Guidelines

Abbreviations

AHH	*A Haunted House*
AROO	*A Room of One's Own*
BP	*Books and Portraits*
BTA	*Between the Acts*
CDB	*The Captain's Death Bed and Other Essays*
CE	*Collected Essays* (4 vols.)
CR1	*The Common Reader*
CR2	*The Common Reader, Second Series*
CSF	*The Complete Shorter Fiction*
D	*The Diary of Virginia Woolf* (5 vols.)
DM	*The Death of the Moth and Other Essays*
E	*The Essays of Virginia Woolf* (6 vols.)
F	*Flush*
FR	*Freshwater*
GR	*Granite & Rainbow: Essays*
JR	*Jacob's Room*
L	*The Letters of Virginia Woolf* (6 vols.)
M	*The Moment and Other Essays*
MEL	*Melymbrosia*
MOB	*Moments of Being*
MT	*Monday or Tuesday*
MD	*Mrs. Dalloway*
ND	*Night and Day*
O	*Orlando*
PA	*A Passionate Apprentice*
RF	*Roger Fry: A Biography*
TG	*Three Guineas*
TTL	*To the Lighthouse*
TW	*The Waves*
TY	*The Years*
VO	*The Voyage Out*

Thoughts on Peace in a Wine Cellar: On Transcribing the 1917 Dinner Party in the Holograph *Years*

Josh Phillips

> Yes, said Elvira, putting her arm round his
> shoulder, we will burn down Oxford, Cambridge
> after the war; & then we will have real education:
> beautiful +impermanent+ homes built of combustible wood
> (Woolf M.42-5 139.135-138)

Arson: not a very peaceful way to begin an article with "Peace" in the title. The image is familiar, perhaps. We may have encountered it elsewhere, in *Three Guineas*' call for "Rags. Petrol. Matches." to burn down the old women's college, and in its place to build a "poor college" out of some "cheap, easily combustible material which does not hoard dust and perpetuate traditions": a call that has to be recanted, be disavowed in order to maintain the "disinterested influence" that educated, independent women "possess through earning their livings" (Woolf, *Three Guineas* 34-35). But this arson attack is perhaps less well-known. I hope to use this article to introduce the curious document in which it appears to a wider audience. This incendiary snippet is taken from Berg M.42-5, pp. 69-142, the holograph MS draft of the dinner party scene in the '1917' chapter of *The Years*.[1] This is far from the only commonality that this portion of the draft *Years* shares with *Three Guineas*: rather, the two texts share enough commonalities that we can fruitfully read this portion of M.42-5 as a key *avant-texte* for *Three Guineas*, as well as for *The Years*. M.42-5 deploys tropes and vocabulary already familiar to us from *The Years* and *Three Guineas*, but in curious forms. This commentary attempts to theorize the status of this peculiar draft and where it sits in relation to both the published *Years* and *Three Guineas*. It examines the act of transcribing this manuscript through a close examination of three points in the document which call attention not only to the ways in which it prefigures *The Years* and *Three Guineas* but to its status as a haptic, hand-written document. These include: a closer examination of the conflagratory imaginary which opened this article; an invocation of Creon and *Antigone*; and a moment which prefigures *Three Guineas*' Outsiders' Society.

My reading of M.42-5 as a key *avant-texte* for *Three Guineas* militates against a certain genealogy that sees the roots of *Three Guineas* in the first volume-and-a-half of M.42, the novel-essay hybrid written in 1931 and transcribed and published by Mitchell Leaska as *The Pargiters: The Novel-Essay Portion of The Years* (Woolf,

---

[1] Pages 143-145 briefly describe Crosby, who by this time is retired and living in a boarding house in Richmond, and her experience of the war. The majority of this portion of the holograph *Years* is excised, and what remains becomes the '1918' chapter of the published *Years*. For a fuller account of this scene, see Eleanor McNees, "The 1914 'Expurgated Chunk': The Great War in and out of *The Years*."

Pargiters). This critical history traces *Three Guineas*' genesis to the "interchapters" that Woolf removed from this early draft, "compacting them in the text" (*D3* 146). It is taken up by early critics of the holograph *Years*, including, inter alia, Charles Hoffmann, in his article, "Virginia Woolf's Manuscript Revisions of *The Years*," and Grace Radin, in her monograph, *Virginia Woolf's* The Years: *The Evolution of a Novel*, which remains the only monograph-length publication devoted solely to the holograph *Years*.[2] As Anna Snaith points out in the introduction to her Cambridge edition of *The Years*, critics such as these have "used Woolf's own terms 'granite' and 'rainbow' as a dichotomous reading lens, and have argued that research sheered off into *Three Guineas*" (Woolf, *TY* lxiii). According to this genealogy, that which was rainbow in this early novel-essay became *The Years*, while what was granite became *Three Guineas*—as if granite and rainbow can be separated that easily.[3] Since Radin's monograph on the draft *Years*, much has changed. James M. Haule's research into the galleys and proofs of *The Years* has revealed much about Woolf's laborious editing process, while the exhaustive textual apparatus and notes to the Cambridge edition of *The Years* have provided the scholarly community with a far greater insight into the many thousands of pages of holograph and typescript drafts that eventually became *The Years*. Meanwhile, Alice Wood has discussed the complex parturition of *The Years* and *Three Guineas* in her 2013 monograph *Virginia Woolf's Late Cultural Criticism* (27-62). Wood provides an account of the documents that became *The Years* and *Three Guineas* in light of the development of genetic criticism. Wood's work on the documents that Woolf produced, both published and unpublished, in the years leading up to the publication of *Three Guineas* and *The Years* provides another narrative. Wood reads historically, placing emphasis on the drafts of "Professions for Women" and the six "London Scene" essays Woolf published in *Good Housekeeping* in 1931-32, and the earlier volumes in the holograph *Years*.

It is important to note that my reading of this portion of the draft *Years* as an *avant-texte* for *Three Guineas* does not diminish its links to the published *Years*, nor to other portions of M.42, nor to the constellation of documents that attest to the development of *The Years*. This portion of *The Years* exists in manifold forms: there are typescript fragments of this scene, galley proofs of *The Years*, galleys of the 1917 scene (Berg M.128), and final page proofs of this portion of *The Years*.[4] I

---

[2] The 1977 edition of *The Bulletin of the New York Public Library* was devoted to *The Years* and contains a significant amount of work on the novel's *avant-textes*. Most pertinently, in her article "'Two Enormous Chunks': Episodes Excluded during the Final Revisions of *The Years*," Grace Radin publishes two facsimiles of material deleted from the draft *Years* at galley proof stage. These excerpts are taken from the passage immediately following the one I present here and depict Crosby in Richmond, and her reactions to the War. The Enormous Chunks have since been reproduced in a number of widely-available editions of *The Years*.
[3] For a fuller discussion of the valences of granite and rainbow throughout Woolf's work, cf. "Materials for Theory: Digging Granite and Chasing Rainbows" in Derek Ryan, *Virginia Woolf and the Materiality of Theory: Sex, Animal, Life*.
[4] As discussed above, Grace Radin's work on the galley proofs of *The Years* has made the latter states of this portion of *The Years* much more widely available.

hope that this commentary is not read as an attempt to sideline these genetic links but rather to examine one of them in depth.

It is also worth briefly interrogating what is meant by *avant-texte* here. My use of the term strays from that of Jean Bellemin-Noël, who coined the term in 1972, describing the *avant-texte* as "the group [of documents] made up of drafts, manuscripts, proofs, and 'variants' which can be viewed as material that precedes a work [...] and which can be seen as forming a system with it" (Bellemin-Noël).[5] In the first instance, this portion of the holograph *Years* is not "material which precedes" *Three Guineas* directly; rather, the scene is more obviously a draft for its counterpart in the published *Years*. But this essay contends that there are grounds for viewing this portion of the draft *Years* as a precursor to *Three Guineas*: the two perform similar ideological work, and in many cases do so using similar language. The boundaries between *The Years* and *Three Guineas* are further blurred in a diary entry that Woolf wrote on June 3rd, 1938, the day after the publication of *Three Guineas*, in which she refers to the two as "one book" (*D5* 148). My work shows that *The Years* and *Three Guineas* remained imbricated in one another well after Woolf abandoned the essay-novel form in 1931.

While the 72 MS pages are heavily condensed and compressed by the time *The Years* is published, there is nonetheless a trajectory common to both versions of this scene. In both scenes, Eleanor Pargiter goes to dinner at the Westminster house where her cousin Maggie lives with her husband, Renny, and their children. The five diners—Eleanor, Maggie and Renny, Sara Pargiter (Elvira in the MS draft), and Nicholas—gather in the house's basement kitchen to eat, to drink wine and to lament the War. Their dinner is interrupted by an air raid, and as anti-aircraft guns take shots at the German aircraft, the five imagine a new world that might yet be born after the War. Raid over, the party moves back upstairs and continues their discussion. Eleanor, Sara and Nicholas eventually say their goodbyes, leaving Maggie and Renny, and disperse. In both the holograph and published *Years*, Woolf uses the space offered by the War as fertile ground in which to plant the seeds of a utopian imaginary—an imaginary that is articulated more fully in *Three Guineas*. In the 1937 *Years*, the five diners drink a toast to the "New World" (*TY* 264) that might yet emerge from the ashes of the War, a new world in which people shall live "adventurously, wholly, not like cripples in a cave" (*TY* 268). In the published *Years*, this New World is a fugitive imaginary, articulated in fits and starts, full of ellipses and dashes where language fails its speakers: "'But how...' she began, '... how can we improve ourselves ... live more ...' —she dropped her voice as if she were afraid of waking sleepers—'...live more naturally ... better... How can we?' (*TY* 267). Eleanor's dialogue here is a far cry from Elvira Pargiter's confidently oracular description of a coming university, which forms part of an imaginary

---

[5] "L'ensemble constitué par les brouillons, les manuscrits, les épreuves, les « variantes », vu sous l'angle de ce qui précède matériellement un ouvrage, quand celui-ci est traité comme un texte, et qui peut faire système avec lui." Translation mine.

that more closely prefigures that of *Three Guineas* than it does the corresponding section of the published *Years*.

Elvira Pargiter's Conflagratory Imaginary

Both *Three Guineas* and the holograph *Years* play with fire. But the call to burn down Oxford and Cambridge that we read in the opening to this article is really three calls, and the fire burns hotter each time. The fire Elvira imagines setting is kindled in a passage that is deleted, scored through with two curving diagonal lines (Fig. 1).

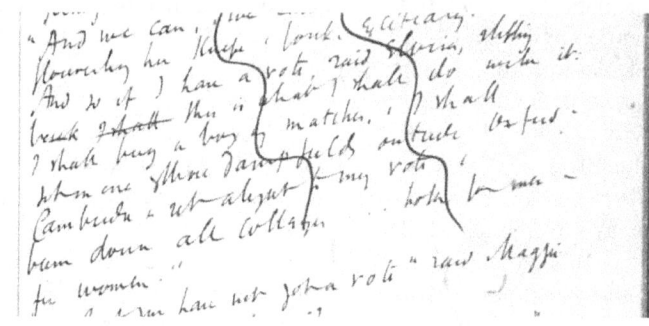

Figure 1 (Woolf M.42-5 81.14-20)

|And if I have a vote, said Elvira, stiffly
back I shall this is what I shall do with it:
I shall buy a box of matches, & I shall
sit in one of those damp fields outside Oxford
Cambridge & set alight to my vote &
burn down all the colleges... both for men &
for women| (Woolf M.42-5 81.14-20)

Shortly after this, the second fire Elvira imagines setting is not deleted, but is articulated only parenthetically, set inside a square bracket (Fig. 2).

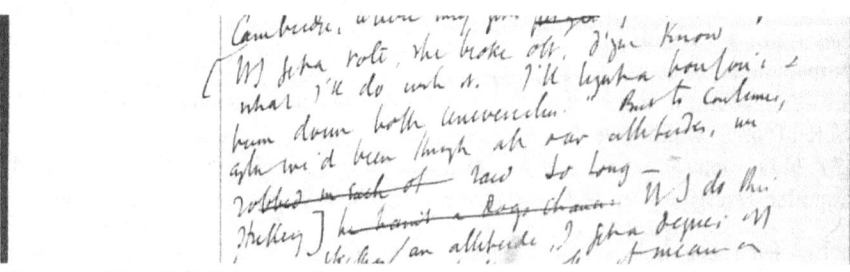

Figure 2 (Woolf M.42-5 83.3-8)

[If I get a vote, she broke off, d'you know
what I'll do with it, I'll light a bonfire &
burn down both universities. But to continue,
after we'd been through our attitudes, we
~~sobbed in each ot~~ said so long
striking] (Woolf M.42-5 83.3-8)

Only far later in the manuscript does Elvira's imaginary fire burn undoused by deletions, unstifled by parentheses (Fig. 3). This is the fire with which this article opened, a fire bright with revolutionary fervor, which anticipates *Three Guineas*' call to "Let the light of the burning building scare the nightingales and incarnadine the willows. And let the daughters of educated men dance round the fire and heap armful upon armful of dead leaves upon the flames. And let their mothers lean from the upper windows and cry 'Let it blaze! Let it blaze! For we have done with this "education"!'" (*TG* 34).

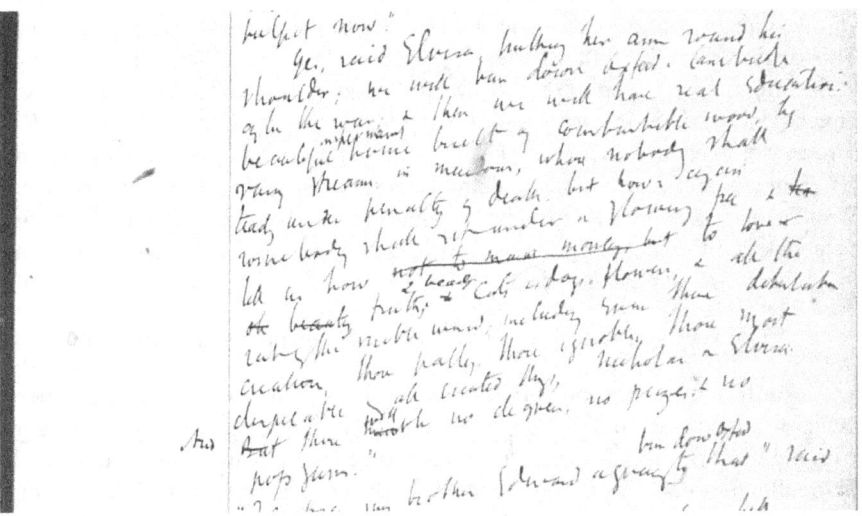

Figure 3 (Woolf M.42-4 139.5-18)

Yes, said Elvira, putting her arm round his
shoulder, we will burn down Oxford, Cambridge
after the war; & then we will have real education:
beautiful +impermanent+ homes built of combustible wood, by
running streams, in meadows, where nobody shall
teach under penalty of death; but now & again
somebody shall sit under a flowering tree & ~~tea~~
tell us how ~~not to make money, but~~ to love &

~~oh beauty~~ truth +& beauty+, cats & dogs, flowers all the
larks of the north wind, including even those detestable
creations, those basest, those ignoble, those most
despicable of all created things, Nicholas and Elvira.
+And+ ~~But~~ there ~~must~~ +will+ be no degrees; no prizes: & no
pop guns." (M.42-5: 139.5-18)

In M.42-5, Elvira's conflagratory imaginary expands, and one stifled flame becomes three fires, but, in *Three Guineas*, the narrator does not quite manage to burn down the old women's college. She never sends the guinea earmarked for "Rags. Petrol. Matches." (*TG* 34). Instead, she backtracks and admits to the undesirability of this desire. To burn down the women's college and rebuild it upon nakedly utopian lines would be to stop women from "earning their livings," and make them dependent once again "upon their fathers and brothers," rendering them "consciously and unconsciously in favour of war" (34). *Three Guineas*' conflagratory imaginary remains just that, imaginary. The two texts conjure similar images, but not the same image: they are analogous, not homologous. This distinction is important. These two sets of imaginaries bear the weight of their different forms and of their different temporal moments, one a portion of a novel's draft written in early 1934, the other an essay published in 1938, as European war became inevitable. These differing forms and temporalities demand different ethical frameworks and demarcate different spaces of possibility. What Woolf can say as Elvira Pargiter in the generic space granted her by a manuscript notebook is different to what Woolf, writing as *Three Guineas*' narrator, can say in a typeset and published essay.

"The very spit & image of our nation": Creons Past and Present

Woolf's invocation of Antigone in *The Years* and *Three Guineas* has been much discussed. Woolf's Antigone tends to be figured as a revolutionary figure with the power to redefine social norms and gesture toward a more sustainable future. But how does the *Antigone* of M.42-5 change these readings of the Antigone of *The Years* and *Three Guineas*? Antigone herself does not appear in M.42-5, but her words are still present, or at least some version of her words. Rather than the five words that appear in Jebb's translation in *Three Guineas* as "'Tis not my nature to join in hating but in loving" (*TG* 154), spoken by Antigone in Sophocles' play and recited by Edward but left untranslated (and indeed un-transliterated) in *The Years*, M.42-5 provides us with a curious variant: "sumφilein oux exthan ephen" (M.42-5 115.128). This mixture of English and Greek characters bears enough of a similarity to positively identify it with the five words of Antigone, "οὔτοι συνέχθειν, ἀλλὰ συμφιλεῖν ἔφυν" (*TY* 372). It would be too simple to just say that Woolf did not have the whole of the *Antigone* memorized, that she was writing in haste with the intent of editing at leisure, and leave it at that. Rather, we need to ask what version of the *Antigone* M.42-5 conjures. It is a peculiar *Antigone*, one where the titular character's words are spoken but she herself is not around to speak them, one where her words are curiously transmuted, uttered not by Antigone, who dies walled in a cave, but by Elvira Pargiter, who shelters from death in a cellar.

And what of Creon? Creon's presence in M.42-5 is more substantial, but no less curious. For Creon appears at a dinner party in 1910, sitting next to Maggie. Elvira describes him first as an "old man in gold thread" (M.42-5 115.131), before narrating a speech she makes to Creon:

> Damn your insolence, Creon, being the very spit &
> image of the old man you sat next at dinner Maggie
> two thousand years ago. But what are two
> thousand years? The flicker of a lizards eye lid —
> gone. Time to come's whats we matters Maggie;
> because I met a man at dinner the other night
> who said to me, Time to come is all Cleopatra's needle
> & this — pointing to the ladies all +dressed up to the 9s+ in every dress
> & the footmen in plush trousers, is but a rose leaf
> on the top. (M.42-5 118.111-119)

Elvira narrates this scene once again, but rather than the lizard's eyelid flickering, the present is but a flicker of a "lizards tongue" (Woolf M.42-5 120.110). Creon's last appearance is in passing, as a substitute for the Prime Minister: Elvira says that Rose is locked up "for breaking the Creon's | window" (M.42-5 125.121-122). M.42-5's Creon is a curious being, not quite ancient, not quite modern. Two thousand years of patriarchal power are elided into one figure.

Compare this instantiation of Creon to that in *Three Guineas*. Here, he is a thoroughly modern fascist: "in embryo the creature, Dictator as we call him when he is Italian or German, who believes he has the right [...] to dictate to other human beings how they shall live; what they shall do" (*TG* 129). In each of these texts, Creon is more than a figuration or metaphor for patriarchal power; he is synecdoche; he is the whole force of the patriarchy condensed into one man. But read them together, and a double articulation of incipient tyranny is at play, one synchronic, the other diachronic; one reaching from the distant past into the present, the other spreading its tendrils across Europe as Woolf wrote. The two articulations intersect, inscribing a micropolitics of incipient tyranny upon the body of Creon. And this double articulation is constantly making its presence felt. It is there in every display of patriarchal power. The model of patriarchal power that arises from reading M.42-5 alongside *Three Guineas* makes clear that present tyrannies are patterned after historical ones. Creon stubbornly refuses to remain in the past: Creon is the "very spit & image of our nation" (M.42-5 115.132).

An Early Articulation of the Outsiders' Society

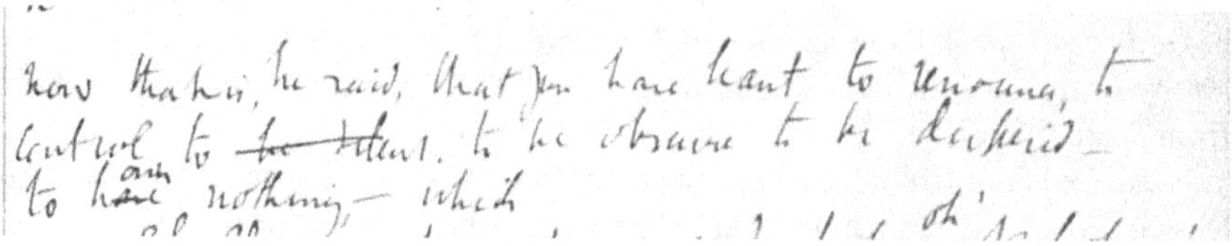

Fig. 4 (M.42-5 134.2-4)

> Now that is, he said, that you have learnt to renounce, to control, to ~~be silent~~, to be observant, to be despised — to ~~have~~ +own+ nothing (M.42-5 134.2-4)

One of the earliest precursors to *Three Guineas'* Outsiders' Society is articulated in this portion of the draft *Years*, spoken by Nicholas.[6] Nicholas's injunction to Eleanor, to Elvira, and to Maggie, his call to renounce, to control, to be observant, to be despised, to own nothing prefigures *Three Guineas'* call for the daughters of educated men to form a society (or perhaps an anti-society) which is "anonymous and elastic before everything," and whose members should "maintain an attitude of complete indifference," going so far as to "train themselves in peace before death" (*TG* 97-100). Nicholas's call for women to renounce and control is, at first glance, not so very different from the call of *Three Guineas'* narrator. But the sexual politics of this moment are very different. Nicholas is a man—for there could be no doubt of his sex. That the genders are swapped from one instantiation to another is not trivial. There is an irreducible difference between these two moments: in the former, a man is telling a woman to renounce and be despised; in the latter, it is a woman telling a man that women should henceforth play no part in silly masculine games of power.

It is worth pausing to discuss just what Nicholas says to the women assembled in Renny and Maggie's cellar. He does not, precisely speaking, ask them to be silent.

---

[6] Note, *one of* the earliest: for discussions of yet earlier articulations that might be productively viewed as precursors to the Outsiders' Society, cf. Anna Snaith's introduction to the Cambridge edition of *The Years*, and Alice Wood's 2013 monograph. Snaith discusses finding the "crucible for *Three Guineas* and the Society of Outsiders" in the drafts of the 1907 and 1910 chapters located in M.42-4 (Woolf, *TY* lxvii), while Wood argues that the letter Elvira drafts in the 1910 chapter of the holograph *Years* provides the site for Woolf to "explore her own contrary opinions on how women might respond to and ultimately enter into patriarchal society" (Wood 91). Jane Marcus also analyzes this scene of the holograph *Years* in *Virginia Woolf and the Languages of Patriarchy* but does not connect it to *Three Guineas*. Marcus writes of this scene that it "reads like a debate that might be going on among present-day feminists. Rose, a male-identified feminist, works for votes for women but does not question the patriarchal system. Maggie and Elvira, international outsiders like Woolf herself, are isolated and ignorant about birth control. [...] Maggie doesn't want a vote because 'Englishwomen in politics are prostitutes. Every patriarch has his prostitute. She comforts him and then asks for favours'" (Marcus 53).

Rather, the word "silent" is deleted, scored through, perhaps just as soon as it is written, perhaps some time after. The injunction to be silent was at one point articulated, before it itself was silenced. And reading Woolf's manuscript makes this apparent: there is a temporality embedded in Woolf's handwriting, in its complex patina of deletions and additions, crossings-out and interlineations. Woolf thinks through her text, textually, and this moment—possibly as brief as an instant—between the articulation of the injunction to be silent and its silencing points to wider difficulties in reading this text. Reading and transcribing, for making a transcription is never just making a reproduction. When I began to transcribe this portion of the draft *Years*, I thought my task was simple: to copy into a .doc file, as faithfully as possible, the marks that Woolf made on her paper some eighty-four years prior to my starting my work. Since then, my view of the task has changed—or, rather, I have found that I was doing a task different than the one I had thought I was doing. Moments like the one I discuss above, like the silencing of the articulation of silence, have shown me this. There is what Edward Bishop calls a "wildness" to Woolf's texts (154) which he says must be preserved, but which I do not believe can be preserved entirely in the move from one medium to another. The resources available to Woolf, writing freehand, with black ink on light blue paper, are not the same as the resources that were available to me as a transcriber in the closing months of 2018. These resources included a desktop computer with a copy of MS Word. Herein lies the difference. Insofar as my transcription was typed out in 12pt Garamond, it follows the logic of the word processor, text unfolding in perfectly straight lines behind a little blinking cursor. If Woolf's manuscript has a wildness to it, my transcription is thoroughly domesticated, a paid-up member of the Spaniel Club in contrast to the "crowd of *canaille*" (Woolf, *F* 74) frolicking merrily across Woolf's manuscript page. The draft *Years* is a physical, haptic document as much as it is a written one. As we have seen, crossings-out and interlineations are temporally imbricated on the page, and my method is not entirely adequate to this.

My transcription was not made, in the first instance, from the original notebooks, held in the Berg Collection at the New York Public Library, but rather from microfilm facsimiles, copies of which are held in the University of Glasgow's library. The bulk of my work was done this way, but a trip to the NYPL gave me the chance to examine the document more closely, and to clarify portions of the draft which did not make the transition from paper to microform transparency (and thence to PDF) well. Joanne Trautmann Banks's 2002 essay on the process of editing Woolf's letters and the difficulties that reproductions offer textual editors invited me to reflect on the shortcomings of my methodology: "We behaved as though the letters that we edited were the letters that Woolf wrote," Trautmann Banks writes. "Yet that was not precisely true" (36). Working on the other side of the Atlantic from Woolf's notebooks, I perforce did the same. I behaved as though I was reading the manuscript that Woolf wrote. Yet that was not precisely true. There were many degrees of separation from me and "my" document. I note this because working this way creates many vectors for mechanical and digital errors to slip in, from dust in the workings of the microfilm machine I used at Glasgow's library to the digital artifacts that inevitably sneak into scanned files—not to mention any human errors on my part. In transcribing this manuscript, I came across page after page of moments like this where my methodology proved inadequate to the document in front of me. Hans Walter Gabler writes of the multiple temporalities proper to the draft manuscript. He writes that "authorial draft manuscripts form a class of their own. What they carry and convey is never only text. Their significance lies equally in the tracing patterns of the writing they evidence" (218). These 'tracing patterns' might take the form of doodles or notes, deletions or interlineations that can't be neatly folded into the body of the 'text,' interruptions in the fabric of the manuscript, or much more besides. Gabler writes, "What we encounter as writing in the pages of original draft documents, therefore, are the traces of how the document space was filled in the course of composition. Analysing and interpreting the traces, we gain a sense of how the writing gradually, that is in time, came into being in three visible dimensions as it spreads randomly over the document's two-dimensional surface" (212). We can see this gradual unfolding at play in the deletion of the injunction to be silent: an unfolding that we can only ever view in hindsight, and whose temporality remains elusive to later readers.

Most likely, we came to the published *Years* long before we did this draft. It is infinitely more likely that a reader's first encounter with the Pargiters and their utopian imaginary was through the published *Years*, and any reading of this draft scene is marked indelibly by its published counterparts. We most likely first encountered a *Years* in which Nicholas does not exhort his female dining companions to renounce or control, to be observant or despised, but these words range below the surface of the published *Years* unseen, anterior but in some sense prior. In the draft, Nicholas cries that "there are no words for what I mean" while Eleanor notices that "her stock of words [becomes] exhausted (M.42-5 113.119; 114.113-114). This loss of words is perhaps apt: this Gordian knot of proliferating temporalities is difficult even to talk about, let alone to unpick. We may have to dwell with it, as a moment of impasse, as an aporia.

Any understanding of M.42-5 is necessarily filled with gulfs, lacunae, aporia. Lacunae between manuscript and transcription, draft and published texts. But these gulfs are not empty. Rather, a hauntology of reading makes itself apparent here, visible in the gaps, a hauntology which is "irreducible, and first to everything it makes possible" (Derrida 63). The time is thrown thoroughly out of joint. Not just time as chronotope, as it unfurls within each individual document and as the Pargiters experience in their collective passage from the 1880s to the Present Day, but also our time of reading, of encounter with the text. The draft *Years* has an affective heft: the published *Years* becomes bent out of its familiar shape by the gravitational pull exerted by M.42-5. Strange apparitions haunt this newly-reconfigured ground. To return to the example with which I opened, Woolf's narrator may never have sent the guinea earmarked for "Rags. Petrol. Matches" (TG 34) but the fire that isn't set is haunted by the fire (or fires) that blazed merrily in Elvira Pargiter's conflagratory imaginary. Once set, these fires are not easily doused. Encountering M.42-5 irrevocably changes our reading of the published *Years* and *Three Guineas*, and discussing the assumptions and contingencies inherent to this transcription helps us to interrogate the nature of the presences whose shadows fall over *The Years* and *Three Guineas*.

My thanks are due to the University of Glasgow's College of Arts for their generous support in publishing this article and the accompanying transcription. I especially wish to thank Drs Maria Dick, Bryony Randall and Helen Stoddart, and Prof. Alice Jenkins for their help in securing funding for license fees. I would also like to thank Carolyn Vega and the curators at the NYPL's Berg collection for allowing me to examine the drafts of The Years. *My thanks also to Sarah Baxter at the Society of Authors, and the Estate of Virginia Woolf for their permission to reproduce this archival material. I would also like to thank my PhD supervisors, Drs. Jane Goldman and Bryony Randall for their help and support in conceiving and undertaking this project. Finally I wish to thank Mark Hussey and the editorial board of* Woolf Studies Annual *for accommodating this resource.*

Works Cited

Bellemin-Noël, Jean. *Le Texte Et L'avant-Texte: Les Brouillons D'un Poème De Milosz*. Larousse, 1972.

Bishop, Edward. "The Alfa and the *Avant-Texte*: Transcribing Virginia Woolf's Manuscripts." *Editing Virginia Woolf: Interpreting the Modernist Text*, edited by James M. Haule and J. H. Stape, Palgrave Macmillan, 2002, pp. 139-157.

Derrida, Jacques. *Specters of Marx: The State of the Debt, the Work of Mourning and the New International*, translated by Peggy Kamuf, Routledge, 2006.

Gabler, Hans Walter. *Text Genetics in Literary Modernism and Other Essays*. Open Book Publishers, 2018.

Haule, James M. "Reading Dante, Misreading Woolf: New Evidence of Virginia Woolf's Revisions of *The Years*." *Woolf Editing/Editing Woolf: Selected Papers from the Eighteenth Annual Conference on Virginia Woolf*, edited by Eleanor McNees and Sara Veglahn, Liverpool UP, 2008, pp. 232-244.

Hoffmann, Charles G. "Virginia Woolf's Manuscript Revisions of *The Years*." *PMLA*, vol. 84, no. 1, 1969, pp. 79-89.

Marcus, Jane. *Virginia Woolf and the Languages of Patriarchy*. Indiana UP, 1987.

McNees, Eleanor. "The 1914 'Expurgated Chunk': The Great War in and out of *The Years*." *Virginia Woolf: Writing the World*, edited by Pamela L. Caughie and Diana L. Swanson, Liverpool UP, 2015, pp. 55-62.

Radin, Grace. "'Two Enormous Chunks": Episodes Excluded During the Final Revisions of *The Years*." *Bulletin of the New York Public Library*, vol. 80, no. 2, 1977, pp. 221-251.

—. *Virginia Woolf's* The Years: *The Evolution of a Novel*. U of Tennessee P, 1981.

Ryan, Derek. *Virginia Woolf and the Materiality of Theory: Sex, Animal, Life*. Edinburgh UP, 2013.

Trautmann Banks, Joanne. "The Editor as Ethicist." *Editing Virginia Woolf: Interpreting the Modernist Text*, edited by James M. Haule and J. H. Stape, Palgrave Macmillan, 2002, pp. 11-24.

Wood, Alice. *Virginia Woolf's Late Cultural Criticism: The Genesis of* The Years, Three Guineas, *and* Between the Acts. Bloomsbury, 2013.

Woolf, Virginia. *The Diary of Virginia Woolf*. Edited by Anne Olivier Bell and Andrew McNeillie, Hogarth Press, 1977-1984.

—. *Flush*. Edited by Kate Flint, Oxford UP, 2009.

—. "[Years, The] The Pargiters; a novel-essay based upon a paper read to the London, National Society for Women's Service. Holograph, vol 5", 1934. Henry W. and Albert A. Berg Collection of English Literature, New York Public Library. Microfilm.

—. *The Pargiters: The Novel-Essay Portion of "The Years"*. Edited by Mitchell A. Leaska, Hogarth Press, 1978.

—. *Three Guineas*. Edited by Naomi Black, Blackwell, 2001.

—. *The Years*. Edited by Anna Snaith, Cambridge UP, 2012.

Thoughts on Peace in a Wine Cellar: A Transcription of the 1917 Dinner Party in the Holograph *Years*

Transcribed by Josh Phillips

EDITORIAL SYMBOLS

/	Line Break
[illeg.]	Illegible text
[text?]	Uncertain reading
~~text~~	Text deleted with a strike-through
|text|	Longer sections of text deleted with vertical or wavy line
+text+	Text added by means of interlineation
<u>text</u>	Text underline in MS
[text]	Text in square brackets in MS
†	Text inserted with a caret or long swooping line
†text †	Text marked with a caret or circled for insertion elsewhere

TRANSCRIPTION

p. 69

1	<u>6th Jan</u>	It was a bitter cold night in the middle of
2		December, & Eleanor, as she emerged from the
3	she was confused/	underground, pulled her shabby moleskin coat
4	for a moment	more closely round her, +&+ she stood still ~~for a~~
5		~~moment un~~ certain ~~for a moment~~ of the
6		point of the compass. There were the Houses of
7		Parliament; there was the river; therefore she
8		must turn to the right. The shrouded lights
9		added to the difficulty. The street lamps,
10		hooded with blue shed only a muffled
11		~~let~~ twilight illumination. All the
12		government buildings were dark. Great
13		fans of light, turning like the sails of a ~~mill~~
14		windmill moved across the sky; revealing
15		little ~~patches a pure yellow-tinted sky~~
16		~~very far away~~; & ~~sometimes they stopped~~
17		stopping sometimes as if to examine some

18		patch of the sky more closely. ~~There~~
19		& then they swept on again. It was
20		probable that there would be an air raid
21		tonight. ~~Eleanor reflected.~~ ~~On the other hand~~
22		~~it was quite four or five nights~~
23		But ~~there had been none~~ ~~The moon would~~ ~~was~~
24		for there was no moon. But there had been
25		no raid this month so far: & next week the
26		moon would be [*penny?*] again. She
27		was dining with Maggie & René; & they
28		lived in one of those rather obscure little
29		streets somewhere behind Deans Yard
30		which was always difficult to find
31		She ~~peered up at it.~~ There were very few
32		people about. She peered up at the corner
33		of streets trying to read the names ~~& the~~
34		huge bulk of the Abbey always made

p. 70

1		seemed to make the streets in its neighbourhood
2		smaller and darker. ~~But~~ she ~~had a little torch~~
3	pocket	look with her ~~little~~ torch, & flashed it on to one
4		door after another. Fifteen was their number
5		~~She found it & knocked~~ Here it was:
6		she rang & at the same time she knocked
7		as if in the darkness the maid would find it
8		difficult to hear. But the door
9		opened almost instantly. It ~~was~~
10		must be Rene himself she thought
11		seeing a tall man instead of a maid.
12		"Come in, come in" he said; speaking
13		perfect English, but ~~rather more cordially~~ there was
14		something foreign in his manner — she did not
15		know what. And he ~~led her to~~ opened ~~the~~ a
16		door ~~into the sitting room~~, & went straight
17		into the sitting room which seemed to her

18		after the blue muffled streets extraordinarily
19		bright. Another man was standing by the
20		fire, & she had ~~not~~ expected to find them alone —
21		My friend Nicholas…—" something or
22		other. She could not catch the foreign sounding
23		name. He was clearly not English. He
24		was large, rather pale, & rather effusive —
25		for, having shaken her hands he went on
26		talking, as if he could not allow the
27		entrance of a stranger to prevent ~~something~~
28		~~that he [paused?.]~~ him from finishing what he
29		~~way~~ was saying, as if the intermission, which
30		would have paralysed an ~~ordinary~~ Englishman, ~~and~~
31		gave him a momentary flinch, a jar; a
32		momentary shock, which could not
33		which was at once swept into to the current of
34		his being. He was relaxed: often then

p. 71

1		[*faint?*] moments of meeting were so embarrassing
2		… & his pulse was never more than seventy, &
3		his temperature was always ~~[illeg.]~~ well
4		below normal. We are talking of Napoleon,"
5		he said, "for whom I have a perfect passion.
6		~~Once I begin talking about Napoleon I cannot~~
7		He was a man altogether <u>sui generis</u> in every
8		way. And I find it extremely interesting to
9		consider these men in the light of science —
10		if science it can be called; for as come
11	more than/	psychology is at present in a state where it
12	child's play	can hardly claim to be more than ~~such tosh~~
13		I will tell Maggie…" said Rene leaving them
14		alone together
15		Eleanor slid off her moleskin coat & laid it on a
16		chair.
17		That's very interesting she said awkwardly

18	on the bank	~~as if~~ conscious that the stream of ideas was
19		running full tilt but ~~felt beyond reach~~. She
20		was cold & dazzled & still & crude.
21	'I come often, he /	It is the only thing that is going to count in the
22	continued'	world ~~that will be born~~ after the war; the
23		man continued. If we do not know ourselves
24		how can we ~~be~~ make laws that have any
25	[*illeg.*]	~~bearing whatsoever~~ +to+ our ~~actions~~ beliefs, our desires?
26		As I see it, we are living today in ~~an obsolete~~
27		[*illeg.*] which is obsolete because it bears no —
28		he stopped, hesitating for a word,
29		Because it doesnt fit" said Eleanor
30		supplying a word that was much shorter than
31		he, with his foreigners ~~for~~ knowledge only of the
32		more formal words, could not use
33		~~It doesnt fit thats just it~~ it doesnt fit
34		it doesnt fit" he repeated ~~using~~ using the
35		phrase gladly "~~it doesnt fit~~ thats just
36		it... She had not given him the idea; only

p. 72

1		word; nevertheless she felt satisfied. In fact she had not
2		followed what he was saying. But she liked him.
3		Then suddenly she realised his meaning
4		"That is perfectly true," she said: how odd that
5		you should say it. Because I was thinking so [*illeg.*]
6		But we are all thinking the same things he went
7		on, only we do not say them
8		The door opened; Rene returned. He was
9		not nearly as foreign as she fancied. ~~His looks~~
10		One might even take him for an Englishman,
11		Eleanor thought: he was tall; he ~~was~~ had a
12		big nose, & very dark eyes. He came from the
13		South of France, but then he had been educated
14		in England. He ~~looked at~~ had the reserve
15	looking round the /	that Eleanor was used to in young men.

16	room /	We ~~have~~ been ~~having an~~ argument, he said brusquely
17	a tea cup /	"The lady" Nicholas began: "I did not catch
18	on the hearth /	your name" he interrupted [*illeg.?*]
19	rug seemed to /	Eleanor Pargiter" said Eleanor, shy at
20	~~explain that~~ explain	naming herself
21	that / they had been /	Eleanor Pargiter ~~he~~ Eleanor Pargiter, he
22	arguing for /	repeated robbing the words of their usual meaning.
23	some time	"~~Call me~~ Eleanor's +the name I like+ such [*illeg.*] she said
24		~~impetuously~~ abruptly:
25		Thats a French name is it not, said Nicholas
26		meaning...
27		The rowing man is so attractive at first,
28		but he becomes an awful bore in time, Eleanor
29		thought to herself, he will explain everything. Yet she
30		liked him. He made her feel reckless. He
31		filled the holes
32		Rene poured out wine, & handed it
33		to them. How have you got wine? she asked
34		him. "Because he is the son of a Frenchman" said
35		Nicholas. And like all Frenchmen, he has a

p. 73

1	vast cellar of the..." again he hesitated "I must be
2	careful to use the right word now" he said as René
3	will be insulted
4	~~I'm not ashamed of being French~~ said Rene.
5	He drank heavily
6	~~I was~~ We were
7	"Dinner will be ready in a moment"
8	He ~~poured out a glass of sherry, handed it~~
9	handed them glasses of sherry.
10	"Wine?" said Eleanor. ~~She had not drunk~~
11	~~wine for weeks~~ "What a luxury!" She
12	sipped; ~~her glass~~ she had not tasted wine for weeks.
13	"Being the son of a wine merchant, being a Frenchman
14	said Nicholas ~~drinking he has a [vast? just?] idea of the~~...

15		he sipped — he drank he
16		This is the sort of man, Eleanor said to herself,
17	an /	who becomes a ~~dreadful~~ bore, after a time; ~~but~~
18	awful	~~she because he talks too much~~ but at first
19		just because he did not mind what he said
20		he was a help. The wine slid down her throat; she
21		~~felt a~~ did not mind so much what he said now;
22		And what was the argument ~~about~~?" she said
23		Politics I suppose?"
24		~~Yes~~ The reasonof the war" said Rene. That was
25		how we came to Napoleon. ~~We were~~
26		What the Allies should have done at the end
27		of the Napoleonic wars" ~~Nicholas added~~
28		But to understand the behaviour of any large
29		body of men ~~the~~ Nicholas began —
30		Magdalena came in
31		"Dinner's ready" she said "We dine
32		in the kitchen" ~~she said~~ if you dont mind"
33		she added ~~taking the~~ showing Eleanor the way

p. 74

1	~~"Wo~~
2	~~But~~
3	But Magdalena, Elvira is coming" said Nicholas
4	but they were already down in the basement,
5	& Magdalena was explaining that they had no
6	servants. She had cooked the dinner herself
7	Eleanor supposed.
8	"We have a nurse" she said, helping them to
9	soup. ~~And~~ so we dine here & +and+ its much
10	~~better~~ +nicer+ having no servants:"
11	~~But Elvira said she was coming~~" said Nicholas
12	~~She said only Saturday, I shall meet you at~~
13	I saw her Saturday, said Nicholas, she said to me
14	~~then we~~ +we+ shall meet to morrow; at Maggies:
15	this time she may have mistaken the day; ~~but~~

16	No, she's coming" said Maggie ~~only she's late~~
17	~~only~~ +but+ we cant wait
18	But I will ring her up..." he said & left the room
19	"+Then+ why did we ever have servants" said Eleanor
20	"When its so much nicer ~~being in the kitchen~~ +doing everything+
21	She told them ~~how she had~~ about Crosby; about
22	coming home at night to her own flat. ~~She had~~
23	The wine, which she had not tasted for so long
24	was removing her silence; & Maggie, she noticed
25	was less silent — perhaps ~~the affect~~ of result of
26	~~h~~ marriage, of children;
27	Of course I have a woman to wash up" said Maggie.
28	And we +only have half a house+ let the top floor; &
29	"And we're dirty" said Rene
30	He poured another glass of wine
31	Nicholas came back. He was grave
32	"She's not there" he said to Maggie: "No
33	answer

p. 75

1		"Probably on her way here" said Maggie
2		He sat for a moment looking at his soup: then he
3		began to drink great mouthfuls. ~~Eleanor~~ But was
4		he in love with Elvira, were they engaged? Eleanor
5		wondered. She liked him ~~much better~~ now that
6		he was silent. ~~If~~ he was without self conscious [*men?*] ~~his~~
7		now that he was anxious; he showed it.
8	superficial cant/	Dining together in this basement room ~~under~~ next the
9	such as 'I love you'/	kitchen ~~with~~ Rene fetching things ~~they were~~
10	'I dont'	feeling developed, she thought; more easily at any rate
12		Ah, said Nicholas, putting down his ~~bol~~ spoon. His
13		face +relaxed & he smiled+ beamed as he looked at the door & Elvira
14		came in:
15		She looked pinched & cold, as the light

16	dazzled her for a moment
17	|*We thought you were dead" said*
18	~~*Rene*~~ *Maggie*| She too had changed, Eleanor ~~had~~
19	thought. As a child she had looked so queer; now
20	~~the~~ she was scarcely crooked; & ~~she was [straight?]~~
21	~~The the she was But~~ |*that she had the* ~~*deformed*~~
22	~~*pe persons char*~~ *look, which even a slight deformity*
23	*brings, of* ~~*uncomfortableness What was it?*~~
24	~~*Remoteness?*~~| ~~take them~~ but the change from the
25	street to the room had numbed her. The [*illeg.*]
26	~~sco~~ hardly smiled: But as she sat down, she
27	gave her hand to Nicholas, who kissed it.
28	"Yes we are dirty" said Maggie, continuing
29	And we dont ~~change~~ +dress+ for dinner any more
30	But you've dressed, said Rene. he had waited on
31	them all. He was now eating himself.
32	No this is not dressing" said Maggie [*I sit?*]
33	Eleanor
34	She was wearing something silver with gold

p. 76

1	threads [*illeg.*] at the ~~sleev~~ wrist ~~where the st~~ the
2	[*stuff?*] was frayed, so that the gold threads were
3	tangled; ~~she pointed at~~ tatters, she said
4	I was thinking how beautiful it was, said Eleanor;
5	Again, again she had looked at her
6	~~But~~ I couldnt dine out ~~like this~~ +in [*illeg.*]+ said Maggie
7	Elvira put down her spoon and touched the sleeve
8	~~which~~
9	I bought it in Constantinople +once+" said Maggie
10	"a turbaned and fantastic Turk" said Elvira
11	~~I met a turbaned~~
12	~~thats how it fou~~
13	dreamily ~~she was~~, as if she was [*illeg.*] still ~~half~~
14	numbed by the cold: but +now+ slowly reviving, as she drank

15	"~~that~~ Thats pretty too" she said, touching the soup
16	tureen. ~~and the plates~~" They were painted
17	with red & purple birds ~~with~~ +&+ baskets of flowers; &
18	it was old China, Eleanor suspected; she
19	thought she could remember ~~seeing~~ it ~~in a~~
20	~~cupboard~~ in Browne street.
21	"It used to be in the drawing room at home" said
22	Maggie "But now we use it
23	"+&+ break it" said Renny
24	~~I daresay~~ It'll last out the war" said
25	Maggie: This is the second year: we've
26	still got fifteen plates.
27	"And why were you so late?" said
28	Nicholas, speaking gently but reproachfully,
29	rather as though she were a child. He had let her
30	finish her soup, Eleanor noticed, before he
31	spoke to her.
32	"Because — Oh because that damned
33	fool ~~Eleanor's nephew~~ came to tea
34	Elvira ~~spoke with~~ suddenly seemed to
35	wake out of her stupor

p. 77

1		|*George has joined up, Eleanor: George wears a*
2		*uniform. George came to tea*| I didnt ask
3		George to come. I was lying on my back reading a
4		book. The bell rang. Thats the wash, I said
5		to myself, & it was George; in his uniform.
6		What the devil are you wearing that for? I said
7		There he was, in the middle of the room ~~looking~~
8		~~every inch a British officer. And he said to me~~,
9		with his hand held to his head like this,
10		so youve gone & done it I said ~~Now why~~?
11		arent you ~~an educated man I said~~ ashamed of
12	striking	yourself, ~~parading the streets like a cult~~
13		~~ea~~ [*carting?*] attitudes like +this+ ~~the duke of Wellington at~~

14		~~Hyde Park Corner. And he said~~
15		|*He was something like the d. of Wellington at*
16		*Hyde Park Corner*| And so we had tea
17		You wouldnt think that a well fed young man —
18		~~red cheeked~~ you know with those very nice eyes that
19		Morris has, upon whose education his parents
20		spent between two & three thousand would go
21		& behave like a... flaunting popinjay on a
22	six lumps/	soup tureen. So I gave him tea —
23	of sugar. I/	& I'd only 26 lumps of sugar left — take them all I
24	said	said, by way of rations
25		"But he didnt see it," said Nicholas
26		|*No,* ~~And thats what irritated me~~; he
27		that was how the argument started. He didnt
28	How many/	see that he ~~[had?] a manner~~ that I was laughing at him
29	lumps of/	Here lumps of sugar when ~~I had~~ +illeg+ only 22 left ~~of my~~
30	sugar I/	~~ration~~ with [illeg.]: ~~A~~ The hero's first [attendant?]
31	said	*I said to myself*|
32		How many lumps of sugar I said by way of [salve?]
33		But he didnt see it
34		George? George who? said Eleanor. ~~She felt~~
35		~~she felt Elvira she felt~~ she felt beneath

p. 78

1		[*illeg.*] flaunting words some anger: ~~that made her~~
2		~~another that this~~ but an of Elvira might
3		suddenly drew her up & hits: but at what?
4		she had ~~her [adventures?]~~ not understood
5		~~George is your nephew, I suppose" said M~~
6	He's joined up/	You mean George Pargiter, Morris's son?" said
7	has he?/	Maggie Hes joined up h ~~I suppose~~
8	Well I'm not surprised	"Lying, hypocritical, damned little humbug."
9		said Elvira
10		They all sat silent for a moment
11		Eleanor did not feel ~~in the~~ angry:
12		"Something has happened to Elvira, she thought: she

13		has grown up..." ~~Irrelevantly~~ she did not
14		think what she was saying. she thought, probably she
15		is in love with Nicholas."
16		"You are being unfair" said Nicholas, still very
17		gently: "You should make allowances.
18		"I said to him; Do you think this is the act of a
19		~~brave man~~ Whatd you do it for
20		~~My king my country~~ he said ~~stood~~
21		~~to~~ standing to attention in the middle of the
22		drawing room floor: looking like an old mule ~~who is~~
23		going to kick. He said My king, my country
24	played a/	~~chanting~~ I pelted him with dead rose leaves —
25	few bars of the/	then helped him to butter. And would you
26	national/	believe me Maggie, he thought I
27	anthem on/	You damned ass I said: & I helped him to butter & to
28	the poker/	cake, to ~~bu cu~~ apologies for no cream, &
29	tongs	he took it all [*illeg.*] as a matter of form,
30		sitting there with his horrid little switch on
31		his knee, in the middle of the sitting room...
32		~~Damned little humbug~~ when I wanted to read
33		~~Elvira~~
34		But Elvira, said Eleanor, you are being unfair

p. 79

1		A boy like that
2		Where was he educated? Nicholas interrupted
3		Perhaps Rugby: ~~Oxford or Cambridge:~~" Eleanor
4		was not sure.
5		"I see" said Nicholas. And after he had been to school
6		he went to college?" He spoke like a doctor,
7		questioning the relatives of a patient
8		"Yes," said Eleanor "And then?" Nicholas paused
9		Then he went into his father's chambers. My
10		brother is a barrister.
11	he turned to/	I see," said Nicholas "~~Then how could~~ How can
12	Elvira	you expect a boy ~~who is not in any way~~

13	who has been educated like that, who is in no
14	way remarkable, who sees his friends go to the
15	war, who is rather bored by his profession;
16	~~who is not~~ a nice ordinary English boy — was he that?
17	Eleanor nodded: it struck +her+ her that Nicholas
18	spoke of him as if he were dead —
19	to take up an attitude that requires a great deal
20	of courage?
21	Eleanor began to ~~think she had been influenced by~~
22	~~Elvira's passion~~ sort out her thoughts, dulled by
23	Elvira's anger.
24	And after all, she said, isnt it natural?
25	Could you allow the Germans to invade us &
26	do nothing?" she addressed Renny at her side.
27	An extraordinary expression of impassivity came over
28	his face. ~~He seemed to conceal~~ Could you? she
29	added, though she knew the question hurt him.
30	I? He said Im one of the hypocrites myself
31	I work ~~for the government I help them to~~ make
32	I am a chemist. I help them to make shells."

p. 80

1	"I'm not ashamed of it"? he added. It is obviously
2	the only thing to do: ~~at the present moment~~
3	"I feel that too, said Eleanor ~~The room~~ of the
4	[Q?] Dorsetshire hills came back to her "~~My~~
5	I love ~~the~~ English country" she added.
6	"No, no, no, that is not what I mean," said Renny
7	~~Thats because youre~~ +He's+ French, she thought, waiting for him to
8	speak. I mean — but we have discussed this so
9	many times, he added.
10	Maggie was changing the plates.
11	Yes let me see how it goes, she said, sitting down &
12	beginning to help them.
13	If nobody fought, if we said to the German

14	~~all right~~ come along, take it, if they took it, if
15	they found... there is nothing that you can take —
16	which of course is a fact... she ~~diff~~ carved as
17	she spoke... nobody can possess anything — she
18	paused, carving the meat carefully so that the
19	helpings should be equal —
20	What an extraordinarily interesting book the Bible is,
21	~~said~~ Elvira interjected ~~she had the~~ she seemed
22	~~look of a person who~~ +to+ dreams, & wakes;
23	while the others talked, she lay back, inattentive;
24	suddenly something found her: "psychologically
25	speaking: she laughed, "as Nicholas would say.
26	Christ ~~was far in advance of all these~~
27	said that. |~~And~~ *meaning obviously.*
28	*love — she held up a fork in one hand: love, she*
29	*repeated*| Being a very great [*illeg.*] scholar, what
30	he meant when he said Love one another, &
31	for he had great possessions, & the other saying
32	I forget exactly how he said it, but the same was
33	only ~~freed~~ happiness in freedom, the only
34	freedom is not to ~~have~~ own things: for which
35	[*illeg.*] of it was King George, I would say
36	Fight if you like but it shall all be done in the

p. 81

1	dark, without medals ~~but George~~ But George didnt
2	see what I meant
3	~~Yes its~~ The argument is this, said Renny;
4	if we were to end war; ~~if we were~~ in the present
5	state of human progress, people would be far more
6	unhappy than they are at present. If every man
7	& woman had five hundred a year, they would
8	not know what to do with it. Therefore let us
9	end the war as [*quickly?*] as possible & then..."
10	|*"Educate ourselves" Eleanor finished his [sentence?]*
11	*Renny said no more.*

12		*"And we can, we can" Nicholas burst out,*
13		*flourishing his knife about excitedly,*
14		*And if I have a vote, said Elvira, stiffly*
15		~~back I shall~~ *this is what I shall do with it:*
16		*I shall buy a box of matches, & I shall*
17		*sit in one of those damp fields outside Oxford*
18		*Cambridge & set alight to my vote &*
19		*burn down all the colleges… both for men &*
20		*for women|*
21		But you have not got a vote" said Maggie
22		Thats one [*illeg.*] she said
23		~~Its~~ "This is only a function of knowing ourselves:"
24		"Psychologically speaking" Maggie used
25		the words as if they were a refrain; something
26		that Nicholas was in the habit of saying:
27		"That is quite true, Magdalena, said
28		Nicholas. ~~When we do not know our~~ |*We live in a*
29		*society which does not fit—|*
30		We do not know ourselves, therefore we
31		do not fit." ~~Eleanor Pargiter was such~~
32		He smiled at Eleanor, acknowledging her word
33		Education does not fit; ~~war does~~ religion

p. 82

1		does not fit; war does not fit. And yet here we
2		are sitting round the table sitting [*comfortably?*]
3	know ourselves	because we tell each other the truth, because we
4		say what is in our minds." And yet" he
5		looked at Eleanor, Eleanor Pargiter is an
6		Englishwoman: Rene is a Frenchman; Magdalena &
7		Elvira are part~~ly~~ Irish & part~~ly~~ Spanish, which
8		I am on my mothers side [*Italian?*], on my
9		father's a ~~Po Jew~~ Polish Jew
10		"That explains it, thought Eleanor: she had been
11		wondering what nationality he was
12		"And then I said to ~~him~~ +George+ said Elvira as if she were

13		going on with a story, +had+ your hat on the [*illeg.*] of
14	our/	~~Grand Papa~~, but & tell the truth: whats all
15	grandfather/	nonsense for, killing Germans for the sake of
16	with coins	~~protecting women, children~~? Poppycock I said
17		using the language of his majestys footguards
18		to help the poor boy to find honesty, without
19		~~success~~. Because I said to myself, if hes come to see
20		me wearing those ridiculous clothes I must
21		try to penetrate his disguise with sympathy; by
22		means of psychology, Nicholas; ~~putting~~ [*illeg.*] for
23		the time into [*breaking?*], frown;. Thats whats
24		done it by war. The nurse maids admiring the
25		Home Guard (thats what I say to King George
26		no medals, no uniform) And I felt come on the
27		the [*feathery? heathery?*] charge; you remember, Maggie,
28		how Mama did it, putting her camellia to her
29		lips to seduce Uncle Abel ~~George I said~~
30		the [*feathery? heathery?*] charge..."
31		"You burst into tears, flung yourself upon his
32		neck" said Maggie:
33		"Yes, said Elvira; I loved him; poor
34		little humbug. He did not want to fight the

p. 83

1	German, but having been educated at Oxford &
2	Cambridge, where they give ~~prizes~~ +money+ for Latin & Greek…
3	[If I get a vote, she broke off, d'you know
4	what I'll do with it, I'll light a bonfire &
5	burn down both universities. But to continue,
6	after we'd been through our attitudes, we
7	~~sobbed in each ot~~ said so long
8	striking] ~~He hasnt a dogs chance~~ If I do this,
9	|*he says striking an attitude, if I get a degree, Ill*
10	*do that he says striking another, it means a*
11	*Fellowship; &*|

12		We flung sobbed in each others arms & he said
13		so long & went off."
14		I don't think many young men want to fight; but its
15		very difficult for them +the young men+ not to" said Eleanor
16		"You should have had more self control
17		Elvira" said Nicholas severely.
18		Yes, yes, yes, she replied impatiently; but you
19	so long, he /	dont understand Nicholas, son of a Jew, the [mind?] of
20	said.' /	[illeg.] words: poppycock; cheerio; so long
21	cheer /	there +a+ +we+ am at the Tower waving to a
22	waving her /	King who rules over the +due+ heal — slain in an
23	hand, & the /	auld cauld dyke. I heard two countries
24	He gave his /	making a man — where shall I fancy & dine today.
25	headgear a /	Theres all that is" she held out her
26	a shake, & — /	Yes, said Maggie. She paused. "Its very difficult, being
27	Adieu forever /	a woman. Elvir. Elv behaves in a very silly,
28	adieu for ever /	irrational, undignified, & sentimental way:
29	now	but its partly her training +[illeg.]+
30		And she imitates her mother" said Nicholas.
31		That was quite true, Eleanor thought, this

p.84

1		was something in the Elvira's feelings, & words that
2		reminded her particularly of Eugenie as if
3		she t only she was a different that there was
4		something ridiculous about it.
5		"Dearest Digby how tired you look let me
6		comfort you take a seat; & tell me just what
7		has been annoying you at the office to day—
8		Digby, my prince of men, my — Sir Digby,
9	& looking the /	of the Board of Trade, G.C.V.O in a tight
10	whole [thread?] /	frock coat looking like a trout in the sea:
11	off her twin. /	sits there purring all once: not seeing the hook
12	They are very /	And Renny still would, Maggie: Renny is
13	difficult at /	still in a state of arrested development,

14	Buckingham /	he, still a peculiar male, a very interesting subject;
15	Palace just now /	for [*illeg.*] Nicholas, because my sister,
16	he would say /	having committed the unpardonable folly of
17	or the Foreign /	having married & having two entirely lovely &
18	Office party is /	beautiful children has to adopt an attitude —
19	at 9 tomorrow /	she stopped & looked at her sister: then at her
20	Dont be late /	brother in law.
21	Eugenie. And /	Renny dear, she said, it would be very
22	there she was, in /	unbecoming if you would tell the truth about ~~your~~
23	full sway /	~~marriage~~ the marriage state.
24	dun, dead /	Yes;
25	in front of /	
26	her looking slain	

p. 85

1		"Yes Nicholas, but you dont understand —
2		she ~~two~~ stopped. Her eyes were full of tears.
3		"He gave his [*bundle?*] [*reins?*] a shake ~~he said~~:
4		& I went back into the sitting room, saw the
5		cups, the chairs where we had put them, &
6		he gave his bundle of reins a shake, adieu for ever more,
7		he said, adieu for ever more
8		|*Yes its very difficult said Eleanor: very difficult for*
9		*the young"*|
10		Its very difficult, its very difficult said Eleanor.
11		"There are so many different feelings in us
12		|*But you should have had more self control*
13		*Elvira Nicholas repeated*|
14		"But some are good & some are bad" said Nicholas
15	Yes. It was /	Oh yes, Elvira agreed ~~I was a damned~~
16	very pleasant /	~~posing hypocritical humbug~~; but it took me
17	at first" said /	fifteen minutes by the clock to find ~~that~~ out:
18	Elvira: & then /	~~that~~ & then only because I remembered Mama
19	not so /	"Dearest Digby, how tired you look: let me
20	[*pleasant?*]	entreat you to sit down, tell me what has
21		been annoying you at the office to day

22	Elvira threw her hand out just as Eugenie
23	used to Eleanor remembered; And he sits
24	down in an arm chair, Sir D P ~~of the~~
25	K.C.V.O in a tight frock coat, looking like a
26	[*pouter?*] [*illeg.*] & picks one white thread
27	off his trouser. Remember Eugenie its the
28	F.O. party [*illeg.*] dont be late dont be late
29	And there she was in full evening dress dead in
30	front as her looking glass."
31	"Because you felt physically uncomfortable
32	at feeling a feeling so sentimental, so
33	disgusting as your feeling; Nature happily

p. 86

1		provides a guide. When we feel bad feelings she lets us
2		know it: sometimes she sends a head ache, sometimes
3		it is merely a little roughness in the [*thighs?*], or the
4		sense of the nerves never standing still. Or it may
5		show itself in a distracted deportment. Ill tempered
6		mood like Elvira's when she came in to night
7		~~And~~ +But+ the poor young man ~~was much in the~~
8		~~same state~~ will go back to the army. He will
9		have no chance of recovery. You should have
10		shown more self control."
11		~~He's been at the front"~~ said Renny, "He's a
12		doctor. ~~His minds full of theories.~~ Thats why he
13		talks +such+ nonsense: — all these theories;
14		"You've been at the front?" said Eleanor.
15		"Yes yes yes" said Nicholas, absentmindedly
16		He was slightly peevish.
17		"Its women like you who make war possible
18		Elvira he said "~~silly sentimental fools"~~
19	She	~~Elv~~ saw [*illeg.*] at the top of a tower, waving
20		a white hankerchief to a knight in armour
21		"And the moon was strong" ~~over the~~ dark hill
22		she continued

23	"And was a nightingale singing?" Maggie
24	[*illeg.*]
25	"No no no. There was a dark bird skimming
26	close to the ground." And something
27	showed in the ~~water~~ +water+ I said to myself,
28	What is the colour of a water lily in
29	moonlight? And…
30	The need of [*illeg.*] in that fact moved you?
31	Nicholas argued
32	~~"It was a very jolly scene" — that was~~
33	No Nicholas I said to myself I dont care about

p. 87

1		this scene. Its a sickly scene. Its a passive, white
2		lily livered scene; theres no blood lust, no life
3		to it; the emotions rule
4		Then you feel physically *[illeg.]?* uncomfortable?
5		Yes & then I made another scene "Dearest
6	Its all /	Digby
7	*[illeg.]*, said /	~~Psychology is a~~ You pretend that psychology is a
8	Renny, abruptly /	science, said René, addressing Nicholas, when it is a
9	but it isn't /	mere toy. You try to explain Elvira's feelings
10	a science its /	scientifically: & there is no explanation. I see a
11	a toy.	Elvira ~~thinks of a lake~~; hears a door slam & thinks of a
12	Out of that memory /	water lily; she sees a chair & thinks of her father.
13	you pretend to /	"I am collecting evidence for what will be
14	make a scene	the greatest & most valuable of all sciences"
15		said Nicholas obstinately
16		Well go on, Elvira, said Renny, what did you
17		think about next?
18		She sat silent, Perhaps, Eleanor thought, she was
19		offended. Renny had been rude to her, in a
20		brotherly way. At last she smiled.
21		The devil fly away with you, Rene, she said
22		at last, and may he dangle you down on the
23		highest peak of the distant mountains in your

24		~~dig waste~~ bleak, wasted land. He's
25		~~come from~~ a Frenchman" she said, addressing
26		Eleanor, a pure, unmitigated Latin. Bred up
27		for thousands of years in the French peasant
28		ancestry. ~~Pure~~ They always owned a
29		little land; & folded the same sheets
30		very carefully, for generation after generation
31	Law, logical;	Unmitigated, un*[illeg.]*, incorruptible
32		she looked at him as she spoke as if to read
33		his *[illeg.]* from the hall, |*he has a mind*
34		*untrammelled by any straight & wandering bell*|

p. 88

1		unmatched by the travelling bees; who go from flower
2		to flower, orchids with *[dance?]* & brambles too: there he
3	few of the	sits & attempts to impose on one — she raised her
4	of her —	glass, who have lain open to every stir & tremor of the
5		~~uneducated~~ free, ~~the~~ solemn humbug like that.
6		If you analyse a feeling you kill it. That
7		explains why Renny is an ass; why Nicholas is an
8		ass; they are both the most lovable &
9		charming of men, she said ~~drink~~ sipping her wine
10		with a gesture ~~that seemed~~ as if the wine
11		drinking ~~their~~ to them: but asses: ~~science indeed!~~
12	un mitigated	~~Maggie, men of education~~ +learning+ asses!
13		~~But~~ You've mixed up two +different+ parties, Elf" said
14		Maggie: who had not been attending: ~~the Foreign~~
15		~~Office party was the night Mama died.~~
16		They used to go out to parties" she explained/
17		~~my father & mother.~~ "There were regular parties
18		~~werent there Eleanor?~~ And if you were in a
19		government office you had to go to them,
20		I remember coming back from one of those parties
21		I came up to the room at the top of the house
22		where Elvira slept: she pretended to be a
23		hump back: it was extraordinarily ~~beautiful~~ +pretty+

24	There were shadows in the garden; & artificial lights;
25	& the moon: & if you looked out of the window
26	you saw an extraordinary mixture…
27	such as I cant explain" she broke off
28	"There were the brandies" she took up a fork as
29	if to: then there was the line of the garden wall:
30	then there were the houses behind, perfectly
31	straight lines:
32	"When I was young I used to dance, Elvira
33	murmured, Everybody loved me when I was young
34	Roses & hydrangeas hung upon the sections &

p. 89

1		bow street was a heart shaped note (thats my mother
2	A waltz /	dancing) round the room. Away the rolls was a
3	playing down /	heart shaped note:…
4	the *[illeg.]*	'she was wearing a green dress, with silver in it"
5		said Maggie. ~~The way she moved was so~~
6		~~lov extraordinary~~. She was rather heavy. She was
7		over fifty then. But her movements — she
8		waved both her hands as if her body were like…
9		she hesitated
10		+whats often, *[illeg.]*+
11		a flag on the bridge, said Elvira, only *[illeg.]*
12		controlled. She sank down on the end of the bed:
13		whereupon Papa said +called+ what about the bathroom
14		door Eugenie
15		~~It's~~ the area door" said Maggie: there'd been a
16		burglary up the street & she'd forgotten to have a
17		lock put on
18		|And then ~~we said~~ Elvira began:
19		Yes, said Maggie:|
20		The bathroom door, the area door, the lock
21		has been left off the area door. Tum tiddy
22		tum tum — Cant you O I cant remember the
23		the Blue Danube? Eleanor suggested

24	They all /	A curious hollow sound echoed in the street outside
25	laughed	Its only a steamer on the river said Renny
26		~~It was a waltz tune they were~~ How does a
27		waltz tune go? They were dancing."
28		As the sisters tried to bring back the scene,
29		~~of their mother dancing~~ Eleanor saw Eugenie
30		once more. She saw her free wild gestures
31		~~Oh it goes~~ +a waltz+ — how does it go? The Blue
32		Danube…" She tried to remember one of the
33		tunes to which she had waltzed as a girl.
34		A long drawn hollow sound wailed ~~out in the~~
35		out
36		"No, no" Eleanor ~~said~~ laughed, as if the

p. 90

1		~~the by accident~~ some foghorn in the river had tried
2		to give her the note: then, in a second, she realised
3		they all listened
4		"It might have been a foghorn" she said.
5		~~But~~ The siren wailed again
6		~~Those damned Germans" said Renny~~
7		There could be no doubt; it was the warning to
8		take cover.
9		"Those damned Germans" said Renny. ~~They~~
10		~~all~~ He got up.
11		~~I must bring the children down" said~~ Maggie
12		you too. She said something to her husband; Al and
		+[illeg.]+
13		~~went out of the room~~
14	~~My dear Maggie~~	"If a bomb falls on this house ~~we are all~~ +smash+
15		~~done for; he said; however" she left the room~~
16	the heart	It wont make any difference" he said: but she
17		left the room. "We bring the children down into
18		the kitchen" he ~~said~~ explained. "Not that it makes any
19		difference" he followed her.
20		Eleanor got up & looked out of the window.

21 ~~The stars were shining with extreme~~ The
22 sky was perfectly clear; the stars were
23 shining with extreme brilliance. She heard
24 a rush of wheels. A taxi drove ~~swiftly~~ that
25 ~~ther~~ very swiftly. Then she heard the patter of
26 footsteps. Two men were walking very fast,
27 ~~almost, but~~ as if they prevented themselves
28 from breaking into a run. A
29   Ought we to ask people in? she said —
30 tentatively. But the men had passed. The
31 street seemed completely empty: all the lights
32 were out in the house opposite. "Or to
33 turn out these lights? she said. She looked
34 at the brightly lit table; they had just
35 finished the meat. Nicholas ~~drew~~ laid
36 his knife, fork together neatly.

p. 91

1 ~~"Are you afraid?~~ Do you mind air raids? he asked
2 her. Some people do; some people dont."
3 "No, said Eleanor "The chances ~~are so very~~
4 of being hit is so very slight. She sat down again
5 They will probably be here in about ten minutes" said
6 Nicholas. |*As he spoke they heard a the dull*
7 *boom of a gun far away.*
8 *That is some way off" he said "in the North"*|
9 "It is more boring than frightening" said Eleanor.
10 ~~She had been in these air raids already~~
11 "Because we were talking of something that
12 interested us" said Nicholas "And now we
13 cannot think what to say."
14   They heard a shuffling on the stairs.
15 There are the children, said Eleanor. Ought we
16 to help?
17   No, said Elvira: +its all arranged+ They put the
    children in

18	then if a /	the kitchen; & we get in the coal cellar
19	bomb drops /	~~so that~~ Maggie can be quite sure that if a
20	Maggie /	bomb ~~does drop~~ +falls+ we shall all be killed at the
21	is sure	same time/ ~~Thats what Nicholas calls~~ That is the
22		~~maternal impulse isnt it Nicholas~~
23		What Nicholas calls the maternal impulse:
24	Plates	As she spoke they heard the dull boom of a
25	Pray your *[illeg.]*	gun far away. Renny came in,
26	& —I"	"They are getting nearer" he said, "Come along" ~~But~~
27		†They followed him out to the little passage; ~~Re~~
28		†Renny turned off the light.† ~~They~~ The
29		basement was dark, save for the glow of the fire
30		in the kitchen grate. ~~They heard~~ In the
31		red glow Eleanor could see some shrouded
32		figures; the ~~ch~~ sleeping children, she supposed. She
33		moved as quietly as possible.
34		~~"In here" said~~ Renny turned on the lights
35		in a large chamber on the right. It was part

p. 92

1		coal cellar, part wine cellar ~~kitchen chairs stood~~
2	Curse those /	"Its all right; you can talk now" he said. With
3	Huns	luck they'll sleep straight through. ~~What a damned bore!~~
4		he exclaimed ~~Indeed~~ the coal cellar had a
5		slightly cheerless & sepulchral look, with its
6		crypt like ceiling, as in the other room. A light in the
7		centre shone on a heap of glittering coal; ~~& on~~
8		two or three alcoves were packed with bottles
9		lying on their sides. ~~Renny Renny had put~~
10		~~brought~~ there were some kitchen chairs: Renny
11		Elvira ~~who had gone upstairs returned with~~
12		came in with her arm full of quilts & coats.
13		Then Maggie came in, she was carrying a
14		plate on which was a large plum pudding. She
15		helped them, as they sat in a circle ~~with~~
16		on kitchen chairs. ~~Everything seemed to proceed with~~

17		~~an orderly common sense that was slightly~~
18		~~forced~~ She spoke with exasperated common sense,
19		Eleanor thought. She was anxious about the
20		children presumably.
21		Are they +*[illeg.]*+ asleep? she asked,
22		~~Now"~~ +Yes+ said Maggie: but if the guns get much
23		louder, ~~they~~ +it+ may wake them"
24		Another gun boomed out; it was closer this time.
25		Theyve reached London ~~all right."~~ said Nicholas
26		They began to eat their plum pudding.
27		Maggie listened
28		Is the nurse ~~at all~~ nervous?" Eleanor asked
29		but she was not sure whether she ought not to
30		talk of something different.
31		"She's got a candle & she's reading a book said
32		Maggie:
33		"What book?" Renny asked

p. 93

1		"some shilling shocker" said Maggie
2		Thats what this feels like" said Elvira.
3		~~Quite unreal, rather~~ exciting: but ~~quite~~ unreal"
4		A gun boomed again
5		Thats Hampstead I should say" said Nicholas
6		They waited. There was silence for some time.
7		"This is a very magnificent cellar" said Eleanor
8	like the /	It looked ~~very~~ almost as if it had been built to
9	crypt of /	stand a siege, from blocks of solid stone & +it was arched+
10	a church	Another gun boomed, over head it seemed; Maggie
11		went into the kitchen
12		Eleanor looked at Renny. Rather ostentatiously she
13		thought he took a mouthful of pudding:
14		Nicholas was looking at his watch as if he were
15		timing the gun *[illeg.]*. There was something priest like
16		in his expression. Elvira sat ~~inte~~ motionless, looking

17	down	at her plate. The ~~Germans~~ +enemy+ must be very close
18		Eleanor told herself that any moment
19		they might be killed. But she could not think
20		of anything appropriate to say, even to herself.
21		It all seems so silly" as if she were
22		apologising to the self which tried to stun her with a
23		vision of sudden death. "Its unpleasant of course" she
24		added. ~~The feel~~ +*[illeg.]*+ at the top of one's head."
25		~~She wondered~~ +looked up at the stone ceiling+ what ~~the feeling would be if the~~
26		~~stone arch suddenly toppled.~~ First there would be a
27		~~roar of~~ & wondered what wd happen if the
28		bombs struck the house. There would be a roar of
29		sound, she thought.
30		~~Again~~ A gun sounded very close. She
31		looked up ~~The stone ceiling rest.~~ A cobweb was on
32		the ceiling. Perhaps it shook
33		Thats St Jame's Park said Nicholas
34		Or Westminster" said Renny
35		~~It was~~ There was dead silence.
36		They heard Maggie say in a soothing voice.

p. 94

1	"Turn over & go to sleep"
2	They waited. The gun boomed again. It was further away
3	~~Yes thats over"~~ They must have been
4	very close, though: I could hear the shrapnel
5	~~I tho thought I could hear the shell" said Eleanor~~
6	Guns boomed far away, dully, distantly.
7	Maggie came back
8	"~~He woke~~ He woke for one moment" she said.
9	But I do think he's ~~gone~~ off again now." She sat down.
10	Now we will all have a glass of wine" said
11	Renny
12	Well I do think that is one of the most
13	disappointing exhibitions ~~It was over~~ of human

14		incompetence ~~I have ever~~ have ever seen" said Elvira
15		You were frightened ~~Elvira~~ said Nicholas "You
16		went quite white"
17		But I ought to have fainted" said Elvira
18		~~They all had felt~~ Eleanor noticed that they all
19		shifted their positions in their chairs, as if
20		they had been sitting in a+n+ ~~strained attitude~~
21		~~of strain~~ an uncomfortable attitude.
22		"They were very close that time" said Nicholas.
23		You could hear the shell."
24	†Eleanor thought /	~~That's the Crystal Palace~~
25	of the aeroplane /	Theyre going away ~~over Kent now~~" said Renny
26	travelling /	"I wonder if they did much damage" said Eleanor. †
27	[illeg.] over /	~~may have killed a cow, or~~
28	the Crystal /	Renny shrugged his shoulders.
29	Palace, out /	You cant tell at that height, in the
30	in ~~h~~ the fields	dark" he said
31	again†	"It was ~~a little~~ pointless +waste of [dignity?]+ [illeg.]"
		she said.
32		Maggie came in, & sat down —
33		"Now we can finish our pudding" she said

p. 95

1	he peculiar /	"He woke for one moment, but he's fast asleep now:"
2	to they /	she said — |*I suppose we must sit here +wait ~~till th~~*
3	Do It did us /	*until we hear the alarm*|
4	wake the baby /	"Now we will all have a glass of wine" said Renny
5	she just started /	~~I think~~ That was ~~one of the most~~ disappointing
6	I dont think she /	exhibitions of ~~human incompetence~~ I have ever seen
7	heard us	said Elvira:
8		"You were frightened" said Nicholas. "You were
9		quite white — at one moment — when the
10		guns were overhead."
11		"But I ought to have ~~fainted she said~~
12		felt much more than I did feel" she said
13		Thats just what I was thinking" said Eleanor

14		And yet we might have been killed in next
15		moment" she said ~~taking~~ holding her glass up
16		to Renny, who stood over then with a bottle of
17		wine: they had made an old box into a
18		table. On it they stood their glasses, & the wine
19		bottles. They sat around in a ~~or~~ circle, with the
20		coal making an avalanche of blackness behind
21		them. Wrapped in *[sheets?]* & ~~overcoats~~ dressing
22		gowns they lurked ~~as if they were coaching~~
23		huddled over the box ~~they looked something~~
24		like a company of old men squatting round a
25		camp fire, or a circle of witches brewing
26	with as if /	some midnight potion; or ~~a~~ — Maggie ~~raising~~
27	the background /	finishing her plum pudding, ~~no could not~~ she
28	of the bare /	~~rose what~~ looked at them, certainly Eleanor ~~her~~
29	cellar walls /	plain blue dressing gown which hid the
30	with the	foolish little ornaments, the folds of velvet &
31		~~gold, brocade, which she~~ in her dress, the

p. 96

1		magnificent ~~blue black or red~~ jewel that hung ~~on~~ firm
2		from her neck. Like all the Pargiters, she improved in
3		appearance as she grew older. +The+ middle aged ~~she was~~
4		her face was ~~wrinkled, lines went in a~~ full of
5		wrinkles; the flush had gone soft now, was such
6		those; ~~the smooth~~ but it was much more
7		expressive than it used to be ~~more~~ & *[nostrils?]*
8		without *[illeg.]* She had a way of
9		wrinkling ~~her~~ up her forehead, & *[illeg.]* & then all the
10		~~wrinkles went~~ she had a way of opening her eyes.
11		Also, before she spoke she would ~~pur~~ hold her lips
12	& then /	tight for a few moments. She looked ~~jolly~~
13	she would come /	~~unco~~ rather like an old Abbess, sitting on her
14	out with /	kitchen chair holding her glass of wine +in her hand+
15	some rather /	"You look like an Abbess, Eleanor," she said
16	sensible yet /	~~I'm afraid~~ I'm very untidy ~~said~~ Eleanor

17	random /	replied, her hands going automatically to her
18	remarks	thick crop of hair
19		~~Please dont" said Elvira You look so~~
20		Dont dont dont
21		But what were we talking about before *[the?]*
22		raid? ~~They~~ She tried to remember
23		"About — about —" the memory of what they
24		had been saying had gone completely
25		"We were all afraid up to a point" said
26		Nicholas. Or one should remember what we
27		were saying:
28		"I expect it was great nonsense" said Renny.
29		|*The things people dont say are very*
30		*interesting" said Elvira*| ~~And that is~~ The
31	said Elvira	real point of talk +is that+ people then say what
32		they dont say. ~~Thats~~ And what they dont say

p. 97

1		is what they are; & what they are — that may be very
2		interesting; although whether it has any importance,
3		seems to me, after tonights exhibition +of human nature+
4	rather	doubtful. Does it matter, in your opinion, she
5		turned to Eleanor, what human beings are?
6		Human beings, do they matter at all? Men &
7		women, wouldnt it be better to drown them?
8		~~What is the King~~ If I were King George & the
9		Kaiser I'd send for one large bucket, line up
10		my peoples on either side, & say jump in,
11		which, both armies, being perfectly trained, would do;
12		& then there would be left about six people in
13		each country who might come together, say,
14		at Hyde Park Corner, & ~~create a new world of~~
15		embracing each other with rapture, create a
16		new world" She waved her glass. They
17		all felt a desire to laugh & talk
18		I will shut the kitchen door" said Maggie. She

19	shut it & came back
20	~~Elv gets so excited~~
21	"Wat is the new world going to ~~lil~~ look like Renny?"
22	said Eleanor, after the war?
23	"There'll be a revolution" said Renny
24	~~In England said I cant believe it"~~
25	My dear friends, said Nicholas. You are all
26	labouring under a ~~very~~ great +delusion+ mistake. You think
27	the war is of some importance; whereas the
28	truth is that this is of no importance at all.
29	None whatever" he said slapping his glass down
30	on the box.
31	"Several millions are being killed" said Eleanor
32	Yes, my dear Eleanor: several millions are
33	being killed; ~~but several millions are~~
34	human suffering is a terrible thing:
35	but as we ~~all have all~~ +were all+ agreed ~~that it is~~

p. 98

1	~~that it did not matter in the least~~; as we
2	~~only~~ as we did not find it in the least terrible
3	until August the 4th 1914, we all engaged
4	ourselves in perfect comfort while ~~people~~ in
5	millions were suffering far more terribly than
6	they suffer on battlefields: to say that the war is
7	terrible seems to me… he hesitated for a word,
8	hysterical ~~cheap, common, vulgar, &~~
9	|*when you say that there will be a new world*
10	*after the war*| say to say that war is
11	terrible; ~~and~~ as it came for at a moment
12	second; as if it came at a moment when
13	people were psychologically unborn, now *[illeg.]*
14	we are not going to learn anything from it
15	~~because we do not know ourselves~~
16	There will be no new world, until we are
17	educated. But we can educate ourselves

18		~~that I firmly believe~~ we can educate
19		ourselves; we can educate ourselves."
20		He repeated the sentence with emphasis, as if he had
21		come to an end of his vocabulary. He sat silent,
22		glaring ~~at~~ ~~in front of his~~: he grasped his wine
23		as if he would break the glass. Then he finished
24		off what remained of the wine.
25		Yes, said Eleanor; I ~~have~~ +ve+ always thought
26		that all of the streets ~~where I~~ in a poor district —
27		up in Notting Hill, — or where you live, Elvira, off
28		the Waterloo Road; I've always thought the lives people
29		live there; the women always having children;
30		never enough to eat; & not for three four five years
31		but all their live; in rooms where you ~~cant~~
32	But thats /	wouldnt keep a dog: thats far worse & *[illeg.]* were
33	why	~~Thats why for war~~ Thats why ~~they~~ the war is
34		~~has been such a godsend: they explain the wars~~
35		war is possible. Its so much better for most
36		people than the lives they are leading: the
37		women can feed their children: the men
38		get excitement, ~~fresh air~~

p. 99

1	And Renny gets Alsace-Lorraine" said Elvira
2	But whats the point of getting Alsace Lorraine if —
3	she stopped. The guns had ~~almost~~ ceased. They were
4	beginning again; ~~they were still~~ but they were still
5	far away.
6	~~"One of the Germans has~~ What has happened is
7	that one of the German ~~air~~ aeroplanes has been unable to
8	find his way through the barrage. He has turned
9	back. The whole thing will now begin over again;
10	unless he is shot down before he reaches us."
11	Or the English have mistaken one of themselves for the
12	enemy" said Maggie: that~~s what happened~~
13	happens sometimes.

14   But ~~the~~ though the guns ~~fired~~ went on firing, it was
15   in the distance.
16   But Renny, do you want Alsace Lorraine?" said
17   Eleanor.
18   He did not answer. Again the mask she had
19   noticed before came down over his face. ~~He looked at~~
20   ~~Eleanor looked~~
21   "Yes, he does" said Maggie, as if thinking
22   for him. "He had an uncle, & he had an
23   aunt, & their farm was burnt by the Germans
24   in whatever year it was"
25   "1870" said Elvira: "And I had a
26   grandmother, or a great grandmother, I forget
27   which; & she was searched by the French in the
28   year 1812, but being a woman of some sense
29   she said, take my body — by all means; only
30   give me a pearl necklace instead; which is what
31   Maggie & I are living off at the present moment.
32   The wages of sin. |*The something [mistaken?] comes*
33   *along, & says Mrs. Pargiter [illeg.]*| &
34   The *[illeg.]* or my drains are out,
35   *[pale?]* or I want to see the *[illeg.]* what
36   do I do? Break off a pearl, sprout it at the

p. 100

1   the jeweller. |*But what does Renny say! The body is*
2   *the body is all; there is no such thing as the*
3   *spirit. Give me Alsace Lorraine!*|
4   Whereas, poor dear Renny, who believes in the body,
5   but not in the soul…
6   Eleanor felt in a flash that she understood why
7   Maggie had married Renny.
8   "He is an extraordinarily loveable man" she said
9   to herself; feeling that he was full of deep &
10   extraordinary feelings; +&+ ~~that was why he puzzled her~~
11   ~~he was very~~ though she had been puzzled by him

12		at first, by his reserve; his dignity; his simplicity; his
13		extreme consistency now all was ~~at her~~ solved
14		by a feeling of affection, sympathy for him.
15		"I have a great feeling for my country." he said
16		stubbornly
17		"And I have absolutely none" said Maggie.
18		~~I think of all In fact I dont understand what~~
19		~~you mean Renny~~
20		Are you quite sure of that Magdalena?" said
21		Nicholas
22		Quite ~~sure~~" she replied "I think its +patriotism+ silly
23		I think its disgusting, I think its barbaric…
24		Here we are sitting in a coal hole" she said.
25		They could hear the guns booming ~~in the a~~ away in
26		the distance
27		That was interesting" said Nicholas
28		"You get two women like Magdalena & Elvira
29		he continued; who are absolutely uneducated;
30		who have received nothing from their country;
31		from the institutions of their country; they cannot
32		inherit titles; they cannot vote; they cannot
33		practice professions; they are kept purely as
34		slaves for the breeding of children: & that
35	system it seems	~~has~~ abolished all feelings of patriotism.

p. 101

1		therefore it would seem"
2		Eleanor interrupted
3		I dont altogether agree" she said. My sister
4		Rose was actually in prison at the outbreak of the
5		war.
6	Which Pitt	(Rose, Elvira explained, is a very fine fellow who
7	rolled up	smashed the Prime Ministers plate glass window as he
8	when	sat eating a kipper with a golden spoon —
9		the fragments fell on the *[inlaid?]* and he *[illeg.]* duty
10		Take that woman away, put her in gaol, he

11		said to the footman who stood behind him
12		with a glass of rum, for I dont believe in
13		force. ~~She wanted a vote~~
14	Well Rose	She went straight to the war office, Eleanor
15		continued, offered her services. I dont know
16		anybody who is more patriotic."
17		Thats what Nicholas is saying: thats what
18		patriotism is: getting something"
19		And we dont want a vote because our great
20		grandmother gave her body to the French Duke in
21		the year 1812, & left us enough jewels to
22		live on/ But how we're going to live when the
23		money, all spent, paying for *[illeg.] [pop?]* seems…"
24		The guns ~~so~~ sounded far away. They could
25		only just be heard now.
26		|*Well lets get out of this cellar & go into the*
27		*dining room" said Renny.*|
28		~~Yet she had no education either~~
29		~~Yes said Maggie~~
30		~~What is R Rose is driving a car~~

p. 102

1		And yet she had no education"
2		That is very interesting." said Nicholas ~~"But~~ he
3		~~slo~~ hesitated. ~~You will not think this offensive~~ I am
4		~~here~~ I do not know your sister. ~~Her mot~~
5		She may be one of those very rare people, whom one
6		meets perhaps twice in a lifetime — who act
7		disinterestedly: of the type of Shelley; — ~~or she may~~
8		~~Oh no~~ Eleanor laughed +No no+ why Rose is not of the type of
9		~~Shelley~~ She's ~~a~~ very active, *[respectable?]* straight trimmed, woman
10		(very like Uncle Abel) said Maggie.
11		~~She~~ One +who+ ~~ought to have been a sea captain; or a~~
12		she would have made an admirable county

13		gentleman" ~~or~~
14		~~riding~~ Riding about the estate on a stout cob" Elvira
15		added. ~~Hullo she found~~ *[illeg.]* to the
16		~~whos that [illeg.] fellow that damning~~
17		little city *[gents?]* who dont know the *[illeg.]* of the hound
18	stem /	from the ~~note~~: & showery *[coppers?]*; a ~~better~~ whole hearted
19	take that/	boys, who hold open the gate/ Here you little ruffian!
20	& learn to /	with a very red face, Maggie, +rather good features+ added, & a buff
21	blow *[illeg.]* /	coloured waistcoat" ~~shout~~
22	now	In that car, said Nicholas, she is probably
23		enjoying the war, because it was her chance to
24		develop faculties which † in peace,
25		would †~~not only~~ remain undeveloped† & ~~therefore~~
26		cause her considerable physical discomfort." was she
27		happy before the war?"
28		Eleanor considered.
29		"There was always ~~rather~~ +a curious+ bitterness… Eleanor
30		began
31		Lets get out of this cellar, go upstairs" said
32		Renny "~~I believe~~ Its all over"
33		They listened again ~~they [carried?]~~ only a very

p. 103

1	they heard only a distant concussion, like the beating of a
2	wave on the shore miles away.
3	Oh right, I'll tell Emily" said Maggie
4	They all rose, stretching themselves, & stumbling
5	over their sheets, dressing gowns,
6	"Hey diddle diddle, the cat & the fiddle, the cow" — ~~she~~
7	Elvira recited, as they went up the kitchen stairs, she *[illeg.]*
8	~~But thats not it~~ "I arrive from dreams of thee, &
9	a spirit in my feet has led me, who knows how
10	to thy chamber window, sweet" Thats more like it,"

11		But Eleanor" she said, putting her arm round her
12		cousin as they went into the drawing room, you must
13		remember how a waltz time goes?" she led her to
14		the +little+ piano. "~~Now~~ play" she said.
15		"Its an age since I touched a piano" said Eleanor
16		sitting down. And ~~Maggie wont like me to play~~
17		~~on her piano"~~ one ought to play on other peoples
18		piano."
19		~~No no It~~ said Elvira, this is the piano the
20		donkey plays on when he's tired of braying; Renny
21		seconds himself from the effort of making shells, by
22		playing Bach with two fugues of the left hand.
23		Well, I'll play" said Eleanor.
24		She played a few bars of an old waltz, but she
25		stopped, aware that the others had come in &
26		were standing behind her.
27		What an extraordinary power music has!" said Nicholas.
28		Even a few bars of a worthless tune."
29		Maggie turned on a light or two. The fire was
30		fire was burning, brightly. The room looked large,
31		spacious, comfortable, after the coal cellar.
32		They could hear the nurse moving about in the
33		room overhead, putting the children to bed again.
34		"They didnt mind the raid?" Eleanor asked,

p. 104

1		sitting down on the sofa by the fire with Maggie
2		"Its so difficult to tell with very small children: ~~what they~~
3		what do they notice? What dont they notice?"
4		Jasper's two, & three months
5	1912	two months they +must have+ heard the guns +is only
		a year &+ ~~in their sleep I suppose~~
6		~~I suppose but only~~ +I suppose+ in their sleep"
7		And they will dream of them all their lives" said
8		Elvira "~~Beautiful~~ +terrible+ dreams or beautiful dreams
9		Or will they perhaps be very silly dreams?

10	said /	~~"Most dreams are silly"~~ said Maggie. I dreamt last
11	Maggie	night I had gone to a party in my nightgown
12		& I woke up & found that the sheet had
13		fallen on the floor."
14		I dreamt last night that I had gone to a party"
15		said Renny "with holes in my socks."
16		~~this is a [peat?] thing~~
17		Maggie ~~picked her~~ dipped +her hand+ into a basket & ~~began to~~
18		~~darn the socks~~ prepared to darn the socks
19		"What were we talking about in the cellar" she
20	slipping a /	asked, ~~"Patriotism?"~~ love, war, politics
21	wooden ball /	patriotism?"
22	into the /	We were saying that Rose drives an ambulance
23	heel of the /	~~on the~~ |*to the amazement of the* [nature?] *where*
24	sock	~~she w~~ *the French see Rose coming, they say...*|
25		said ~~El~~ Elvira. And Nicholas says she is not
26		patriotic because she *[illeg.]* driving an ambulance"
27		was that it?" she asked rather +shyly+ ~~they to how~~
28		~~called him~~ that she had called him by his Christian name
29		But he had called her Eleanor: & she had not heard
30		what his surname was. Oh, thank you so
31		much" she said, taking the cigarette he offered her.
32		"That is just what I was looking for." She
33		noticed that his ~~finger~~ forefinger was stained deep
34		yellow. He smoked incessantly.
35		"Have a cigar Eleanor" said Renny, getting
36		up a *[illeg.]* a box

p. 105

1		a cigarettes ~~is~~ +are is+ ~~a [memorable?]~~ +memorable little+ ~~ma [illeg.] [makeful?]~~
2		but shant I be sick?" she said. She let him snip off the
3		end & placed it, rather gingerly, in her mouth.
4		There may be such an emotion as a pure & disinterested
5		passion for ones country" said Nicholas. "All I can

6		say is that I have never met with it" Never,
7		never ~~never~~
8		But then what passions are disinterested" Eleanor
9		asked, taking a pull at her cigar.
10		Magdalena's for her children" he replied
11		For what other reason, after all, did we get in the
12		coal cellar, when we should have been so much
13	he looked at /	happier in the dining room |*except that we*
14	Maggie	*felt — I profound respect; mixed with pity; mixed with*
15		*[illeg.]*	But when Magdalena said I wish to
16		die with my children, we all felt she has
17		not been paid for saying that, she has nothing to
18		gain by saying that. Although it is a very
19		~~sil~~ silly thing to say. Therefore we went into
20		the coal cellar.
21		"Im ~~very~~ sorry Nicholas" said Maggie "But I
22		cant help it." ~~Its the maternal instinct~~
23		"Its a thing to struggle against with all your
24		might" Elvira exclaimed, Its a horrible thing
25		its a ~~terrible thing~~" ~~beauty~~ its a terrible thing
26		~~the maternal instinct~~ but very beautiful of
27		course. Maggie holding the baby in her arms,
28		saying; with the guns going over head ~~"Thats~~
29		~~nothing at all, go to sleep"~~ — & saying
30		come here, poor puss, come poor puss" That is
31		how I knew she that she was in love with you,
32		Renny, the night the King died.
33		|*"They were calling out in the street, a man*
34		*went with a barrow"*| ~~said Maggie~~
35		"But in a hundred years she will feel it much

p. 106

1	less" said Nicholas
2	I feel it much less than my mother felt it after all" said
3	Maggie: +Nothing will induce me to+ I am not going
	to have +another *[illeg.]*+ more than two

4		children —
5	we have /	"And we are +going to say to our children, when ~~they are~~+ not going to let our children depend
6	taught them /	upon us" said Renny; & we are not going to depend on
7	to can their /	them. We shall divide up the family fortune,
8	[hubs?] /	—which +if there is any [fortune?]+ will be extremely small" said Maggie
9	This is your /	~~& we shall drive them +go away+ out of the house. My~~
10	shame	~~father" he continued~~
11		But surely family feeling is a very valuable
12		thing? said Eleanor. The cigar was drawing. She
13		noticed the richness of the flavour, compared with a
14		cigarette.
15		"Very valuable" said Elvira The only education
16		I ever had was that I hated my father... A
17		~~man who fitted completely~~ "Eugenie Eugenie
18		~~the Duchess~~ dont be late for the Foreign Office
19		Party. +And+ ~~also~~ the Duchess doesnt use fish knives
20		~~a man who fitted completely, Nicholas.~~ Thwe
21		man who is responsible for the European war.
22		The man who believed, actually believed,
23	[humourless?] /	Eleanor, that it is an honour to be given a
24	[unless?] half /	degree by one of our universities. And called
25	without /	himself Sir Digby Pargiter, K.C.V.O, K.C.M.G,
26	stood [sword.] /	K.G., M.P., W.C.L, & L.L.D."
27	his legs	"He was a very handsome man in a half light," said Maggie
28		You have only to make a law, said Nicholas
29		~~Elvira is very~~ that war shall be carried on
30		in complete privacy; without ~~ho medals~~; without
31		honour; without monuments; without
32		— these damned newspapers" said Renny.
33		~~without~~ +[illeg.]+ setting women like Elvira flinging themselves
34		upon George's neck & saying —
35		"Protecting chastity" Elvira suggested. ~~"or is it~~

p. 107

1	giving white feathers to the men who are really courageous
2	"& red roses to the men who are cowards" Elvira added,
3	only mine was a lily —"
4	"And you would have no more war"
5	Eleanor puffed at her cigar. It did not make her feel
6	sick. On the contrary it filled her with a balmy
7	feeling of content & rest. She felt at ease, *[illeg.]*
8	contemplative.
9	"I'm afraid theyre very expensive?" she said to
10	Renny.
11	No ~~I've given you~~ +thats+ a cheap one" he said
12	I keep them for beginners" ~~[he said]~~
13	You would have no more war," she repeated
14	the ~~last~~ Nicholas's last words, ponderously.
15	But without some sort of negotiation would
16	people do anything, Renny? she asked. He interested
17	her very much: she wanted to make him talk
18 *[illeg.]* reminded /	"~~Do you~~ remember what Lord Salisbury said +making a+ when he
19 him of?	had to form a ministry? Feeding day at the zoo."
20	|*I wonder — she repeated "I dont think that was*
21	*true of Gladstone, or of Parnell"*|
22	My dear Eleanor, its always true, of all politicians
23	said Renny. ~~They'd eat their grandmot~~
24	~~You dont suppose that a man~~ |*Thats what*
25	*makes men politicians"* he said.
26	*You dont think that any politician really loves his*
27	*country disinterestedly?" I mean, would*
28	*work without the sort of privilege, the sort of*
29	*patronage* ~~that~~ *+of+ being in office* ~~means~~|
30	I dont think that was true of Gladstone, or of Parnell," she
31	said
32	He is not altogether to blame" said Nicholas —
33	a young man, going into politics. He must start with

p. 108

1		the most sincere conviction; but then his brother comes to him &
2		says, Look here old chap —
3		the imitation of English slang was so coarse that
4		Eleanor ~~began to laugh~~ smiled — "it would be
5		very convenient to me, Nicholas proceeded, to
6		have that little spot ~~under the~~ for which I am
7	just as well	~~admirably~~ fitted ~~just as~~ anybody else; which may
8		be true; & the duchess of… the duchess of…
9		says "come & dine with us, just among friends… &
10		he has never dined with a duchess before… &
11		the footmen all wear white waistcoats &
12		plush trousers, ~~Eleanor~~ & he says to himself
13		Pitt was Prime Minister ~~when he was~~ +at the age of+ was 27;
14		& in short" — he held out his hands
15		expressively. This is the fault of the system."
16	Think	Gold lace on a hot summer's night" ~~said~~ +murmured+ Maggie
17		"Power, he said, Elvira added, power Miss
18		Pargiter, & he turned to the lady on his right
19		who was all covered with diamonds. ~~And the~~
20		~~little Oxford don, the~~ whereupon the toady, —
21		a wretched little man from Oxford, says
22		what did the toady say Maggie? —
23		~~Oh he always~~ +that+ he read Milton ~~before breakfast~~ in his
24		bath—
25		"I dont think Gladstone was like that" said
26		Eleanor. She puffed at her cigar. Renny,
27		smoking too. had blown a perfect ring through his
28		nose.
29		How did you do that? she asked. He
30		did it again. ~~Thick~~ a perfectly formed
31		ring of thick smoke hung for a second in the

32	air. She tried to imitate him, but
33	without success.
34	Suddenly ~~they heard~~ +they heard+ ~~a~~ a clear
35	flute like sound broke +*[say all?]*+ in the street below.

p. 109

1	What on earth, Maggie exclaimed, ~~holding~~ +stopping+ the ~~sock~~
2	needle.
3	Its the boy scouts" said Renny. "The All Clear.
4	The raid is over."
5	Well we knew that some time ago, said Maggie
6	Now they'll wake the children." The bugles
7	sounded again more loudly under the window.
8	Then they heard them dying away down the street.
9	~~Renny went to the win~~ Almost directly
10	afterwards, they heard again the hooting of
11	cars, & the rolling of wheels, as if traffic had been
12	returned, & the ordinary ~~nig~~ life of the night ~~began~~ had
13	begun again.
14	Isnt it getting late?" said Eleanor. She looked
15	at her coat lying on the sofa, as if she ought to go.
16	"It is exactly thirteen minutes past ten" said
17	Nicholas, looking at his watch.
18	On January 14th 1917" said Elvira:
19	19th cant even get the ~~day of the month~~ +day+ right, said
20	Renny
21	And is it 1917?" Elvira asked. "not that it
22	matters. Not that it matters a straw. If
23	I had to teach a child English history I should
24	begin by saying dates dont matter. And accents
25	dont matter, in Greek. And only very few facts
26	matter. Very few ~~things~~ +facts+ matter, I should say, if I
27	were addressing a vast assembly of human beings,
28	collected to hear the words of wisdom that flowed
29	from my lips, standing up on a platform in a

30	great hall. What matters, I should say,
31	sticking an attitude, is… ~~Go on~~
32	~~Nicholas~~
33	The audience is getting impatient, Elvira"
34	Eleanor

p. 110

1	"~~Let~~ Tell us — you —" said Elvira, looking at Eleanor
2	who felt suddenly newborn: she felt herself ~~getting~~ a blushing: it
3	was ridiculous.
4	"I'm not an interesting person" she said. "I used to
5	ask myself," she saw herself brushing her teeth; again, she
6	saw herself going slowly down stairs: its all so
7	higgledy piggledy I said to *[them?]*: & one — how odd the
8	mind is! — I see before me a dogs bowl with a
9	lump of sulphur in it: & I'm saying to myself something
10	about love & money," & I ~~seem to be on the verge of a~~
11	revelation; & then I go on upstairs (it was the night
12	mama died), I say to *[myself?]* with absolute conviction
13	thats the secret: But I couldnt put it in to words:
14	I'm so ordinary. "Thats why" she sighed, "I've done so
15	little" I think thats what matters, she said after a
16	pause: not to mix up love & money." Only one, of
17	course" she added. And you, Renny?" she asked.
18	Another thought struck her.
19	Perhaps thats why — one always tries to find excuses for
20	*[oneself?]* — but I never felt so strongly as if *[illeg.]* felt,
21	~~They said~~, so did Bobby — my brother; ~~she~~ — about
22	politics: ~~votes for women~~, you see, she explained to
23	Nicholas, my family is one of those large
24	Victorian families. And we all take different views.
25	And my brother went to school, college; my
26	sisters stayed at home. And I remember
27	thinking when there was all that talk about

28		~~women's~~ education; — one of my sisters wanted to go
29		to college, but my father wouldnt let her — a
30		man's education is all mixed up with money.
31		Thats wrong. One of my brothers, she explained,
32		was very brilliant boy. He got all sorts of
33		prizes: He's a fellow of his college."
34		He translated Sophocles into rhyming verse"
35		said Elvira.

p. 111

1		But then of course if men have to make their livings?"
2		she stopped. Now Renny' she repeated
3		My dear Eleanor, I have nothing whatever to say" said Renny
4		A *[illeg.]* which compels four educated people to sit in
5		a coal cellar while German & Englishmen try to
6		kill each other overhead is obviously so childish
7		that ~~an educated man ought to we ought to~~ —
8		~~drown ourselves~~ that there is nothing to be said —
9		But we can educate ourselves, we can, we can"
10		said Nicholas. He spread out his hand
11		~~What matters is this, he said~~ Elvira asks ~~us to~~
12		~~say~~ what matters: & I say this is what matters:
13		He touched the first finger" Eleanor reflected with
14		alarm that he had ten; In the first place
15		we are none of us remotely educated. Eleanor
16		talks of 'education'. The nineteenth century was
17	not of /	the age of the +learned+ specialist. The men were educated in
18	education, but	one way: to make money; the women in another:
19		to bear children. The result is the war (I will
20		explain that later) The war has no ~~meaning~~ +importance+
21		~~because we have not had~~ whatsoever. The war
22		is simply naughty children letting off fire works in
23		the back garden. — But now we say to you
24		to ourselves, Look here Eleanor, Renny, Magdalena,

25		Elvira, it is time to grow up; I ~~Nicholas~~
26		say to you ~~try to know yourselves~~ | *You*
27		*laugh at me."*
28		*Yes, said Maggie, we think you* | You have
29		~~every~~ like you what matters is to
30		develop not this faculty which makes
31		money, not that faculty which breeds
32		children; it is to develop the whole
33		soul, the whole body. The whole of this

p. 112

1		at present rudimentary organism ~~which has in it the~~
2		~~seeds of completeness — the human~~ of which we
3		know nothing, or next to nothing."
4		But how? said Eleanor. If you had children ~~how w~~
5		would you send them to college?"
6		Poor George Pargiter, said Elvira; his parents spent
7		two or three thousand on his education ~~with what result~~
		+& produced+
8		a docile sheep." A ~~sheep dressed~~ up in
9		mud coloured clothes. a man who goes
10		through every attitude correctly. ~~Thats education"~~
11	now the /	My King, my country."
12	excitement has /	The soul being of course, ~~the~~ all our faculties, the
13	coming out of	soul body & brain (they are mixed) will." He
14	the *[illeg.] [illeg.]*	paused. His pale flexible face worked curiously.
15		He frowned as if he could not find words.
16		How can I make this plain to you?" he said.
17		But I will try. The soul grows, spreading in
18		rings like those you see in water when a stone has
19		fallen. The only way in which we can educate
20	is to stand /	ourselves, at the present moment (when we are so
21	aside	immature, so barbaric) ~~is not to~~ killing ourselves
22		as Renny says for a ~~bit~~ +piece+ of land) is not to impede
23		those rings: ~~when we~~ to let them spread
24		when we ~~interrupt the soul & say~~ this is right,

25		not knowing what is right, we interrupt the soul;
26		when we give a prize to the soul — say a
27		peerage, say a *[illeg.]*, or Edinburgh or Oxford
28		*[illeg.]*; ~~then~~ we freeze the soul; we fetter the
29		soul; ~~hanging~~ +And+ the soul repeats the same rhythms
30		again & again & again: ~~like a this~~ like a
31		~~gramophone when~~ the needle ~~has stuck~~ of a
32		gramophone which has stuck.
33		Whereas we want the soul to sweep" he
34		swept his hands round & round & round —
35		to expand & to expand — mixing together

p. 113

1		everything, always adventuring, always experimenting ~~for~~
2		And ~~then we go & shut ourselves in little boxes:~~
3		~~We~~ And ~~we should~~ forming new combinations,
4		~~We do not want the emphasis laid on "I":~~
5		~~Whereas now~~ we do not want the
6		emphasis laid on "I." "I" is
7		And that is what is wrong with education as it is
8	he screwed his /	today. The emphasis is laid on I; and the soul
9	fist up in to /	cannot bear being "I." The soul shivers
10	a tight ball	the soul screws itself up into a horrid little…
11		he stopped, unable to find a word—
12		But if people have to earn their livings?
13		Eleanor asked. ~~Roughly speaking, she added~~
14	If people have /	|~~a degree and honours My brother, she added~~
15	got to /	Then they've got to be ~~hedgehogs, or~~ whatever
16	earn their /	the animal is that Nicholas cant find a
17	livings then /	word for" said Maggie| "horrid ~~little~~ —
18	they are /	shrivelled, screwed up — little —
19	the [vegetables?] /	there are no words for what I mean!
20	the animals /	Nicholas exclaimed. None whatever!
21	the herd	Language is in its infancy. Language is the
22		still unborn. I can not say what I feel. But
23		I feel it! He was all lines and contortions.

| 24 | |French is always said to be such a beautifully
| 25 | ~~clear & [illeg.]~~ language ~~said~~ for explaining things, said
| 26 | Eleanor.
| 27 | My dear Eleanor, said Nicholas, if I had the
| 28 | whole French, the whole German, the whole English
| 29 | language at my finger ends I could not say
| 30 | what I mean" said Nicholas.| But no
| 31 | matter, he went on; in time to come ~~we shall~~
| 32 | when the soul has learnt to sweep everything

p. 114

| 1 | everything into one rhythm, forming new wholes — but
| 2 | what does that mean to you? — nothing whatever —
| 3 | there will be born a language, which will
| 4 | be music, poetry, & painting. Whereas now we ~~are~~
| 5 | ~~sitting in little boxes giving each other~~
| 6 | set like this" he drew himself up primly
| 7 | & ~~say~~ putting his feet neatly together; ~~& say~~
| 8 | ~~At~~ in our separate carriages, each with his own
| 9 | little cross, or holy book — each with his own ~~child~~
| 10 | ~~dog, chair, mat, child, fire, mantelpiece, wife, lock~~
| 11 | mending his lock…
| 12 | But if we have to earn our livings — Eleanor repeated
| 13 | noticing that once more her stock of words was
| 14 | becoming exhausted
| 15 | when all the time, Nicholas continued, paying her
| 16 | no attention, I know you know we all know
| 17 | from the sensations ~~upon~~ at the base of our
| 18 | necks up our flights — he touched her body
| 19 | lightly — that this is an outrage to the soul;
| 20 | that the soul resents such treatment & longs to
| 21 | be altered, say two three hundred years,
| 22 | all — & that whatever *[300?]* years? — only the
| 23 | flick of a lizards tongue — to be allowed
| 24 | privacy, obscurity, anonymity in which to
| 25 | flow. ~~What was that book you were~~

26	~~reading yesterday~~ Elvira?"
27	He turned to Elvira. She had fallen fast
28	asleep, ~~& was with her~~ +in the *[illeg.]*+ with her head
29	resting on ~~the sofa~~ cushion.
30	~~Eleanor got up.~~ |*He took her hand +very+ ~~gently~~*
31	*gently +as if+ Tell me Elvira, what was the*
32	*book*| She woke with a start.

p. 115

1	at the sound of her name.
2	~~I was fast asleep"~~ she said. I ~~had~~ was dreaming — I
3	she saw going here *[illeg.]*
4	Its time to go" said Eleanor. She looked at her
5	watch. It was eleven. She got up.
6	You were reading a book two days ago, when I came to
7	see you, Elvira," said Nicholas. He addressed her
8	as if she were a child, "And you ~~said to me, that it~~
9	~~when I came in~~ you ~~said~~ read a passage, a
10	sentence from that book aloud, & you said
11	~~I wish I had written that. Now~~ Psychologically
12	speaking, Nicholas… for Elvira makes mock of me
13	always, that is very +*[wholly?]*+ fine. What was it?
14	I was reading a book. I was reading a book when you
15	came in, Elvira began, ~~but my dear Nicholas I am~~
16	~~so tired, I am so sleepy.~~ But I'm so ~~tired~~ +*[illeg.]*+ Nicholas;
17	~~I'm so~~ two days ago ~~Do you know what I was~~
18	"And there was a bowl of red flowers on the table; &
19	a — what do you call those things — long slim
20	*[tapers?]* with blue lights in them?" for candles? —
21	~~Oh yes, I remember~~ on the table by the book?
22	& you said —
23	"She was standing, Elvira ~~said~~ began on the
24	Greek hill side, & the horsemen had galloped
25	away & there were clouds of dust. It was moonlight
26	& the little ~~of~~ red flowers were growing in

27	[cracks?] of the earth. And she said to Creon,
28	sumφilein oux exthan ephen" ~~to which~~
29	& Creon said, Go with her. ~~And Creon said~~
30	& shut her up in her tomb. Very like the
31	old man in gold thread Maggie: Creon.
32	The very spit & image of our nation, Creon.
33	Whereupon I shut the book, & said to

p. 116

1	|Creon, I threw it in your face. That was what we
2	said the night the King died, wasnt it Maggie;
3	~~I said to Rose~~ she spun around, laughing, as
4	~~Yes, trying to warm [hands?]~~
5	That is the feeling" said Nicholas at the base of the
6	spine when the soul expands. He threw out his
7	hands. When it [contracts?]. He made a noise
8	like a dog barking
9	I wish I had heard such said Eleanor. She
10	took her coat|
11	Yes, yes, yes, said Nicholas. That is quite enough
12	That is what I was trying to say: I was born
13	to love, not to hate: hence the sensation. Grrrrr
14	he made a noise like an a rusty brake —
15	~~hat which is~~ hated — & the sensation — he like an enormous kitten?
16	beamed all over & made a soft purring noise —
17	love "Look ~~all~~ +now+ my muscles are relaxed: I am
18	~~happy~~: I am warm: I am at ~~peace~~ +rest+." And in that
19	state alone can I create: Yes, because in that
20	state the rings spread, forming new combinations,
21	new patterns, new ideas: ~~are you~~ well it is
22	time to go." He
23	"Yes, said Eleanor, "I've got a long way to go."
24	~~The Tube will be crowded~~ I suppose the buses
25	run as usual, in spite of the raid? she asked
26	Renny put down the paper

27		Better let me call you a cab" he said
28		"I really prefer walking" she said "And its
29		cheaper." She ~~looked~~ sat for a moment
30	wood? coal?	looking at the fire. How ~~have~~ +do+ you +manage to get+ got such a
31		wonderful fire? she asked. In my flat I've only
32		got gas. & thats been cut down lately.
33		"I met a man with a barrow" said Maggie

p. 117

1	& made eyes at him" ~~Bribery & corruption~~
2	Bribery & corruption" said Renny. "War"
3	My dear Renny: said Nicholas, you poison yourself…
4	He picked up the evening newspaper which Renny had been
5	reading:
6	"Renny reads six papers every day" said Maggie
7	~~I cant stop" he replied.~~ +Well+ "They do for lighting the fires"
8	he said.
9	"I ~~find~~ +do+ that too" said Eleanor. I ~~used buy~~ cant stop
10	~~a newspaper every time I go out"~~ buying newspapers…
11	But they never have anything to say. She took the
12	sheet & glanced at it ~~Its going to last~~
13	~~another year?" she~~ And theres no news… she
14	But when you see people standing in queues hour
15	after hour to buy half a pound of
16	margarine…
17	Have you tried this?" said Renny. He produced a
18	glass tube filled with white pills. The latest
19	substitute for sugar" he explained.
20	|We shall starve the Germans before they starve us
21	said ~~Elv~~ Maggie:
22	"Their children are dying like flies" said Renny.|
23	~~Uncle Abel just shot off a few of his fingers said~~
24	~~Maggie "That didnt matter so~~ It's the

THOUGHTS ON PEACE IN A WINE CELLAR *Phillips*   63

25   ~~meanness of this war I hate — said Maggie~~
26   ~~Its just a~~ Having Uncle Abel just shot off a
27   few of his fingers +said Maggie+ That didnt matter. The
28   spirit of war is sheer meanness." ~~Lies; [illeg.];~~
29   ~~harming~~ —" she stopped
30   But the German mother is extremely prolific"
31   Maggie, said Renny
32   ~~And I said to Creon" said Elvira~~
33   "And I shut the book & said to Creon…"

p. 118

1   Damn your insolence, Creon, being the very spit
2   image of the old man you sat next at dinner Maggie
3   two thousand years ago. But what are two
4   thousand years? The flicker of a lizards eye lid —
5   gone. Time to come's whats ~~we~~ matters Maggie;
6   because I met a man at dinner the other night
7   who said to me, Time to come is all Cleopatra's needle
8   & this — pointing to the ladies ~~all~~ +dressed up to the
       9s+ in every dress
9   & the footmen in plush trousers, is but a rose leaf
10   on the top. ~~A Roses, those sharp spines being gone~~
11   ~~Gather ye rosebuds while ye may. Any leaves like a~~
12 |~~red red rose, thats newly sprung in June Oh this time~~
13   ~~Theres~~ +Thats+ far ~~on that~~ log Maggie ~~that's why it~~
14   burns
15   Yes its wood paving" she said. "Part of the
16   Brompton Road. Call that a rose leaf I said.|
17   I shouldnt mind women painting their faces," said
18   Maggie, if they did it well.
19   "In my mothers time," said Eleanor, ~~we were~~
20   powder was allowed; but not paint. As her
21   "~~And~~ Cigarettes, she smiled, ~~shou~~ I should have
22   been turned out of the house if my father had caught me
23   smoking one. ~~And now~~ Renny has given you a cigar.
24 |~~I'll send~~ +give+ ~~you a box of those cigars" said Renny~~

25		~~Theyre cheap."~~
26		~~You dont mind women.~~ ~~You~~| How things have
27		changed! ~~In twenty years!~~ ~~She~~
28		You know Eleanor used to sit at a large
29		round table pouring out tea; & the kettle wouldnt
30		boil; ~~& she'd take out a hair pin~~ & ~~say to the~~
31		Crosby brought in hotcakes & ~~Eleanor said~~

p. 119

1		Crosby said, I'll boil it on the kitchen fire Miss; Eleanor said
2		No it was a wedding present & you cant boil a ~~kettle~~ +wedding+
3	present	on the kitchen fire, she said; or the whole sanctity of
4		marriage would be dissolved; |whereupon Uncle Abel
5		came in, with his horrid little shiny knuckles on the
6		where he'd ~~d~~ cut off the head of a blaspheming
7		Turk. ~~But he was~~ & said; what did Uncle
8		~~And now~~ Abel say, Eleanor?
9		~~What have you all been doing?~~ Papa ~~would~~ +had always+ to say
10		What have you been doing? today?
11		~~And you lied" said Maggie~~: "And +what+ did you ~~tell~~
12		~~tell the truth?" said Maggie~~: say to him?" said Maggie
13		~~Sometimes one thing: sometimes another~~" said Eleanor.
14		If you'd been walking down the Burlington Arcade — ?
15		~~That was~~ "Yes, that was a problem" Eleanor agreed.
16		It was a bad system in many ways" she agreed. It
17		suddenly struck her that Mira had lived, perhaps in
18		this very street. Had he come rather surreptitiously
19		~~when they were~~ at night, to this very house?
20		It was a horrid system" she said. "I was
21		very fond of my father, she said. And yet I lied to him."|
22		"Its the meanness of this war" said Maggie. She
23		put her hand into the sock, twisted it round, &
24		dropped the sock into the basket. "Uncle

25		Abel shot off half a dozen *[fingers?]* & it didnt
26		matter. But this war. Starving…"
27		She stopped.
28		"But the Germans are extremely
29		prolific Maggie" said Renny "For every
30		baby we starve to death they bear another."
31		"And I shut the book" said Elvira

p. 120

1		folding herself up like a long legged bird & sinking on to the
2		floor, in front of the fire, & said to Creon…
3		~~Never heard of him" said Maggie~~ "Who's Creon?" said
4		Maggie.
5		|*The man you sat next to at dinner Maggie, two thousand*
6		*years ago*| ~~Oh~~ the man you sat next at dinner
7		Maggie, two thousand years ago:
8		Seven years ago, Maggie corrected her.
9		"Whats seven years, whats two thousand years? The
10		flicker of a lizards tongue. Time to come's what
11		matters; +he said+ time to come is all Cleopatra's needle, ~~&~~
12	& this, he	~~this — so~~ he said +to+ (I was dining with the
13	said	Wilkinsons +a night ago of+ last night) ~~is~~ +*[illeg.]*+ pointing to the ladies
14		painted like bright poppies & the footmen in
15		plush trousers, us but a rose leaf +~~laid~~+ on +the+ top of time
16		~~Paul Wilkinson is what they call a scientist~~
17		+Who said that — Paul?+
18		"Dining with the Wilkinsons wore furs?" said Maggie:
19		And the women painted?
20		"Blobs of red in the middle of their cleeks, &
21		~~black rings~~ +*[circles?]*+ round their eyes"
22		"I like painted faces" said Maggie: "if they do it
23		well"

24		"No, no," Eleanor exclaimed, No, Maggie; not
25		paint
26		~~If they~~ +If they use+ powder, why not paint?" ~~Ma~~ said
27		Maggie:
28		~~"Perhaps" said Eleanor~~
29		"Stars & Garters" said Elvira, "The order of
30		St Michael & St George hung round the neck of a
31		blue gibbon. Rings through the nose. And she
32		shall *[illeg.]* wherever she goes."

p. 121

1		"I suppose its largely habit +custom+" said Eleanor "When I was a
2		girl powder was allowed, but not paint. As
3		for cigarettes" she smiled, "my father would have
4		turned me out of the house if he'd caught me
5		smoking one. Whereas now Renny gives me a cigar…
6	†[given me a /	She threw away the stump of the cigar which she had
7	cigar?]†	finished. † "How things have changed" she said. "Even
8		in my life time!"
9		"Yes said Elvira: "Once you poured out tea, at a
10		~~round table~~ +at a round table+; & Crosby brought in the hot cakes; & the
11		kettle wouldnt boil, & Crosby said "I'll boil it on
12		the kitchen fire Miss; & Eleanor said, You cant
13		boil a wedding present on the kitchen fire or the whole
14		sanctity of marriage would be destroyed; &
15		took out her hair pin: whereupon Uncle Abel came in,
16		with horrid shiny knuckles on his ~~right~~ +left+ hand ~~whose~~ +which+ had
17	with which /	~~head~~ cut off the head of a blaspheming Turk &
18	he had	said — what did Uncle Abel say Eleanor?"
19		~~"Papa used to say~~ — Elvira loves the story of the
20		Pargiters" said Eleanor, she never grows up — well
21		Papa would say, what have you all been doing
22		today?

23	"And if you'd been walking down the Burlington
24	Arcade," said Maggie "or driving in a hansom
25	without shutting the flaps
26	Yes, that was the problem, said Eleanor.
27	"I lived in a very typical Victorian family" she
28	explained to Nicholas. He had drawn up
29	over the fire too. The log, which had still
30	some remains of tar on it, burnt brightly.
31	"That is very interesting" said Nicholas.
32	"You lied" said Renny +Maggie+ All women lied.

p. 122

1	"I was very fond of my father" said Eleanor. "But I lied."
2	She thought how she had never dared to tell him of her
3	about the her houses; in Rigby that she had lied about
4	Duffus the builder;
5	"Well he lied to you" said Maggie.
6	Eleanor suddenly +[illeg.]+ remembered Mira's letters, hidden away
7	in a corner of her father's drawer. Bobby had found
8	them when they were cleaning out the house. She
9	suddenly thought that Mira had lived somewhere
10	here, in Westminster. She thought her that perhaps
11	this had been the room where street, the house,
12	perhaps her father had visited her in this very room. What
13	was the address on the letters? She looked round
14	almost dazed for a moment. There was a picture of a
15	French hill side.
16	What make you of that, Maggie? she asked
17	Well, said Maggie — He never of he had a mistress —
18	would he have told you? He lied
19	"I never knew it" said Eleanor, flushing: "How did
20	you?"
21	"By the pricking of my thumbs" Elvira murmured
22	"By his manner +look+" said Maggie: "He used to come
23	to tea with mama. He gave me a necklace —

24		~~a very ugly necklace~~ — blue with gold shots. And
25		~~I liked him He was~~ she hesitated — I was
26		very fond of him
27		Every Victorian husband had a mistress" said
28		Nicholas. This is nothing to be ashamed of
29		~~he said~~
30		That was why we liked Uncle Abel, said Elvira,
31		jumping over the bonfire; up he went
32		*[whether?]* & all; coat tails flying: My
33		dear Abel, said my father, coming in from
34		the office, *[illeg.]* you with *[illeg.]*

p. 123

1	†round the /	your waistcoat? And the dear old boy washed
2	*[comb?]* to†	his hands at the pumps, & cut off † to his Times
3		Did you ever see her Eleanor?
4		~~I believe I did~~ once" said Eleanor. "A very vulgar
5		*[blowing?]* woman came to the house ~~as a~~ when he was
6		dying, to ask for money. Morris saw her."
7		It was a horrid system" she ~~said~~ added. ~~"Why~~
8		A daughter lying to her father; a father lying to his daughter.
9		~~Why she does one mind?" she asked Nicholas~~
10		I was very fond of him" ~~she said~~, & he of me.
11		~~"In the end, it was like brother & sister.~~ And yet he left
12		me to find it out after his death; from a
13		~~horrid~~ bundle of vulgar letters"
14		"My dear Eleanor, said Nicholas, what was I telling you?
15		~~We are not educated therefore~~ we can not
16		tell each other the truth. We are not educated.
17		We all ~~conceal~~ have things that we dare not say.
18		I myself" he smiled
19		~~That man~~ +Nicholas+ ought to be in prison, said Elvira; ~~she~~ +putting+
20		put her hand on his knee. "In the cell next Rose
21		~~Criminals~~ she ~~for asking~~ for breaking ~~the~~ Creon's

22	window, & he for..."
23	"I take good care not to break her window"
24	said Nicholas
25	~~And~~ Thats ~~the~~ what I hate about you" said
26	Elvira "A hole, corner, basement. Very bad for
27	the soul. Otherwise how much better in many
28	ways — No *[feathery? heathery?]* change comes over me, ~~with you~~
29	~~Nicholas, How I am, only a brain~~; To you I am
30	only — what?" she turned & looked up at him:
31	A brain a soul, Elvira, he said, taking her hand &
32	~~kissing~~ in his

p. 124

1	"Thats all damned rot" said Renny
2	It is a very great timetable *[sent only? sentencing?]* said Nicholas
3	but it may be a necessary stage in human education"
4	I look at it this way" he spread his hand again
5	& touched the first finger. As I have said, the
6	~~ase~~ & *[assess?]* again the medical, or priestlike air
7	which Eleanor had noticed. "As I have said,
8	the ~~age~~ nineteenth century was the age of
9	specialisation: +Renny & I+ I, made to make bridles, railways,
10	~~war~~ guns, cannons, aeroplanes, underground tubes.
11	Great ships with lavatories swimming baths & worthless
12	equipment complete ~~the~~ developed here" he touched
13	his forehead: "Magdalena, Eleanor & Elvira
14	in order to bear children +work for+ teach them train them
15	~~pour out tea~~ boil the kettle, +cook the cakes+, pour out tea
16	developed here" he put his hands to the back
17	of his neck. Therefore I can not marry Elvira:
18	Elvira can not marry me +complicating issue+ being ~~the~~
19	(but I will explain that later) ~~I say to~~ Elvira,
20	~~You are the most hysterical~~

21	~~We bore each other to death" said Elvira~~
22	~~Are~~ We ~~saying things that~~ +dont+ shock you Eleanor?" said
23	Maggie
24	+Oh+ no," said Eleanor. ~~After all~~ We are only saying
25	what we think. And the Victorian lady, she
26	added +was not so very ignorant+ visited among the poor. I was ~~not~~
27	allowed to walk down Bond Street alone," she
28	said, "but I knew the Levys. It was an
29	odd mixture. "I remember…" she saw
30	the house in Canning Place again, & the
31	drawing room of Abercorn Terrace. "But
32	why can't you marry?" she said to Nicholas.

p. 125

1		We should ~~bore~~ +kill+ each other ~~to death~~ said Elvira +we shd. die of exhaustion+ Think
2		Eleanor when the bell rings & theres Nicholas, come to
3		tea or to dinner, ~~or to spend the evening talking~~ I say to
4		myself thats very nice. And half way through the evening
5		I say to myself, I am dying: ~~I'm so bored I~~
6	If I couldnt /	~~dont know what to do with myself.~~ |*I walk up, down*
7	sleep I /	*the room. I touch little china ornaments. And I*
8	shd. die	*sink back into my chair again. It goes on & on & on:* |
9		~~with boredom~~: with the stale fumes of —" she
10		sniffed:
11		~~Male egotism~~ Nicholas interposed ~~"I talk about~~
12		~~myself. I cannot help it.~~ Every time I go to see Elvira
13		I say to myself on the doorstep, learn to think of
14		other people, Nicholas. Learn to live with your
15		whole being.
16		And I say to myself, every time I hear Nicholas on the
17		stair, Cease to be impatient, Elvira. Cease to be
18		sentimental. What is the date of the Battle of
19		Waterloo? ~~I say to myself.~~ & ~~for what reason is the~~

20	*[Insurance?]* act desirable? I say to myself?
21	But when we have been sitting for a very short time
22	together" said Nicholas, "I am talking about
23	myself; & Elvira is ~~fast asleep fast asleep~~ exhausted.
24	Nicholas is a very clever man" said Elvira
25	"That is to say I have developed a certain faculty here" he
26	touched his forehead "out of all proportion"
27	And Elvira is the most feminine of women.
28	~~What is a date? What is an accent?~~ |*If*
29	*Elvira reads a book she reads it with her*
30	*whole body: I read it with my* ~~*brain*~~ *whole brain*|
31	She thinks ~~with her~~ with the palms of her hands,
32	with the soles of her feet, she has eyes in the
33	nape of her neck. But you ought to cultivate
34	your brain Elvira.

p. 126

1	|~~"Thats how we go on," said Elvira~~ +*Thats how we go on:*+ +*And I say*+ *I hate clever men* + said Elvira+ *I*
2	~~*Of all deliberate frauds of all incomplete sterile*~~
3	*of all deliberate frauds* ~~*of all*~~ *the most intolerable,*
4	*the most dangerous, the most corrupt, the dullest*|
5	"But we are very fond of each other. We cannot
6	live with out each other. And yet —" he sighed
7	"Its all damned rot" said Renny.
8	Eleanor again thought she ought to go. And yet if
9	people wished to talk, if they tried to say what they
10	thought, if in spite of all the exaggerations, the
11	foolishness of their language, they ~~d~~ tried to ~~let~~ set
12	free ~~what~~ the secret within them. And it is not
13	necessarily a little foolish, confidence, she added:
14	it does not matter whether Nicolas ~~or~~ &
15	Elvira are in love or not; ~~no~~ but the state of
16	mind, the true balance, the living thing which
17	~~m~~ makes them themselves; if they try to communicate
18	that to me, that is generous; humane; & ~~we~~

19		I must ~~annih~~ annihilate little timid defences,
20		self protective warding off boarding up — she stopped.
21		"I was shocked for one second" she admitted. But only
22		just as a knife cuts the skin: he should be in
23		prison: But that is only the *[sentence?]* relationships
24	locates /	she thought: The State is on +*[illeg.]*+ the skin. It does
25	not fit /	We dont fit the state any longer. Otherwise
26	what is /	I should hate them both, she added. She looked at
27	under the /	~~hand~~ clasped her hands round her knees:
28	skin	I like Elvira: I like Nicholas, she said,
29		who ought to be in prison:
30		"The only objection +I can see+" said Maggie, answering her
31		husband, "is that if every man was like
32		Nicholas, ~~we~~ the human race would end.
33		Which it will do, one of these days," said Elvira, by

p. 127

1	nature's own heat, when the sun fails; when the flowers
2	wither; when the stars shrivel, when very old men & women
3	crawl to the ~~spring~~ well for water & it is *[illeg.]*; &
4	they sink ~~back~~ +down by the well side ~~in the~~ & the ~~frost~~ snow
5	covers them; & they sleep" she shut her eyes.
6	She suddenly opened them "When the Lord Chief Justice
7	puts you in prison, Nicholas, I should say to him:
8	I am only anticipating the natural decree, my lord duke,
9	which has brought you from the swamp to the Bench, and
10	sends us back to the ~~Earth~~ +swamp+. Nature, I should say
11	if I were defending Nicholas at the Bar or the House
12	of Lords, nature, gentlemen. She sank in to silence.
13	Its a +*[mere?]*+ fashion" said Renny. "Its not nature"
14	What do you think Maggie? said Eleanor.
15	"~~Oh that I dont~~ +wont+ think," said Maggie. Yet I think this

16	a good thing to ~~talk of if it helps people to~~ know their
17	~~own minds Yet~~ I often think of something
18	else when Nicholas is talks: I was thinking
19	how beautiful you looked Eleanor in your
20	dressing gown in the coal cellar; & Renny,
21	she looked at them "~~He is not beautiful~~ I
22	like watching him when people talk. He is so —
23	~~violent. And~~ she hesitated, "uncomplaining"
24	"And prejudiced" said Elvira. "And hide bound
25	And foreign. And English. And manly. And childish/
26	And — like an eagle with golden eggs, & a
27	rat in his claws for his young.
28	Yes said Nicholas. He is profoundly patriarchal.
29	Paternal. A lover of his kind: but he will grow,
30	he will expand. The rings of his soul —"
31	Elvira jumped up.
32	Thats it she cried. "Why I dont
33	marry Nicholas: Because that man ~~will be a bore~~
34	that man will preach: that man will

p. 128

1	veer about from house to house with his creed with his
2	art A B C D on foolscap paper. "I will now deliver
3	my message" that man will say: to a select
4	company of English aristocrats: of pale faced
5	little men from the universities. They'll whip out the fire,
6	tame down his words; following the master:
7	the master the humbug; the master the beadle the
8	preacher, the humbug." She gathered her clothes together
9	as she spoke; picking up gloves, hat, coat from different
10	chairs. The gramophone needle will stick, she said
11	to him: I'm sorry Maggie, I'm very *[sleepy?]*, I'm going home
12	to ~~plunge into the deep waters~~
13	Eleanor got up. Nicholas helped her on
14	with her coat.

15	We will all go together" he said. "As far as the
16	Underground station."
17	
18	"Its all damned rot" she imitated him. Now an
19	~~Englishman would tell a lie~~ He simply +says+ I feel this
20	he doesnt say, because it is right." Now an Englishman
21	wld. tell a lie.
22	And if I dont tell lies, said Renny, it is ~~simply~~
23	because Maggie breaks the water jug over my head if
24	I do. Not from any moral feeling: one hears
25	less bore her"
26	"It would be very dull, marriage to a man who ~~told~~
27	lies" said Maggie "[Johnny?] came to lunch" she added.
28	Thats my brother, at the War Office. He told lies
29	for two hours. So did I. Pretending to feel
30	what we didnt feel.
31	"He used to take us for rides on an elephant" said
32	Elvira: But he went to Judea. He married.
33	And the effort to bring up a family ~~on the~~
34	leading to success in his career landed him ~~in~~
35	~~the~~ it ~~I~~ *[illeg.]* it would not be more fine to say.

p. 129

1	numb him: sometimes he comes up to breathe, struggling horribly
2	Thats a nice picture he'll say to Maggie: like a fish on a hook
3	~~Good good good" said Maggie imitating him~~
4	~~No struggles today said Maggie" Talks, talks, talks…"~~ +It was talks
5	"Whereupon Renny says "This is all damned rot:" said Eleanor
6	"I dont pretend to ~~feel~~ have reasons for my feelings" said
7	Renny. He stabbed his knee with a paper knife.
8	I am sufficiently exucated to know that ~~if I give a~~
9	reason+s+ ~~I~~ +are+ almost invariably ~~tell a~~ lies ~~Thats all~~

10	~~You say to me Women ought to have votes I say no~~
11	|*All Renny is ~~women~~ Rose ought to have a vote"* said
12	*Maggie:*
13	*~~"I say at once No~~ [illeg.] I do not want women to*
14	*have votes. I ~~should~~ hate women to have votes. I|
15	What I say is, I think this is all damned rot."
16	
17	Now Renny ~~to~~ play us a tune & let us say: Three
18	blind mice, see how they run
19	Yes, said Eleanor, play us something before we go."
20	& we argue, we spend hours arguing: & the men
21	always give reasons for their feelings: but if they
22	simply said like Renny I want —
23	"Women to be slaves. ~~Thats~~ +which is that+ what I want
24	said Renny
25	Yes but they say "for their own good. To
26	~~influence~~ us: which takes up so much time" said
27	Eleanor. "And then we lie to them" she added.
28	And so it goes on.
29	When shall we be able to tell the truth
30	Nicholas? she said getting up.
31	In about three hundred years" said Nicholas

p. 130

1	But that is a very short time
2	Then we shall none of us be alive," said Eleanor, putting
3	on her coat.
4	"Not in the body" said Nicholas
5	But I'm afraid I dont believe in a life after death" said
6	Eleanor.
7	~~You~~ Nor do I" said Nicholas. But I do believe in
8	life here, on earth; ~~that goes on~~
9	Yes, but if I am not conscious of my life here on earth —
10	"'My life:' no: 'Our life,' yes. ~~We live in each other~~
11	~~We co or when we have learnt com~~ We

12	have only to educate ourselves; we have only to
13	learn to communicate…
14	Stop ~~stop stop~~ cried Elvira jumping up:
15	He had She put her hand over his mouth
16	~~You've talked just enough~~ That'll be your
17	death, Nicholas. A dead man marching. He'll
18	lecture" she said, hooking herself into her cloak
19	to a select company of English aristocrats &
20	pale faced prigs from Oxford & Cambridge: Follow me:
21	follow me: & they'll whip out their pens, &
22	they'll imitate his hands: touching first one finger
23	then another, Psychologically it is
24	Cease to laugh at me for once Elvira, said
25	Nicholas, holding her hand.
26	No, Nicholas, come to think of it, I'm not a
27	& *[upon?]* to our *[forms?]*" said Elvira "Where we
28	meditated in nature for two thousand years?
29	That was what
30	Yes I was going to say, said Maggie, getting up

p. 131

1	We may be slaves, Nicholas, but I think you're worse!
2	Slaves.
3	"We dont have |to kill people I'd rather on the whole|
4	have children: |though that's bad enough" she added.|
5	We're all slaves" said Renny. He got up & stood
6	balancing himself on the fender. Every one in this room is
7	~~is~~ a slave. Except perhaps Eleanor" he added
8	suddenly
9	She felt a glow of pleasure; as if she had said that he
10	liked her.
11	"Why do you say that?" she asked.
12	Because, he spoke very slowly. She hoped nobody
13	would interrupt him; happily Elvira was looking for
14	her gloves. "You're not shocked: he said: And thats rare,
15	in ~~an~~ a man or woman of —" he ~~looked at~~ stopped

16	Of ~~fifty eight~~" she added
17	Well people of that age +are+ generally ~~afraid~~ +shocked+
18	~~But~~ |Oh but ~~the Victorian lady~~" said Eleanor
19	~~visited the poor~~ It was a very queer ~~educa~~
20	bringing up, said Eleanor|
21	~~You see~~ +But+ I visited the poor" she said "~~One~~
22	~~were supposed to have a district do~~ +did+ that:
23	~~And~~ a queer kind of education, she reflected:
24	~~We werent allowed to~~
25	"Better than ~~none~~ +others+" he said
26	Oh no Renny" she replied I'm ashamed of my
27	ignorance. ~~I often dread talking to a clever man~~
28	I used to feel so stupid with my brothers'
29	friends. ~~I still do~~" I used to dread
30	being left alone in the room with them
31	Its a great pity, not being able to talk
32	about the things that interest them." Dont
33	you feel that Maggie?

p. 132

1	"No" said Renny "Maggie doesnt." ~~Maggie thinks~~
2	~~most~~ politics dull:
3	~~"I want attending"~~
4	"I think politics dull" said Maggie" ~~On the other hand~~
5	And ~~I think~~ talks deadly. Otherwise lots of
6	subjects seem to me interesting." And then I will
7	talk about them or I dont."
8	"And Elvira, said Renny, talks about everything whether
9	she knows about it or not."
10	I go to the public meetings said Elvira, "I write on a
11	slip of paper, Hammond on the Leg of a *[Central?]*
12	Asses — thats all Education is, ~~Eleanor~~ +Nicholas+" Or
13	|~~Oh~~ when I was a girl, said Eleanor, I used to feel
14	so ~~inferior~~ +ignorant compared with+ my brother's friends — & to|
15	~~so terribly~~ *[loves?]* or the New Testament

16	*[illeg.]*.
17	~~You~~ +But if+ in ~~our~~ +my+ time, we were taught that we
18	were ~~inferior~~ — that +what+ was the word: inferior to men"
19	said Eleanor. "Morally superior; mentally —
20	inferior. That was how I was brought up" she smiled.
21	"And you visited the poor, you had to be
22	back at five to pour out tea; & you never walked
23	down Bond Street alone" said Maggie:
24	It was the finest education in the world" said
25	Nicholas "Or I should say the finest
26	preparation for education in the world.
27	Not to be able to add up ones sums or to
28	write a letter in French?" ~~she asked~~ Eleanor
29	laughed
30	"~~You could not earn~~ money: you could not
31	~~go into~~ Not to earn money; nor to own
32	+To be+ ~~have a profession~~ +*[illeg.]*+; nor to be famous; nor to
33	Obliviously, inferiority, to be duped — not to

p. 133

1	powers: that was the finest education in the world +or *[proper?]*+ he said
2	Rather a depressing one, for some people. My sister Delia
3	didnt *[illeg.]* it at all; & Rose — well, Rose went to
4	prison. You & Elvira never knew that ~~bitterness~~
5	she said: the bitterness of the woman who feels all her
6	gifts wasting within her: who is compelled to
7	fritter her life away: ~~you created the [illeg.]~~
8	You never felt that it was a curse, being a woman.
9	You and Elvira never felt that did you *[illeg.]*"
10	If a man despises me, I dont ask him to ~~come to~~
11	dinner — ~~thats~~ all" said Maggie:
12	Ah but Maggie, said Elvira, ~~you dont offend~~ you dont

13	listen to what people say. Politics ~~politics al~~
14	bother about talks. Maggie looks at this round bowl:
15	Now I,
16	Oh, I dont complain of it
17	~~That is~~ "he was going on. But she halted in her
18	flow.
19	~~And~~ I've enjoyed my life immensely" she said.
20	~~Perhap~~ I didnt ~~want to~~ envy my brother at all, she
21	said. Poor little boys — sent off to school at
22	ten or eleven. +How+ Bobby hated it."
23	But now you must learn to smoke cigars" said
24	Nicholas.
25	|*Cigars by an Englishman" said ~~Elv~~ Maggie.*
26	*We do not need to undermine that, said*
27	*Nicholas.*|
28	But theyre expensive" said Eleanor
29	Thats the real problem, said Maggie. "If
30	Nicholas means by cigars, experience: for one
31	they experience is ~~costs~~ means money: &
32	then which experience?

p. 134

1	~~of a combination of experiences~~
2	Now that is, he said, that you have learnt to renounce, to
3	control, to ~~be silent~~, to be observant, to be despised —
4	to ~~have~~ +own+ nothing —
5	~~El Elvira interrupted, cried~~ Nicholas, +oh+ Nicholas
6	~~I will~~ Elvira cried
7	Please Elvira, let me finish one sentence, & then
8	~~not~~ I will be silent ~~Then we will all go~~ — he continued
9	~~Now that you have learnt to give up~~ which is the
10	finest education of all, now you must learn to enjoy.
11	Cigars, love, wine, knowledge, that's all," he said.
12	"Yes" said ~~Eleanor~~ Maggie. Thats all. But thats the
13	problem.
14	"To tell a woman that she's got to smoke cigars, said

15	Renny, when we're all going to be penniless, seems to me
16	~~poppycock" what Elvira calls~~ poppycock, as
17	Elv calls it:
18	Thats what his majestys footguards call it."
19	Elvira corrected him, the Kings Guard, you know,
20	the guard dies but never surrenders; & the old
21	goat always walks with *[illeg.]* feet; his
22	horns wreathed with violets: ~~thats life~~ that's
23	real life" she ~~said~~ added, spinning round on her
24	toes.
25	~~"We've got to pay~~ Yes, how are we going to
26	have experience, if thats what Nicholas means,
27	when we haven't any money?" said Eleanor.
28	And which experiences?" said Maggie
29	"I am not allowed to speak" said Nicholas: so
30	that I can only reply, in one word: all
31	experience; +but+ mixed." That is your problem,"
32	he said to Eleanor. "Now we will go. Now it is
33	very late."
34	The only good result of the war, said Maggie

p. 135

1	looking at her watch, is that theyve stopped the church bells
2	so that we dont know the time. My watch is always
3	wrong: Rennys is broken
4	And a mouse ran up the kitchen clock" said
5	Elvira, Hickery dickery dickery dock. Play us a
6	tune Renny before we go. Let us say Three Blind
7	Mice ~~in the lydian mode~~." see how they run"
8	in
9	"Yes do play" said Eleanor. He was very musical
10	she knew.
11	"I should wake the children" he said.
12	"Dreaming of guns" said Elvira
13	But how much love?" said Maggie. "Suppose

14		we do this, after the war, to educate ourselves; how
15		much love ~~would you all advise~~ Eleanor? You see,
16		my mother, being always married to the same man,
17		hadn't any ~~experience~~ +love+. Not like men, I mean, which is
18		a pity (look at Rose for example.) But
19		then men have too much. ~~Cant let little girls~~
20		Its silly: to say experience +*[illeg.]*+, not being able to let a
21		girl walk about the streets. |*I shall have to keep a*
22		*~~maid, or go with~~ Myself, when she's*
23		*~~& experience. I shall~~ have to keep a maid*
24		*When my daughter goes to school*| have to keep
25		a maid
26		"Yes said Elvira, I once lunched with Bobby in a
27	City	chophouse ~~in the city~~: & I said to myself:
28		If I ate, drank what these good fellows eat &
29		drink (the bill came to 18/6 counting the tip)
30		I should be the scourge of the neighbourhood
31		chefs. Steak, cheese, butter; with fine old
32		brandy & a glass of stout every day of my
33		life Maggie: Naturally ~~the~~ Aunt

p. 136

1	Isabella spent the final ~~months~~ days of the year sitting in the
2	drawing room waiting for the maid lest she should be —
3	what was the word, assaulted, accosted, insulted
4	by the ~~male~~ gentlemen in hats & sponge bag trousers.
5	~~That's~~ [Measure for Measure] ~~An~~ But what
6	would comedy be without *[chastity? charity?]*, or tragedy for the
7	for the matter of that?"
8	Things are much better than they used to be" said
9	Eleanor. When I was a girl she but
10	~~but~~ its too late, ~~its too late~~ +to go *[illeg.]*+ she protested

11		~~Its a very difficult problem.~~ ~~th~~ How will you
12		educate your daughter Renny? she asked. "Send her
13		college?"
14		To be educated like a man?" said Renny
15		The objection to that is, said Elvira, that
16		there isnt enough land to go round unless of
17		course they came to an agreement: men fought
18		for five years: then women for five years: then they
19		parcelled out their possessions, & started fighting
20		again." Or they might discover a new race to conquer
21		|No, said Maggie +but more races having already been
		[illeg.]+ we don't believe in Oxford &
22		Cambridge|
23	We shall have /	~~Its very difficult"~~ said Maggie You cant keep
24	to send her /	~~children at home~~, because they're such a nuisance, at
		home
25	[illeg.]	~~But where are you to send them? I dont~~
26		~~believe in Oxford & Cambridge — not for~~ but
27		where?
28		Boys have a very good time at Oxford & Cambridge"
29		said Eleanor, if you can afford it."
30		And they get all sorts of prizes, fellowships," said
		[Maggie? Renny?]
31	Fielding came /	~~said Elvira~~ "Thats the worst of Oxford,
32	before Scott /	Cambridge: ~~she added~~
33	(the other ones /	Its going to be a great problem" said
34	row)	Eleanor. ~~I shall~~ Its a fine night

p. 137

1	She ~~was~~ looked out of the window.
2	Its a perfectly fine night" she said. I shall
3	walk.
4	They
5	I was once walking along a street, & ~~by mistake~~ I went
	in to a

6		swoon, / there was an old man in a Gown, ~~saying~~ +& he said+
7		Fielding came before Scott; & he had been saying that
8	30th Jan	for fifteen years."

p. 138

1	18th Feb	No, no, no, exclaimed Elvira: I dont want to eat in
2		a chophouse, eat rump steak, & then wash
3		my hands like Bobby, in a desolate great hall
4		~~club~~ full of bald headed men, wearing stars &
5		garters; & then for all women to cry here comes a
6		woman, & hide their little bags; & then
7		*[illeg.]* or Sophocles year in year out.
8		Fielding came before Scott, all that rot, its a
9		beautiful education, a man making ~~all that~~
10		money, & getting diamonds *[illeg.]* to
11		wave this pocket handkerchief, from particular
12		which one forces off pop guns. I'm for the
13		British institution of chastity.
14		She went to the piano.
15		"No no, no" said Maggie stopping her. "You'll
16		wake the children."
17		One of these days I shall suffocate your children,
18		while they sleep" Elvira exclaimed "dreaming of
19		guns."
20		"But the question of education" said Eleanor. "
21		Its going to be very interesting, after the war…"
22		~~My dear Eleanor~~ after the war, said Renny
23		†we shall merely have to make money† there'll be
24		no education †
25		"It cant be worse than it was before the war"
26		said Maggie. ~~She always contradicted her~~
27		~~husband.~~ After all it was the educated people
28		who made the war."
29		"Thats what I say" said Eleanor "We have got

p.139

1. learn to educate ourselves differently — as Nicholas says."
2. She looked at him. He shrugged his shoulders.
3. "I speak no more" he said. "Elvira will mount the
4. pulpit now."
5. Yes, said Elvira, putting her arm round his
6. shoulder, we will burn down Oxford, Cambridge
7. after the war; & then we will have real education:
8. beautiful +impermanent+ homes built of combustible wood, by
9. running streams, in meadows, where nobody shall
10. teach under penalty of death; but now & again
11. somebody shall sit under a flowering tree & ~~tea~~
12. tell us how ~~not to make money, but~~ to love &
13. ~~oh beauty~~ truth +& beauty+, cats & dogs, flowers all the
14. larks of the north wind, including even those deplorable
15. creations, those basest, those ignoble, those most
16. deplorable of all created things, Nicholas and Elvira.
17. And ~~But~~ there ~~must~~ +will+ be no degrees; no prizes: & no
18. pop guns."
19. I cant see my brother Edward agreeing to +burn down Oxford+ that" said
20. Eleanor.
21. But we will put Edward under a ~~large~~ bell
22. shaped dome of ~~gl~~ smoked glass where ~~he will~~
23. breathing the stale fumes of exhausted Greek & +he will+ die of
24. it." said Elvira. Except that Edward is dead
25. already," she added. ~~"So; [John?] thats the~~
26. without knowing it. "*[They? My?]* wasted life he said to me,
27. taking down his translation of Sophocles ~~into~~ —"
28. ~~chatter, chatter, chatter +you've [bathed?] [such?]+ said Maggie.~~
29. Poor old Edward" said Maggie
30. It wasnt their fault," she added.
31. No, said Eleanor: thats what I felt. They

p. 140

1 drifted & drifted" she said buttoning up her coat. "It
2 all seemed so safe. It seemed so nice, on the
3 surface. And then suddenly." She saw again
4 the terrace, & the downs like blue mounds
5 across the meadows & heard Alice the maid
6 saying that the postman said the soldiers were
7 guarding the railways with fixed bayonets.
8 She turned to go
9   "Who had this house before you did?" she
10 asked Renny, as they went downstairs.
11 It was a ~~common~~ lodging house" he said; A
12 ~~how~~ thats why we got it cheap. It was not
13 ~~home of~~ what they call 'respectable'."
14 "I was wondering if it was the house
15 my father used to come to" she said, "It was
16 this street; it may have been this very house,
17 where Mira lived."
18 She paused, looking round her. Now there were
19 pictures; there ~~were~~ was a hoop in the hall.
20 They went out into the street. The door shut
21 behind them. They walked in the direction of
22 Victoria Street. She still felt as if the wine
23 ~~talking~~: she felt that ~~the bodies of~~ Renny
24 Maggie, were ~~was~~ still with them: she felt a
25 physically the presence of oddly shaped objects,
26 peoples minds, quite real, half hidden, but
27 bulky, & the presence excited her: she wanted to
28 know more, more about them; she felt
29 that she had encountered something ~~real solid~~
30 hard, but half hidden. She wanted to go on
31 talking. But now they had reached the

p. 141

1 broad, open street. ~~Taxi~~ The traffic was passing
2 much as usual; there might never have been a raid

3	~~she stopped, where~~ when ~~she was~~ they reached the corner
4	she stopped. It was here that she would get
5	her ~~b~~ omnibus.
6	"And you? she said to Nicholas. She
7	expected that he & Elvira would walk on together,
8	leaving her.
9	I shall wait for my bus here" she added.
10	Then good night Eleanor, good night Nicholas"
11	said Elvira. She waved her hand, & ~~walked~~
12	~~off,~~ dismissing them
13	Eleanor looked at Nicholas.
14	"She ~~does not want~~ likes to be alone" he
15	said, understanding ~~Eleanor's~~ that Eleanor expected
16	them to leave her. He spoke ~~as a matter~~
17	as if it were a matter of course. Yet for some *[reason?]*
18	Eleanor felt a great feeling of pity — for him? for
19	Elvira? It was for herself too, she felt, &
20	the great omnibus slowed down, came to a
21	halt. She waved to Nicholas, who stood
22	with his hat in his hands, a queer looking man,
23	but there was something impressive about him.
24	He was so ~~big~~ +tall & now+ so silent

p. 142

1	She figured her father slinking in, ~~& t~~ rather guiltily,
2	& the woman with the tousled fair hair
3	hanging over the bannister.
4	Good night Renny she said shaking him by the hand.
5	
6	~~It excited~~ Come & see me, she said; ~~wishing~~ *[impact?]*
7	as her bus swanned to a halt in front of them.
8	She got on, & waved, rather absurdly, to Nicholas,
9	who stood on the pavement with his hat raised.
10	There was something impressive about him. He
11	looked tall & silent; +but+ she felt that she knew him.

"Unacted Part[s]": Subjunctive Science-Fictional Identities in Virginia Woolf's Later Work
Catriona Livingstone

Writing in her diary on Sunday, September 8 1918, Virginia Woolf recorded her memories of the preceding week:

> I remember lying on the side of a hollow, waiting for L. to come & mushroom, & seeing a red hare loping up the side & thinking suddenly "This is Earth life". I seemed to see how earthy it all was, & I myself an evolved kind of hare; as if a moon visitor saw me. A good life it is, at such moments; but I can't recapture the queer impression I had of its being earth life seen from the moon. (*D1* 190)

I would like to suggest that this passage is one of multiple moments across Woolf's oeuvre in which her writing shifts into the realms of science fiction. Not only does the mention of a "moon visitor" immediately recall novels such as H. G. Wells's *The First Men in the Moon*, but the passage can easily be aligned with the foundational definition of science fiction by the influential critic Darko Suvin: that science fiction is that genre which produces "cognitive estrangement" (Suvin 4). In this remembered scene, already distanced in being associated with an emotional state that cannot be recaptured, Woolf projects herself imaginatively into an even more distanced perspective: that of the "moon visitor" observing the earth from another world. From this distance, she gains an estranged view of her surroundings, which lose their particularity and become part of a generalized "Earth life." The triangulation of perspective, with the version of Woolf remembering the scene, the version lying in the hollow, and the imagined perspective of the "moon visitor" being placed in relation to one another, has the effect of defamiliarizing Woolf's everyday life, rendering it "queer".[1] Crucially, moreover, this triangulation allows Woolf to adopt an alternative identity; shifting from the human world to the animal, she becomes "an evolved kind of hare," thus taking on for a moment the imagined animal identity of the characters in her fantastical story "Lappin and Lapinova" (*CSF* 351-61). Holly Henry argues that, in this passage, Woolf draws upon contemporary astronomical depictions of the Earth as viewed from the Moon (73-4). Here, then, Woolf is applying a science-fictional perspective in order to open up a new, counterfactual form of identity.

This essay is concerned with tracing multiple moments in which Woolf offers fragmentary glimpses of a science-fictional world and, in doing so, provides an estranged view upon the world of reality. I demonstrate that, within these fragmentary

---

[1] It should be noted that when this diary entry was written the word "queer" did not have the associations with identity politics that it has today; Woolf's use of the term refers to something strange or odd, thus tallying with Suvin's definition of science fiction as characterized by "estrangement."

glimpses, alternative modes of being become, for a moment, possible. Over the past twenty years, there has been a significant amount of work demonstrating Woolf's interest in science, and her deployment of scientific concepts in her works.[2] Despite the evident range of Woolf's scientific engagement, however, Woolf scholars are still inclined to view science as a peripheral aspect of her works, certainly not as central to our understanding of her as, for example, feminism, left-wing politics, or queerness. This paper conducts an experimental reading of her works, a reading that considers what it might mean to read Woolf's work through a science-fictional lens. Of course, it is possible for a text to engage with scientific concepts without being science fictional (equally, there are many works of science fiction which contain little scientific content). However, as this essay demonstrates, Woolf's works employ scientific concepts in order to create the estranging perspectives that are characteristic of science fiction. To read them through a science-fictional lens is thus to reveal the centrality of science to Woolf's narrative technique.

In conducting this reading, I am by no means suggesting that we should view "science fiction" as a classificatory label to be stuck upon Woolf's works, or a generic box in which to squeeze them. Throughout her oeuvre, Woolf adopts and experiments with a multiplicity of genres: the biography, the Bildungsroman, the polemic, the family saga, and many others. This paper argues that we should view science fiction as one of those genres, and the science fiction writer as one of Woolf's multiple writerly identities. Drawing upon Frederic Jameson's concept of a utopian hermeneutic, it suggests that science fiction can function as a hermeneutic lens upon her works, one which enables new and illuminating readings. In particular, it demonstrates that such a lens allows us to read her novels in relation to a new set of texts, and to elucidate more fully how her writing is oriented towards the future. Ultimately, it identifies a form of utopianism in Woolf's writing that is located not in programmatic, fully-realized visions of the future, but within her depiction of latent, unexplored aspects of her characters' identities—the lives they might have led, the paths they might have taken—aspects which point the way towards an improved way of being. Her works exhibit what might be called a subjunctive utopianism, one that resides in the might-have-been, in the might-be: a utopianism that runs counter to narrative and emerges only in glimpses.[3]

---

[2] See Michael Whitworth, *Einstein's Wake*; Rachel Crossland, *Modernist Physics*; Christina Alt, *Virginia Woolf and the Study of Nature*; Holly Henry, *Virginia Woolf and the Discourse of Science*.

[3] The focus in this essay is on Woolf's later novels, for the reason that they have a more pronounced utopian character than her earlier works, and are consequently particularly suited to a science-fictional reading. However, as the examples from *The Voyage Out* and "On Being Ill" demonstrate, moments of estrangement occur throughout Woolf's oeuvre, and further work is needed to determine if the texts not featured in this essay can also be read through a science-fictional lens. The animal realities explored in "Kew Gardens," "Lappin and Lapinova," and *Flush* seem particularly ripe for such an analysis, as do Septimus's visions of an alive, communicative natural world in *Mrs Dalloway*.

To place Woolf's writing in relation to science fiction at all may seem counterintuitive, even absurd. After all, Woolf's novels do not adopt obviously science-fictional premises: space travel to alien worlds, for example, or time travel to futuristic societies, or transformative new inventions. Clearly, to consider Woolf as a science fiction writer requires a reconsideration of the boundaries of the genre. However, even here qualifications arise. Woolf does not depict space travel, but in *Flush* she does transport the reader to the very alien consciousness of the dog. She does not attempt to represent a future society, but what is *Orlando* if not a time-traveller? And, finally, while she may not introduce her readers to an entirely new invention (as in, for example, Wells's *The Invisible Man*), critics are becoming increasingly alert to the way in which she engages with radio as a transformative technology that has the potential to remove the boundaries between individuals.[4] As with all acts of generic negotiation, to read Woolf science-fictionally must be part of a complementary process, in which we at once recognize the affinities between her work and other examples of the genre, and extend the boundaries of the genre to encompass her own particular contribution.

I am not the first to draw a connection between Woolf and science fiction. Holly Henry and Charles M. Tung have both identified commonalities between Woolf's preoccupation with vast, inhuman timescales, and the science fiction of Olaf Stapledon. Tung connects Woolf's "recurrent interest in the distant view" with Stapledon's cosmic visions (525). In her book on Woolf and astronomy, meanwhile, Henry identifies a common pacifist, utopian orientation in *The Years* and Stapledon's *Star Maker* (137). Elsewhere, critics have identified elements in her works that have resonances with political utopianism (rather than utopian fiction as such); Youngjoo Son, for example, characterizes Woolf's representations of space as utopian. More generally, as the publication of Alice Reeve-Tucker and Nathan Waddell's edited collection *Utopianism, Modernism, and Literature in the Twentieth Century* indicates, critics are becoming more alert to the ways in which "twentieth-century experimental writers thought u-topically" (6). In reading Woolf's works as a form of utopian science fiction, I am building on these critics' insights into the commonalities between modernism, science fiction, and utopianism.

At the same time, my reading counters the pervasive narrative of Woolf's later works as oriented towards a future of personal and national destruction. Readings of *Between the Acts*, in particular, often contain the suggestion that any nascent utopianism in this novel is fatally compromised by Woolf's consciousness of the political realities of the war and the ascendancy of fascism. Such readings frequently center on Woolf's depiction of identity, concluding that, while Woolf does gesture toward a conception of self as multiple and expansive, identified with and dispersed among the community, she is held back in this endeavor by the need to shore up liberal individualism against the encroachments of a fascist, organicist model of nationhood. Ben Harker, for example, argues that the "hesitant collectivism of Woolf's last novel

---

[4] See especially Michele Pridmore-Brown, "1939-40: Of Virginia Woolf, Gramophones, and Fascism."

ultimately yields to the overpowering barbarism of contemporary history" (451), while Steve Ellis argues that Woolf's sense of the "irreconcilable divisions" between "the collective and the individual" lead her to an "impasse" (189). My reading, in contrast, reveals the ways in which Woolf's construction of identity in her later works evades the deterministic narrative of impending war. By exploring subjunctive forms of identity—the lives that might have been led—she draws attention to the fact that the trajectory of contemporary history is not the only possible reality. As J. Ashley Foster argues in relation to *Between the Acts*, "Different potential historical trajectories from the one that was taken—the possibilities of what might have been—silhouette the text" (65). I suggest that it is this attentiveness to "what might have been" that produces the novel's utopian impulse—that points the reader toward what might be: an improved world beyond the war.

In 2011, *The Guardian* newspaper asked various science fiction writers to discuss "their favourite novel or author in the genre." Ursula K. Le Guin, widely regarded as a central figure within feminist utopian science fiction, selected Virginia Woolf. Though part of the point of her choice was that science fiction writers could learn much from reading "outside the genre," she nevertheless identified Woolf as a "model" for sci-fi. Her short article discusses *Orlando* and *Flush*, identifying in both texts an interest in otherness—in the alien—that she relates to science fiction. The scene in *Orlando* in which the Elizabethan Thames freezes over, she comments, is one of "marvellous strangeness," which conveys "the authentic thrill of being taken *absolutely elsewhere*." Le Guin's comments on *Flush* are worth quoting in full:

> In her novel *Flush*, Woolf gets inside a dog's mind, that is, a nonhuman brain, an alien mentality—very science-fictional if you look at it that way. Again what I learned was the power of accurate, vivid, highly selected detail. I imagine Woolf looking down at her dog asleep beside the ratty armchair she wrote in and thinking *what are your dreams?* and listening ... sniffing the wind ... after the rabbit, out on the hills, in the dog's timeless world.
> Useful stuff, for those who like to see through eyes other than our own.
> ("The stars of modern SF")

For Le Guin, Woolf's writing is science fictional in its occupation of otherness, in its vivid evocation of alternate, alien perspectives.

The history of science fiction has been traced as far back as ancient texts like Lucian of Samosata's *True Story* (Swanson). However, the taxonomy of the genre has largely been undertaken retrospectively. As John Rieder argues, the genre was "somewhat inchoate" until the late 1930s, when it began to be self-consciously defined in American magazines. Rieder notes that many writers associated with science fiction in the early twentieth century, including Wells, also wrote in other genres (30). From this point of view, Le Guin's identification of Woolf as an influence on her own science fiction ought to be taken seriously as another retrospective negotiation of the genre. Another artist who has responded to the science-fictional aspects of Woolf's novels is Wayne McGregor, a choreographer whose work often employs scientific themes. The second section of McGregor's 2015 ballet, *Woolf Works*, adapted *Orlando* as a time-travel fantasy, using lasers and futuristic costumes. McGregor, like Le Guin, responded to the representation of alterity in Woolf's works, commenting that he felt the "alien aesthetic" of the piece chimed with Woolf's interest "in science fiction, in astronomy, and things other" ("Why Virginia Woolf?"). The fact that the science-fictional aspects of Woolf's works have become part of her artistic legacy suggests that they deserve more critical attention than they have hitherto received.

Le Guin's focus on the alien and the "elsewhere" in drawing a connection between Woolf and science fiction is in keeping with critical definitions of the genre, particularly Darko Suvin's concept of "cognitive estrangement" (4). Though aspects of Suvin's description (particularly the signification and tenability of the word "cognitive") have been contested by later theorists, his idea of "estrangement" remains key to critical understanding of the genre.[5] For Suvin, and for theorists such as Tom Moylan who have extended his work, estrangement has a critical, and hence a political, function. By estranging the reader from the society they ordinarily inhabit, science fiction facilitates a critical view of that society. Moylan introduces the useful concept of "triangulation" to discuss this critical process; there is, he argues, "an enlightening triangulation between an individual reader's limited perspective, the estranged re-vision of the alternative world on the pages of a given text, and the actually existing society" (xvii).

The process of taking the reader to an alternate world which then provides a critical perspective on the actually existing world is one that Woolf employs at several points in her oeuvre. One chapter of *The Voyage Out* begins with a description of the ship, the *Euphrosyne*, viewed from the decks of nearby ships. In this view "From a distance," the Dalloways, Ambroses and Vinraces shrink to "insect-like figures," while the learned Mr. Pepper is "mistaken for a cormorant, and then, as unjustly, transformed into a cow" (*VO* 85). The shift from "mistaken" to "transformed" is notable here; there seems to be a transfer of epistemological authority from the *Euphrosyne* to the inhabitants of the passing ship, who provide a belittling, estranging perspective on the main characters of the novel. *The Voyage Out* can be read as an examination of the way in which the mores of British imperialist society become so ingrained within the psyche that they persist even after the individual has become physically detached from Britain; the alien worlds of the nearby ships, however, reveal the actual insignificance of those mores.

Eventually, the *Euphrosyne* is reduced to "a few beads of light," providing the passing ships with "an emblem of the loneliness of human life" (*VO* 85). Given that loneliness, and the failures of understanding between people in physical and social proximity to one another, is a central theme in *The Voyage Out*, the reduction of the characters to an "emblem" of this quality suggests that the passing ships provide an

---

[5] Patrick Parrinder, for example, has argued that the term "cognitive estrangement" is overly prescriptive, used by Suvin to exclude the fantastic from science fiction.

estranging perspective on the narrative as a whole, one which at once reveals the universal applicability of its themes, and the relative insignificance of its action. A similar estrangement occurs in Olaf Stapledon's later science fiction novel, *Star Maker* (1937), a novel that Woolf read and admired (Crossley 29). This novel begins on Earth, but the narrative lens zooms outwards in sequential steps, taking in the galaxy, the cosmos, and eventually other universes. Through these shifts in perspective, the political and existential struggles of the inhabitants of 1930s Europe are at once recognized as modeling a multitude of similar struggles that occur throughout time and space, and are dismissed as insignificant in relation to the vast spiritual vicissitudes of entire galaxies and universes. In both novels, the addition of a triangulating lens performs an objectivizing, contextualizing function.

Woolf's most elaborate exploration of the estranging effects of an alien perspective is, perhaps, her essay of 1926, "On Being Ill." In this essay, illness becomes an alternate reality, a defamiliarizing, critical perspective that exposes the activities of "the army of the upright"—"to communicate, to civilise, to share, to cultivate the desert, educate the native"—as being a mere "genial pretence" (321). The ill person, moreover, is thrust forward into the science-fictional world of the distant future, in which "the heat will leave the world [...] ice will lie thick upon factory and engine; the sun will go out" (*E4* 322). This description is once again reminiscent of Stapledon's vast astronomical timescales, and serves a similar function: to reveal the futility of the constant activity of industrialized cultures. From this rather bleak perspective, however, a utopian glimpse of the future emerges. The ill person, removed from the demands for action and the restricted perspectives of the world of the well, is able to engage in the task of "Heaven-making," and can, through their own imaginative flights of fancy,

> revert again to earth and choose, since there is no harm in choosing, to live over and over, now as man, now as woman, as sea-captain, court lady, Emperor, farmer's wife, in splendid cities and on remote moors, in Teheran and Tunbridge Wells, at the time of Pericles or Arthur, Charlemagne, or George the Fourth – to live and live till we have lived out those embryo lives which attend about us in early youth and have been consumed by that tyrannical "I," who has conquered so far as this world is concerned but shall not, if wishing can alter it, usurp Heaven too, and condemn us, who have played our parts here as William or Amelia, to remain William or Amelia for ever. (*E4* 323)

Within the utopian "Heaven" imagined by the ill person, the individual is able to encompass many selves, and occupy multiple times, places and genders. This alternate reality, moreover, provides a critical view upon ordinary definitions of identity. The demand to play a single part in society as "William" or "Amelia," to live a life in which the limitless potential of "early youth"—the multiple paths that might have been taken—is eventually foreclosed by the requirement to live as a single

"I," is revealed to be inessential. The essay gestures forwards towards a more plural understanding of identity. The science-fictional, triangulating depiction of illness thus allows room for utopian glimpses, glimpses that center on the emergence of unexplored aspects of identity: the latent "embryo lives" that exist within the individual self.

It is notable, moreover, that Woolf uses the word "embryo" to refer to these latent aspects of the self. Woolf could just as easily have used the word "embryonic" here, a word which, despite its obvious etymological connection to "embryo," is essentially a dead metaphor (its literal meaning, "Of or relating to an embryo," having largely been obscured, within non-scientific contexts, by its figurative meaning, "That is at an early stage of development; rudimentary; incipient" [*Embryonic, adj.*]). The fact that Woolf uses "embryo" instead implies that she intends the scientific resonances of the word to be activated for her readers. In the scientific discourse of the period, embryos were associated with plasticity and with a lack of specialization. A series of experiments on newt embryos by Hans Spemann and Hilde Mangold demonstrated that early embryonic cells were unspecialized; that they could be grafted onto another embryo, or that the embryo could be split in half and made to form two separate individuals (Keller 6). These experiments, part of Spemann's work on embryonic induction, featured prominently in the popular biology of the period; in 1925, the year before "On Being Ill" was published, Julian Huxley gave a popular series of radio broadcasts on biology entitled "The Stream of Life," in which he discussed Spemann and Mangold's experiments. Huxley noted that early embryos were "very plastic," and contrasted this plasticity to the later process whereby the cells of the embryo became specialized ("The Stream of Life"). Woolf's evocation of "embryo lives" as a means of escape from being only "William or Amelia" resonates with this scientific conception of the embryo as a site of potentiality: as a state prior to specialization. She suggests that an imaginative reversion to the embryo might be a way to resist the social requirement to occupy a single identity. In the manner of a science fiction writer, she employs a defamiliarizing scientific concept (the embryo) to transport her reader to a counterfactual, utopian realm ("Heaven"), a realm in which an individual can take on multiple identities.

To characterize Woolf's writing as utopian is not to imply that she constructs fully realized models of a future society, in the manner of Thomas More. In fact, the tendency of modern utopian studies has been to move away from the literary utopia as a genre, and toward the analysis of texts from multiple genres which contain utopian elements. Following Ernst Bloch, Karl Mannheim and Frederic Jameson, Marxist critics have tended, in Károly Pintér's terms, to

> employ "utopia" as a hermeneutical method to uncover layers of contemporary social-cultural critique from literary texts in general, and from modern science fiction in particular, while remaining relatively uninterested in literary utopias. (6)

In *Archaeologies of the Future*, Jameson identifies two "lines of descendency" from Thomas More's *Utopia*: the "systemic" utopia which "aims at founding a whole new society" characterized by "closure," and "an obscure yet omnipresent Utopian impulse finding its way to the surface in a variety of covert expressions and practices" (3-4). The lack of a fully-articulated utopian state in Woolf's works thus does not prevent us from reading them as utopian texts, nor from relating them to the utopian aspects of science-fictional texts which themselves are often fragmentary glimpses rather than programmatic visions. The fragmentary glimpse in "On Being Ill" of a "Heaven" in which the individual can occupy multiple identities is, moreover, entirely in keeping with Carl Freedman's characterization of Ernst Bloch's utopianism: as involving a "dialectic of immanence and transcendence" (Freedman 74). For Bloch, utopias exist "in the dimension of futurity," but at the same time have an existence within the present self, as "the object of *hope*, of our deepest and most radical longings": "utopia, which in one sense is always *elsewhere*, always escaping our actual horizons, is in another and no less important sense inscribed in the innermost core of our being" (Freedman 74). Because Blochian utopias are at once aspects of the present and of the future, Freedman argues, "utopian plenitude can be apprehended only in the most elusive and fragmentary anticipations […] utopia emerges only in the teeth, as it were, of the mundane" (77). The applications of such a scheme to modernist literature are noted by Freedman, who argues that Joyce's *A Portrait of the Artist as a Young Man* is a utopia in the Blochian sense, because its depiction of both Stephen's life and his society is structured by "the fractional anticipations" of the future works of art that Stephen will create (78-9). "On Being Ill," with its portrait of an ill person temporarily freed from the restrictions of modern social life, able to engage in "elusive and fragmentary anticipations" (Freedman 77) of a more expansive form of identity while at the same time aware of the demands of mundane existence and of the "tyrannical 'I'," is another modernist text in which the utopian elements are at once immanent (the product of an actually existing imaginative experience and desire) and transcendent (located within another space, "Heaven," that is *not* here).

Another defining feature of Bloch's utopias, according to Freedman, is that they are fundamentally collective in nature:

> Utopian hope or longing, in other words, possesses an inherently collective character and at bottom has nothing in common with individualist impulses like greed. Indeed, it is only the dimension of collectivity that guarantees the future-orientedness of utopia. (74)

This description of a collectively formed utopian longing is an apt characterization of the later sections of Woolf's last two novels, *The Years* and *Between the Acts*. In both novels, characters gather together as a community—for a party in *The Years*, and to watch the pageant in *Between the Acts*—and experience glimpses of an improved future and a more unified form of community. Eleanor in *The Years* catches sight momentarily of "another life," less "broken" than this one (385), while the gramophone in *Between the Acts* gestures towards a "Unity" that must be gathered out of "Dispersity" (144). These glimpses are, however, fleeting, fragmentary, and continually interrupted. In *Between the Acts*, the vicar's expression of unity is interrupted when aeroplanes fly overhead (138). In *The Years*, Eleanor repeatedly expects Nicholas to give a speech in which he will express what she has been thinking, but he is interrupted and never manages to complete it. The characters' utopian glimpses emerge, in Freedman's terms, "in the teeth [...] of the mundane" (77), struggling against its demands and distractions. Moreover, like Bloch's utopias, they straddle present and future. "There must be another life, here and now," thinks Eleanor in *The Years*. "This is too short, too broken. We know nothing, even about ourselves. We're only just beginning, she thought, to understand, here and there" (385). This passage invokes a more complete reality that is at once in the future (it is now "only just beginning") and in the present ("here and now"). Similarly, in *Between the Acts* the unity of the audience of the pageant is at once part of a potential, projected future ("Surely, we should unite?" asks the Reverend G. W. Streatfield [138]), and a feature of present existence ("We live in others," declares Lucy Swithin [51]). It is the ambiguous temporality of Woolf's utopian glimpses that provides their radical impetus; they erupt into the present community, tugging it towards the future.

The utopian longings of *The Years* and *Between the Acts* center on their depictions of identity. In *The Years*, Eleanor and Nicholas's repeated question, "if we do not know ourselves, how then can we make religions, laws, that [...] fit" (254), suggests that any future, improved society must be predicated upon a fuller understanding of identity. In the party scene, the characters begin to form such an understanding, with Eleanor realizing that "My life's been other people's lives [...] my father's; Morris's; my friends' lives; Nicholas's ..." (*TY* 331), and North recognizing the necessity of being "the bubble and the stream, the stream and the bubble—myself and the world together" (369). Any utopian future, such passages imply, must center on a utopian conception of selfhood, in which the radical multiplicity of the self, and its continuity with those around it, is recognized. In *Between the Acts*, meanwhile, a utopian conception of identity can be traced in the concept of the "unacted part" (110). Lucy Swithin, presumably inspired by the pageant's depiction of community and by the fluidity of identity implied by its actors occupying multiple roles, approaches the director, Miss La Trobe, to thank her: "'What a small part I've had to play! But you've made me feel I could have played... Cleopatra!' [...] 'You've stirred in me my unacted part,' she meant" (*BTA* 110). This notion of an unlived, unexplored identity that lies dormant in the self and can be "stirred" by a communal enterprise like the pageant partakes in the dialectic of immanence and transcendence characteristic of Blochian utopias. The word "unacted" has a double meaning: it refers both to a role that has been missed—an identity that is elided by the necessarily limited nature of experience—and a part that has *not yet been acted.* The pageant in *Between the Acts* deliberately confronts the audience with both these meanings, causing them to realize both the limited nature of their own experience—their existence as mere "Scraps, orts, and fragments" of a larger whole (136)—and the possibility of overcoming that limitation by uniting with one another. It offers a utopian vision of an expanded form of self that exists at once as an imaginary state of things that runs counter to the actual conditions of life, and as a potential future state of being. Evelyn Tsz Yan Chan argues that *Between the Acts* is a novel that resists specialization (154). Lucy Swithin's "unacted part" functions as part of this resistance; evading the demand to occupy a single role suggested by the rhyme quoted by Mrs. Manresa, "Tinker, tailor, soldier, sailor" (*BTA* 37), it instead gestures towards a reality in which the individual can take on multiple identifications.

Woolf's "embryo lives" and "unacted part[s]" evade the indicative certainty of narrative time. They exist, instead, in the subjunctive mood: they describe lives that *might have been* lived, that *might* be lived. They disrupt the dominant temporality of the narrative, drawing a radical link between the imaginary alterity of the present and a potential future. This radical, disruptive effect is reflected in the figures with which they are associated. The ill person, as an outsider in relation to the rest of society, is able to achieve an estranged, critical perspective upon it. Lucy Swithin, meanwhile, is a disruptive figure in *Between the Acts*; stereotyped, dismissed and misunderstood by those around her, her associative thought-processes and fanciful musings represent the novel's most consistent attempt to create a vision of a unified community. The countercultural imaginings of these figures construct a utopian form of selfhood that exists neither wholly in the present nor wholly in the future and hence retains its radical potential; it is presented neither as a *fait accompli* nor in some impossibly remote future state, but as always on the cusp of coming into being.

By locating her utopianism within the latent, unexplored identities of her characters, Woolf shares a common project with two contemporary writers of science fiction, David Garnett and Muriel Jaeger.[6] Garnett's novel *Lady Into Fox* (1922), which Woolf read and enjoyed (*L2* 574-5), tells the story of Sylvia Tebrick's sudden transformation into a fox, and her subsequent more gradual transition from the modes of respectable living to more and more wild behavior, until eventually she abandons her human husband to pursue a disreputable relationship with a dog-fox. Mr. Tebrick, though initially shocked by his wife's behavior, eventually comes to accept it, renegotiating their relationship along platonic lines, and helping to care for her cubs. Their new, happy relations are cut short, however, when Sylvia is killed by fox-hunters. The story is an obvious parable of sexual deviancy: of the struggle between social norms and natural sexual desires.

Most notably for my analysis, the supernatural aspect of the story—Sylvia's transformation—originates as an alterity within her identity; she is described as having a "disposition to wildness" that has been repressed through a strict upbringing

---

[6] It might seem contrary to associate Garnett with science fiction, when he is more often linked to the fantastical. However, the overlap between these genres in the interwar period is made evident by the fact that H.G. Wells's Preface to his *Scientific Romances*, upon which Darko Suvin draws heavily in his influential theorizations of science fiction, refers to Wells's own stories as "fantasies," and compares them to Garnett's *Lady Into Fox* (vii).

(Garnett 11-12). This latent vulpine quality triggers the science-fictional element of the story. The novel is in this way comparable to Woolf's short story "Lappin and Lapinova" (1939), in which minor physical resemblances to a rabbit and a hare allow a married couple to construct a fantasy realm in which they occupy alternative animal identities (*CSF* 351-61). Moreover, like Woolf's "embryo lives" and "unacted part[s]," Sylvia's alterity is utopian. Although the book ends tragically, the relationship that Sylvia and her husband negotiate post-transformation points the way toward a liberated sexual politics that prioritizes tolerance and mutual respect. Youngjoo Son argues that Woolf's utopian project resides in the creation of "otherness" within present space (148). My corresponding argument is that, for Woolf and Garnett, a utopian future emerges from the otherness within the self.

Muriel Jaeger's *The Man With Six Senses* was published by the Hogarth Press in 1927 (meaning that Woolf very likely read it, or was at least familiar with its central conceit). It tells the story of Michael Bristowe, a man who has an innate ability to sense the molecular and subatomic structure of materials, and of Hilda Torrington, his friend, who becomes obsessed with ensuring that his abilities are recognized and made use of by his society. However, although Michael enjoys a brief period of celebrity after his abilities cause him to discover the buried corpse of a murder victim, his talents fail to find a practical outlet. As Michael's health begins to fail, Hilda, still convinced that he is the forerunner of an evolutionary advancement in the human species, resolves to marry him in the hope that he will pass on his genetic superiority to their children—to the despair of Ralph, the narrator, who wants Hilda to marry him instead. The novel ends after Michael's death, with Hilda caring for their daughter, but still uncertain whether she has inherited Michael's abilities.

Michael's ability to view objects at a subatomic level causes him to perceive the insubstantiality of the world described by contemporary quantum physics, in which matter could be thought of as constructed entirely of waves: "the ocean of movement ... Shifting formations ... lines of energy ... the great waves ... ripples crossing ... patterns coming and going ..." (Jaeger 104). He applies this insubstantiality to the identities of those around him, asking one man, "Are you solid, do you think, Mr. Horace G. Plumer? [...] You're a ghost, I tell you ... A ghost, if you only knew it" (Jaeger 104). Ralph, too, perceives a shift in his conception of identity as a result of his knowledge of Michael's ability: "Reality had become vague and wavering; the bounds of personality were moved" (Jaeger 128). Michael is thus associated with an alternative conception of selfhood as fluid and insubstantial. His perceptions, moreover, are depicted as being at once countercultural, and prefiguring an improved future. His talents are belittled and rejected by those around him because of their lack of financial value, and he ultimately dies a social outcast. At the same time, the novel hints that his talents could, via his daughter, be spread through the human species, producing an evolutionary advancement. Like Sylvia Tebrick's vulpine tendencies, and like Woolf's "embryo lives" and "unacted part[s]," there is an alterity within his identity that is unexplored within the present and that is at odds with current definitions of selfhood, but that gestures towards a possible expansion of the self in the future.

The form of utopianism shared by Woolf, Garnett and Jaeger, in which visions of the future are located within latent alterities in their characters' identities, does not have an obvious connection with the advancement of the Marxist historical process that is, for some theorists, the sole function of cultural utopianism. For Darko Suvin, for example, the "novum" of a work of science fiction (its estranging element) "is fake unless it in some way participates in and partakes of what Bloch called the 'front-line of historical process'" (82). It could perhaps be argued that, in advocating a more expansive conception of identity, these writers are resisting the capitalist division of labor and its alienating effects. However, the connection with the Marxist historical process would, in this reading, be indirect, and the writers do not obviously foreground a restructuring of the economic basis of society. Some theorists have, however, questioned the equation of utopianism with Marxism. In particular, Ruth Levitas has argued that utopianism is an impulse that encompasses the whole of the political spectrum. Levitas advocates an exceedingly broad definition of utopianism, as "the expression of the desire for a better way of being" (9). It would be easy to fit the latent, unexplored identities we have been discussing into Levitas's definition; they can be read as expressing the desire for another life beyond the one currently being lived. However, to relate these forms of identity to Levitas's broad, apolitical concept of "desire" would be to erase their critical, estranging function: their role in critiquing current social definitions of identity.

I suggest that the form of utopian science fiction written by Woolf, Garnett and Jaeger can more profitably be associated with a third mode of utopianism: one associated with queer theory. This characterization is in keeping with our knowledge of the biographies of all three writers.[7] In her book *Queer Phenomenology*, Sara Ahmed discusses the importance for queer subjects of "deviating" from socially prescribed "life-courses" (20-21), of refusing to follow "conventional scripts" (177). Deviant, unconventional courses can, she argues, emerge through a retrospective survey of one's own life, of the "fork[s] in the road" where we have followed one path but not another:

> So at one level we do not encounter that which is "off course"; that which is off the line we have taken. And yet, accidental or chance encounters do happen, and they redirect us and open up new worlds. [...] It is usually with the benefit of "hindsight" that we reflect on such moments, where a fork in the road before us opens up and we have to decide what to do, even if the moment does not present itself as a demand for a decision. The "hind" does not always give us a different point of view, yet it does allow those moments to be revisited, to be reinhabited, as moments when we change course. (Ahmed 19)

---

[7] Though little biographical information on Jaeger is readily available, her entry in the *Dictionary of National Biography,* which notes that she never married, that her friends referred to her as "Jim," and that she had an intense friendship with Dorothy L. Sayers, is certainly suggestive of a queer identity (Morse). Woolf and Garnett's queerness is well documented.

If we read Woolf's "unacted part[s]" and "embryo lives" as representing such deviant lines—paths not taken, which can be retrospectively "reinhabited," leading us to "new worlds"—their queer potential becomes apparent. Like Sylvia's wildness and Michael's sixth sense, they are aspects of a person's identity that are at once outside existing social definitions, and productive of new potentialities. In unearthing these unaccessed aspects of her characters' identities, Woolf makes ways of being that are socially illegible seem possible. Apparently impossible identifications—the elderly widow Lucy Swithin becoming Cleopatra; the ill, bed-bound person becoming a sea-captain and a court lady—are opened up and made imaginable.

This queer, utopian project of opening up countercultural, deviant paths is certainly a far cry from what was undoubtedly the dominant form of science fiction in the period: the enormously popular and influential utopianism of H. G. Wells. In the 1930s, Wells was associated mainly with the social prognostications of novels such as *The Shape of Things to Come* (1933), which provides a detailed description of the "historical" events of the next one-and-a-half centuries, including an account of a utopian global society. Wells's works have formed the basis for much subsequent theorization of science fiction; Darko Suvin's concept of the "novum" as a defining feature of science fiction, for example, closely resembles Wells's discussion in the "Preface" to his *Scientific Romances* of the "fantastic element" or "strange property" that characterizes a work of science fiction (vii). According to Suvin, "An SF narration is a fiction in which the SF element or aspect, the novum, is hegemonic, that is, so central and significant that it determines the whole narrative logic—or at least the overriding narrative logic" (70). *The Shape of Things to Come*, in which the entire narrative is defined by the novel's shift into the future, is an example of such a fiction. By contrast, Woolf's "embryo lives" and "unacted part[s]" are certainly not hegemonic, nor do they define "the whole narrative logic"; on the contrary, by their very nature they run counter to narrative, emerging as disruptions of narrative time. That being so, surely it is impossible to view them as in any way science fictional?

However, if we accept, with Bloch, Mannheim, and Jameson, that utopias can emerge in glimpses within texts, rather than necessarily determining their entire narrative, then we need not adhere to the view that the science-fictional element of a text must be hegemonic. Instead, we can view the "cognitive estrangement" performed by science fiction as similarly existing within the text in fragmentary form. For Frederic Jameson, it is the role of the critic to apply a utopian hermeneutic lens to a text, to illuminate the ways in which it gestures towards the future. I suggest that it is equally productive to apply a science-fictional hermeneutic lens to Woolf's writing. In all of the texts we have viewed so far, we have seen that Woolf takes up a science-fictional, estranging perspective only for a moment—temporarily considering, for example, what her surroundings might look like from the Moon, or what the patterns of industrialized culture might look like when viewed from a future in which the Earth has frozen over—before setting it down again. To read Woolf through a science-fictional lens is to become alert to the moments in which an alien perspective, or a scientific concept, is used to estrange the self and to open up queer ways of being.

To identify Woolf, Garnett, and Jaeger's writing as sharing a queer utopianism, meanwhile, is to begin to establish an alternative, queer tradition of early-twentieth-century science fiction. Clearly, more work is required to determine whether other writers of the period similarly employ a science-fictional perspective to explore queer, countercultural modes of existence. Such work has the potential to transform our understanding of interwar utopianism. Wells's visions of worldwide pacific governments, while influential, are, as Aaron Worth has demonstrated, imperialistic in their promotion of a global technological hegemony. As such, they fail to counter the widespread contemporary fear that the development of science was doomed to foster state-sponsored violence and oppression.[8] By uniting queer theory and utopian theory, however, we can uncover an alternative tradition of science-fictional novels that gesture us towards ways of being that run counter to, and exist outside, the structures of global capitalism, nationalism, and heteronormativity.

In the last part of this essay, I would like to give an indication of what it might look like to read Woolf's novel of 1931, *The Waves*, science fictionally. In particular, I would like to suggest that the six main characters' use of elaborate systems of images to describe their own identities can be read in terms of the bodily transformations and counterfactual situations associated with science fiction. For example, in a pivotal scene early in the novel, Louis describes himself in terms of a plant: "My roots go down to the depths of the world, through earth dry with brick, and damp earth, through veins of lead and silver. I am all fibre" (*TW* 7). Evidently, this description serves a metaphorical function. Elsewhere, Louis describes his feeling of continuity with past generations; the image of roots extending into the earth can be read as a metaphor for such continuity. On the terms of the novel itself, however, there is no requirement to view Louis's description as anything other than a literal statement of his corporeal existence. After all, the soliloquies of the novel offer a tissue of similar images, and the characters are absent from the apparently more objective world of the interludes. There is therefore no literal level against which to test Louis's assertion, and to conclude that it must be metaphorical. There is no reason why we should not assume that Louis has literally grown roots. When read in this way, the science-fictional aspects of the novel become obvious. It immediately becomes clear that we are in an alternate, alien world in which human and plant forms have merged: that we are, in short, in the realm of science fiction. Olaf Stapledon's novel *Star Maker* contains a description of a planet in which the intelligent species is half plant, half animal; here, Louis appears for a moment to take on the characteristics of a similarly alien species.

Rhoda, meanwhile, repeatedly describes herself as merging with the world around her: "Month by month things are losing their hardness; even my body now lets the light through; my spine is soft like wax near the flame of the candle. I dream;

---

[8] The philosopher and mathematician Hyman Levy voiced this fear in a radio broadcast of 1934: "the society we have developed has called into being scientific possibilities for good or ill that in the near future may certainly lead to Man's undoing" (25).

I dream" (*TW* 34). Again, if we interpret such statements literally, rather than viewing them as metaphorical statements of her imaginative escapism or her lack of a sense of self, then we find ourselves in science-fictional territory. As Michael Whitworth has discussed, Rhoda's descriptions of the matter around her as insubstantial have much in common with contemporary popular scientific accounts of modern physics, particularly of Ernest Rutherford's discovery that the atom consists mostly of empty space (160). If her statements are taken literally, Rhoda becomes a figure like Michael in *The Man With Six Senses*: able actually to perceive the insubstantiality of matter and of her own body. Her declaration that "things are losing their hardness" (*TW* 34) expresses the same scientific concept as Michael's question, "Are you solid [...]?" (Jaeger 104). Rhoda and Michael share a scientific, estranged perspective in which they and the objects around them become translucent ghosts.

It is only our insistence upon reading the self-descriptions of the characters in *The Waves* as metaphorical that prevents us from immediately recognizing the novel as science fiction, an insistence undoubtedly founded upon a preconception that Woolf is a writer who makes heavy use of symbolism, and that any instance of particularly incongruous language is merely an extravagant use of imagery. To read them literally, however, is to reveal the extent to which Woolf employs science-fictional perspectives in order to produce an estranged vision of identity. In both Louis and Rhoda's descriptions, moreover, the resulting vision can be characterized as utopian, since it depicts a radical continuity between self and world. In becoming insubstantial, Rhoda merges with the world around her. Similarly, by turning into a plant, Louis's selfhood takes on a global scope. These transformations, however, are not, to use Suvin's term, "hegemonic," determining "the whole narrative logic" (70); instead, they are fragmentary and temporary. Rhoda does not remain in her insubstantial state, but must continually touch something hard "to call myself back to the body" (*TW* 33). Louis's transformation, meanwhile, is interrupted when he is seen and kissed by Jinny, and becomes "a boy in a grey flannel suit" (*TW* 8). Ordinary, conventional modes of identity are thus eventually restored. They do not, however, constitute a literal level against which Louis and Rhoda's transformations can be measured and dismissed as metaphorical. By touching a hard object, Rhoda does not *reveal* herself to be a body, nor does Jinny prove that Louis is *really* "a boy in a grey flannel suit". It is rather that one state is succeeded by another: Rhoda is at one moment transparent, and at the next a hard "body"; Louis is at one moment a plant, at the next a boy. Their transformations, moreover, recur at several points throughout the novel. They occupy lacunae in the narrative, subjunctive moments in which ordinary conceptions dissolve and alternative, counterfactual modes of being become, for a moment, possible.

It is significant that it is Louis and Rhoda, the outsiders of the novel, who experience these estrangements of being. It is true that a science-fictional lens can be applied to the other characters' self-descriptions; Jinny, for instance, appears to transform temporarily into a water-plant while dancing with a young man (*TW* 80-1). Bernard, meanwhile, appears, through his imaginative reach and powers of sympathy, to undertake science-fictional voyages to the distant past and to the outer reaches of the universe: "to hear vague, ancestral sounds of boughs creaking, of mammoths" (*TW* 89), and to project himself onto "the verge of things" (*TW* 234). Moreover, like Rhoda, he experiences the insubstantiality of the universe described by modern physics, having "to tap my knuckles smartly upon the edges of apparently solid objects and say, 'Are you hard?'" (*TW* 231). However, Bernard's experiences of estrangement can be ascribed to his ability imaginatively to take on the identities of the other five characters; in his final soliloquy the "division" between him and his friends is removed, and he feels "I am you" (*TW* 231). After all, it is Louis who initially undertakes voyages to the past (seeing "women carrying red pitchers to the banks of the Nile" [*TW* 75]), and Rhoda who perceives "fishermen on the verge of the world" (*TW* 178-79). It seems to me—though more work is required to verify this assessment—that Louis and Rhoda experience estrangement with more frequency, and in a manner that is more central to their identities, than the other four characters. In this way, *The Waves* is consistent with "On Being Ill" and *Between the Acts*, in which, as we have seen, it is outsider characters who experience an estranged, expansive form of selfhood. Louis and Rhoda, who refer to one another as "conspirators" (*TW* 181), constantly find themselves on the margins of social gatherings. As in Garnett's and Jaeger's novels, their estranged identities occupy the margins of society, are unrecognized by social definitions, and often serve to isolate the characters still further. At the same time, they point the way towards a more expansive form of identity that could, at an unspecified future time, exist.

The aim of this essay has by no means been to conduct a taxonomic identification of Woolf as a science fiction writer, to pin her down under a particular label. It has rather been to demonstrate the insights that arise when we read her works through a science-fictional lens. Just as Woolf's "embryo lives" and "unacted part[s]" exist within the subjunctive mood, running counter to the main sweep of narrative time, so my reading of her works as science fictional has involved being alert to subjunctive, latent aspects of her use of language. In much science fiction there is an aspiration toward linguistic transparency, and the scientific terms or concepts employed tend to serve a singular function. In Woolf's use of science, however, there is no such transparency. To read her texts science fictionally is to read them in a specific way, to conduct one possible reading among many. To do so, however, is to reveal multiple moments in which a fragmentary glimpse of an alternate world estranges the self and opens up deviant paths. Read in this way, the science fiction writer emerges as one of Virginia Woolf's many "unacted part[s]".

Works Cited

Ahmed, Sara. *Queer Phenomenology: Orientations, Objects, Others*. Duke UP, 2006.
Alt, Christina. *Virginia Woolf and the Study of Nature*. Cambridge UP, 2010.
Chan, Evelyn Tsz Yan. *Virginia Woolf and the Professions*. Cambridge UP, 2014.
Crossland, Rachel. *Modernist Physics: Waves, Particles, and Relativities in the Writings of Virginia Woolf and D. H. Lawrence*. Oxford UP, 2018.
Crossley, Robert. "Olaf Stapledon and the Idea of Science Fiction." *Modern Fiction Studies*, vol. 32, no. 1, 1986, pp. 21-42.
Ellis, Steve. *British Writers and the Approach of World War II*. Cambridge UP, 2015.
"Embryonic, adj." *Oxford English Dictionary.* www.oed.com/view/Entry/61084.
Foster, J. Ashley. "Writing in the 'White Light of Truth': History, Ethics, and Community in Virginia Woolf's *Between the Acts."* *Woolf Studies Annual*, vol. 22, 2016, pp. 41-73.
Freedman, Carl. "Science Fiction and Utopia: A Historico-Philosophical Overview." *Learning From Other Worlds: Estrangement, Cognition, and the Politics of Science Fiction and Utopia*. Edited by Patrick Parrinder. Liverpool UP, 2000, pp. 72-97.
Garnett, David. *Lady Into Fox and A Man in the Zoo*. Penguin, 1980.
Harker, Ben. "'On Different Levels Ourselves Went Forward': Pageantry, Class Politics and Narrative Form in Virginia Woolf's Late Writing." *ELH*, vol. 78, no. 2, 2011, pp. 433-56.
Henry, Holly. *Virginia Woolf and the Discourse of Science: The Aesthetics of Astronomy*. Cambridge UP, 2003.
Huxley, Julian. "The Stream of Life—Development." Transcript. BBC Written Archives Centre, 19 Nov. 1925.
Jaeger, Muriel. *The Man With Six Senses*. HiLoBooks, 2013.
Jameson, Fredric. *Archaeologies of the Future: The Desire Called Utopia and Other Science Fictions*. Verso, 2005.
Keller, Evelyn Fox. *Refiguring Life: Metaphors of Twentieth-Century Biology*. Columbia UP, 1995.
Levitas, Ruth. *The Concept of Utopia*. Peter Lang, 2011.
Levy, H. "The Web is Spun." *Listener*, 4 Jul. 1934, pp. 23-25.
Morse, Elizabeth J. "Jaeger, Muriel." *Oxford Dictionary of National Biography.* 23 Sept. 2004, https://doi.org/10.1093/ref:odnb/73622. Accessed 5 Dec. 2018.
Moylan, Tom. *Scraps of the Untainted Sky: Science Fiction, Utopia, Dystopia*. Westview Press, 2000.
Parrinder, Patrick. "Revisiting Suvin's Poetics of Science Fiction." *Learning From Other Worlds: Estrangement, Cognition, and the Politics of Science Fiction and Utopia*. Edited by Patrick Parrinder, Liverpool UP, 2000, pp. 36-50.

Pintér, Károly. *The Anatomy of Utopia: Narration, Estrangement and Ambiguity in More, Wells, Huxley and Clarke.* McFarland & Company, 2010.
Pridmore-Brown, Michele. "1939-40: Of Virginia Woolf, Gramophones, and Fascism." *PMLA*, vol. 113, no. 3, 1998, pp. 408-21.
Reeve-Tucker, Alice, and Nathan Waddell, editors. *Utopianism, Modernism, and Literature in the Twentieth Century.* Palgrave Macmillan, 2013.
Rieder, John. "Fiction, 1895-1926." *The Routledge Companion to Science Fiction.* Edited by Mark Bould et al., Routledge, 2009, pp. 23-31,
Son, Youngjoo. *Here and Now: The Politics of Social Space in D. H. Lawrence and Virginia Woolf.* Routledge, 2014.
Stapledon, Olaf. *Star Maker.* Gollancz, 2004.
"The stars of modern SF pick the best science fiction." *The Guardian*, 14 May 2011,theguardian.com/books/2011/may/14/science-fiction-authors-choice. Accessed 09/03/2018.
Suvin, Darko. *Metamorphoses of Science Fiction: On the Poetics and History of a Literary Genre.* Yale UP, 1979.
Swanson, Roy Arthur. "The True, the False, and the Truly False: Lucian's Philosophical Science Fiction." *Science Fiction Studies*, vol. 3, no. 3, 1976, pp. 227-39.
Tung, Charles M. "Baddest Modernism: The Scales and Lines of Inhuman Time." *Modernism/modernity*, vol. 23, no. 3, 2016, pp. 515-38.
Wells, H. G. *The First Men in the Moon.* Penguin, 2005.
—. *The Invisible Man.* Penguin, 2005.
—. "Preface." *The Scientific Romances of H.G. Wells.* Victor Gollancz, 1933, pp.vii-x.
—. *The Shape of Things to Come.* Penguin, 2005.
Whitworth, Michael. *Einstein's Wake: Relativity, Metaphor, and Modernist Literature.* Oxford UP, 2001.
"Why Virginia Woolf? Wayne McGregor on the Inspiration Behind Woolf Works." *YouTube,* uploaded by Royal Opera House, 8 February 2017, www.youtube.com/watch?v=otgRonIR1Ic.
Woolf, Virginia. *Between the Acts.* Edited by Mark Hussey, Cambridge UP, 2011.
—. *The Complete Shorter Fiction.* Edited by Susan Dick, Triad, 1987.
—. *The Diary of Virginia Woolf.* Edited by Anne Olivier Bell and Andrew McNeillie, Penguin, 1979-85. 5 vols.
—. *The Essays of Virginia Woolf.* Edited by Andrew McNeillie (1-4) and Stuart Clarke (5-6), Hogarth Press, 1986-2011. 6 vols.
—. *The Letters of Virginia Woolf.* Edited by Nigel Nicolson and Joanne Trautmann Banks, Hogarth Press, 1993-94. 6 vols.
—. *The Voyage Out.* Penguin, 1975.
—. *The Waves.* Edited by Michael Herbert and Susan Sellers, Cambridge UP, 2011.
—. *The Years.* Edited by Anna Snaith, Cambridge UP, 2012.
Worth, Aaron. "Imperial Transmissions: H. G. Wells, 1897-1901." *Victorian Studies*, vol. 53, no. 1, 2010, pp. 65-89.

Woolf's Bioethics: Animals and Dependency in "The Widow and the Parrot"
Sebastian Williams

Introduction

Virginia Woolf's "The Widow and the Parrot" is one of the rare examples of her children's storytelling, providing valuable insights into a more didactic strain of her writing as well as her understanding of human-animal relations. The story, likely penned in 1922 or 1923, follows a "lame" and elderly widow as she goes to collect an inheritance left to her by her recently deceased brother, which includes his parrot, James. The story was written for a family newspaper edited by her then twelve-year-old nephew Quentin Bell, and it has a clear moral: "kindness to animals" is rewarded by happiness (24). Quentin nearly rejected it for publication, referring to it as an "'improving story' based on the very worst Victorian examples," but after careful consideration with his coeditor Julian, decided they should include the story to save face with their aunt ("Afterword"). James the parrot is not simply a pet in this story: at various points he guides Mrs. Gage to treasure, saves her life, and—as implied by the end of the narrative—helps her to find comfort and contentment.

This essay analyzes the relationship between the lame Mrs. Gage and her parrot to illustrate the significance of interspecies interdependence in Woolf's writing. Woolf foregrounds for her younger readers (limited though they were) an interdependent relationship between nonhuman animals and a disabled and elderly individual, ultimately emphasizing the networks of interdependence that interweave our societies. The story argues against frameworks that reduce nonhuman animals to their functional use, while at the same time exposing parallels between anthropocentrism and ableism, as Woolf's portrayal of Mrs. Gage undermines cultural narratives about disability and old age.

"The Widow and the Parrot" was not copyrighted until 1982 by Quentin Bell and Angelica Garnett, and the illustrations, done by Julian Bell (Quentin's son—not to be confused with Woolf's nephew), were copyrighted in 1988. It also appeared in an edited collection of Woolf's short fiction in 1985, though without illustrations.[1] The story opens in a small village, Spilsby in Yorkshire,[2] and it centers on a poor, lame, and elderly widow who lives with her dog, Shag (a name borrowed from one of Woolf's former pets). Mrs. Gage receives news that her brother Mr. Joseph Brand has died and left her an inheritance in the village of Rodmell, including a small cottage and £3,000. The lame widow receives a ride to Rodmell only to learn that her brother's home is run down and that the money cannot be found; one of the few

---
[1] The full title of the children's story in *CSF* is "The Widow and the Parrot: A True Story." In the 1988 individual edition by Harcourt, though, the subtitle was inexplicably dropped.
[2] For reference, Spilsby is located roughly 208 miles (335 km) north of Rodmell.

things left is a parrot named James. Gage leaves Rodmell and begins to journey home on foot when she nearly dies trying to cross the river Ouse,[3] and it is only by the light from what would later turn out to be her brother's burning home that she is saved. (When retelling the story, Gage insists that James had tipped over an oil stove and burned the house intentionally to alert her to the fortune.) While staying with a friend that night, Gage hears the parrot tapping on the glass outside her window. He leads her to her brother's hidden treasure—gold sovereigns buried beneath the floor of the now-razed home—and Gage, her dog, and James the parrot live in happiness thanks to the fortune.

While my primary focus is Woolf's bioethical concerns—including the ethical value we place on the varieties of human and nonhuman life in our societies—I also suggest that "The Widow and the Parrot" extends our understanding of Woolf's oeuvre more broadly, including Woolf scholarship on disability and animal studies. For instance, Carrie Rohman shows how Woolf's investment in nonhuman life is made apparent in one of Woolf's other children's stories, "Nurse Lugton's Curtain." Rohman, who is well aware of shifting conversations about human-animal relationships following the rise of Darwinism and Freudianism in the late nineteenth and early twentieth centuries, suggests that aesthetics, for Woolf, is not "quintessentially human" but necessarily inhuman (*Choreographies* 64). "Nurse Lugton's Curtain," for Rohman, represents the Deleuzean concept of becoming-animal, opening possibilities that extend beyond traditional storytelling and human-animal relations. In other words, Woolf provides a framework for thinking through animality and the body in the context of art and literature, and her children's storytelling foregrounds the degree to which Woolf challenges normative, humanistic theories of aesthetics. Kristin Czarnecki notes that many saw "Nurse Lugton's Curtain" as freeing Woolf of certain highbrow "constraints" (224), though Czarnecki is quick to point out that the story, which was later revised, is not exactly what we might consider "child friendly" (222). "The Widow and the Parrot," however, is a finished narrative, with a clear ethical stance that makes explicit the various ways Woolf understood disability and animality, precisely because the story was written for a small, adolescent audience. There are, nevertheless, potentially problematic issues to note in "The Widow and the Parrot," such as James the parrot's eastern origins and the tendency of some modernists to link animality with the colonized Other, as well as Woolf's emphasis on material wealth—suggesting money, especially inherited wealth, is important in establishing comfort and happiness. Nevertheless, this essay works to illustrate the complex attitudes Woolf harbored toward nonhuman life, including the ways children's literature plays a significant role in shaping ethics and ideology.

---

[3] While Gage's near-drowning in the river Ouse will certainly appear ominous to any Woolf scholar, the story also features a reference to Leonard: "No lights were visible anywhere, for, as you may be aware, there is no cottage or house on that side of the river nearer Asheham House, lately the seat of Mr. Leonard Woolf" (11).

The term "bioethics" refers to a wide category of ethical concerns, including abortion, gene therapy, euthanasia, caretaking, and so forth, but in this essay I use it to refer to disability and animal ethics specifically, including their intersections. Sunaura Taylor writes in *Beasts of Burden* that there is an inherent link between anthropocentrism and ableism, one that is deeply embedded in the ways we see and understand living creatures (human or otherwise) around us: "So much of what we understand of ourselves as 'human' depends on our physical and mental abilities—how we move (or cannot move) in and interact with the world [. . .] and so much of our definition of 'human' depends on its difference from 'animal'" (1). Here, Taylor points to the primary intersection of disability and animal studies without suggesting that disabled people are somehow the same as or less than nonhuman animals; instead, Taylor suggests that both ableism and speciesism are connected by how our bodies and minds are culturally coded by others—what it means to be a "normal" human is often to look, behave, move, and think a certain way. And, such categories are similarly used to reify the human-animal divide in ways that posthumanist philosophers have illustrated. For example, Cary Wolfe suggests that there is an important connection between disability and animal studies when he writes that "both animal studies and disability studies show us something about the limitations of [liberal humanism] and in doing so call on us to rethink questions of ethical and political responsibility" (127). As Derek Ryan aptly summarizes, the value of such approaches to modernist texts is that they "open up nonanthropocentric worldviews *in the present*, in order to address the range of pressing concerns—whether the mistreatment of animals, climate change and the environment, or the issues around bioethics" without "turning its back on humanity altogether" (emphasis in original, "Following" 268).[4] Centering the ways disability, animality, and other bioethical concerns coalesce in Woolf's children's story allows us to better understand the ways literature shapes ethics, yet it also helps us to see the "nonanthropocentric worldviews *in the present*" to which Ryan refers.

The intersections between ableism and speciesism are key for developing what philosophers such as Kelly Oliver refer to as an ethics of proximity based on interspecies interdependence. As Oliver explains,

> Rather than a utilitarian ethics based on intelligence as the criteria [*sic*] for membership in the moral community, or a feminist ethics of care that acknowledges only dependency relations between human beings [. . .] I propose an ethics based on interdependence, particularly emotional interdependence and companionship. (242)

An ethics of proximity suggests that we must recognize the ethical value of nonhuman animals because we rely on them as resources for food, clothing, energy, entertainment,

---

[4] In this sense, "bioethics" and "posthumanism" are not necessarily synonymous, as the former refers to an object or field of study, while the latter is more aptly defined as a theory or approach.

experimentation, and—most importantly in the context of Woolf's writing—companionship and emotional support. For Oliver, "if our dependence on other humans for our very being obligates us to them, then it also follows that our dependence on nonhuman animals morally obligates us to them" (248). While it is important not to conflate human and nonhuman animals, or to conflate all animals as *the Animal*,[5] Oliver redefines human-animal ethics on the basis of interdependency. Throughout "The Widow and the Parrot," Woolf develops a similar ethics, in which Gage is resistant to sell James the parrot as a material asset and in which she cares for her dog, Shag, beyond her own needs. At the core of such ethics is the recognition that we cannot reduce animal bodies (human or otherwise) to mechanical machines or functional assets—a perspective that works to reframe the ways we view disability as well. According to Oliver's model, Gage's ethical value is also not rooted in her functional abilities, but rather her care for the human and nonhuman animals around her.

Woolf and Children's Literature

"The Widow and the Parrot" shares many similarities with other children's literature from the late nineteenth and early twentieth centuries. For example, it has a didactic tone and style, yet it is also unique in that it can help to contextualize some of Woolf's more popular works. Critics such as Lissa Paul assert that children's literature often constructs the child *qua* child (186)—particularly in the context of gender identity—while Peter Hunt writes in *Criticism, Theory, and Children's Literature* that we may understand children as "colonized" by adults, as adults tend to speak for children. Woolf, though, is not necessarily speaking for or even depicting children in "The Widow and the Parrot"; her writing reflects what Marah Gubar, borrowing from Wittgenstein, calls the "family resemblance" that tenuously constitutes children's genres (212). Woolf's story is, in other words, children's literature on a generic level—a highly fraught stylistic category of writing composed in a simple language and tone to advance (wittingly or unwittingly) various ethical and ideological concepts. In this sense, Woolf is trying to *teach* her readers to be more ethical, to adopt renewed perspectives of nonhuman animals and, to a degree, disability, even if the distinction between children's and "adult" literature is ultimately unstable. Analyzing the story in the context of children's literature is helpful for understanding Woolf's own thoughts on animal ethics,[6] especially what she likely would have wanted to pass on to younger generations.

Woolf herself was well-versed in Victorian children's literature and fairytales from her youth, and her mother, Julia Duckworth Stephen, and her aunt, Lady Anne

---

[5] See Derrida's *The Animal That Therefore I Am*.
[6] While beyond the scope of my argument, several other modernist authors wrote children's literature. See, for instance, Gertrude Stein's *The World is Round*, T. S. Eliot's *Old Possum's Book of Practical Cats*, and Aldous Huxley's *The Crows of Pearlblossom*. For more information on modernist children's literature, see Hodgkins. Interestingly, Hodgkins does not mention "The Widow and the Parrot."

Thackeray Ritchie, wrote children's stories as well. Writing primarily on the pervasive influence of fairytales in twentieth-century Britain, Ann Martin asserts that Woolf's own allusions to stories such as "Cinderella" in *Night and Day* and *Orlando* reflect "a resurfacing of culturally latent imagery and diction, including but not restricted to works of literature," imagery and diction that represent a "cultural common ground" that bridges so-called high art and popular culture (35). "The Widow and the Parrot" in this sense also engages the Victorian legacy that served as an essential reference point for a broader cultural imaginary. Martin suggests that Woolf's allusions to the Victorian children's story reflect her ambivalence toward individuals such as her aunt—Annie Ritchie, who adapted several fairytales in *Bluebeard's Keys and Other Stories*—as well as Woolf's modernist experimentation with the literary tradition as it existed up to the early twentieth century. In line with what Martin suggests about Woolf's references to fairytales, "The Widow and the Parrot" extends Woolf's voice into the perceived lowbrow genre of children's literature, while consequently expounding a more ethical perspective of nonhuman animals.

Woolf's mother also penned several stories for children, many of which illustrate the pervasiveness of animals in children's literature. Titles include "The Monkey on the Moor," "The Wandering Pigs," "Cat's Meat," and "The Black Cat or the Grey Parrot." In "The Black Cat or the Grey Parrot"—which is perhaps the most relevant for understanding Julia's influence on her daughter—a little girl named Poppy is guided by a parrot, Polly, to an animal hospital after a little boy injures her dog, Tray. The little boy, Jack, learns to reevaluate his cruelty toward the dog, as well as his selfishness: "Jack ran to her and for the first time felt how cruel he had been to them all" (136). Animals play an important part in Stephen's representation of the world, especially because she was writing at a time when works such as Anna Sewell's *Black Beauty* (1877) impelled readers to reevaluate their attitudes toward nonhuman life, representing, as Elizabeth Steele writes, the "rallying cry of the newly-formed Society for the Prevention of Cruelty to Animals" (32). The Stephen family, including the young Virginia, commonly assigned animal names to each other (Virginia was often called "Goat"), and Steele asserts that Julia shared her extensive knowledge of and attitudes toward animals with her family: "We hear echoing throughout her pages [. . .] exhortations not to kill, not to hunt, not to harm, not to deprive members of the animal kingdom" (34).

Woolf's juvenilia also expands the ways we might understand "The Widow and the Parrot," including the working-class focus of her story "A Cockney's Farming Experience" and its sequel, "The Experiences of a Pater-familias." Composed when Woolf was ten years old, these works show the young writer's romanticized view of the laboring class as well as domestic squabbles. There are cows and horses in the stories, as well as the sympathetic dog Lick, who in one scene is rescued from a runaway horse by the protagonist, John (3). The stories, much like "The Widow and the Parrot," center on protagonists from outside of Woolf's own upper-middle class station—a station she would turn her attention toward for much of her later writing career—as characters receive inheritances from family members, reflecting what

Suzanne Henig suspects is an "English upper middle-class condescension toward money earned by the sweat of one's brow" (iii). "The Widow and the Parrot" in many ways parallels Woolf's juvenilia, in that both are about low- or working-class individuals who inherit wealth as a means of securing social stability and happiness.

"The Widow and the Parrot" carries over much of its focus on animals from Julia Stephen's children's stories, and we see in Woolf's children's story a rags-to-riches narrative like those that had interested her since her childhood. "The Widow and the Parrot" features a grey parrot, much like the one in Julia Stephen's "The Black Cat and the Grey Parrot," and we also learn that Gage's brother was cruel toward animals when he was young, like Jack in Stephen's story. In "The Widow and the Parrot," Joseph Gage "was always a cruel little boy when we were children [. . .] he liked worrying the poor insects, and I've known him to trim a hairy caterpillar with a pair of scissors before my very eyes" (10-11). Mrs. Gage, by contrast, is affectionate toward all animals, which the story openly privileges by rewarding Mrs. Gage with wealth and happiness by the end. And, much like characters in Woolf's juvenilia, the working-class Mrs. Gage in "The Widow and the Parrot" has only a "few shillings a week to live on," but she shares her meals with her dog due to her "devot[ion] to animals" (3). Woolf uses simple syntax and a moralizing tone to demonstrate for her younger audience that we should treat animals as companions rather than tools or assets, and the characters who behave best toward animals are clearly rewarded with material wealth and happiness. Like Martin suggests about Woolf's use of fairytales in other works, "The Widow and the Parrot" illustrates how Woolf reworks or builds on the common cultural aspects of the children's literary genre and frames the story in a narrative clearly set in the early twentieth century (as references to her and Leonard's home in the story illustrate). While the didactic tone of a story with a clear moral is notably distinct from the modernist style we may often attribute to Woolf's writing, it illustrates that her experimentation with various forms of writing (and her subsequent engagement with major political and ethical issues) was not necessarily restricted to the stream-of-consciousness style of many of her major novels. As Rohman describes "Nurse Lugton's Curtain"—which applies equally well to "The Widow and the Parrot"—"Framing this narrative for children allows Woolf to be less rigid or prescriptive in her artistic and high modernist expectations of herself, as a stylist and a thematic innovator" (66). While, as authors such as Derek Attridge suggest, "formally innovative" works often ask readers to make the "most challenging [. . .] ethical demands" (130-31), it is also true that Woolf's use of the children's literary genre provides a unique space for her bioethical attitudes to come to the foreground, concerns that carried over from the Victorian era and into the modernist period.

Interdependency in "The Widow and the Parrot"

Woolf's interdependent ethics is represented by an interspecies relationship built on networks of dependency. Mrs. Gage, for instance, is described as "lame" several times throughout the story, emphasizing her dependency on others (especially regarding her travel and mobility): "Mrs. Gage, as I have already said, was lame in her right leg. At the best of times she walked slowly, and [. . .] with her disappointment and the mud on the bank her progress was very slow indeed" (8). She nearly drowns when trying to cross a river at a deep spot, and is only saved by the light from her brother's burning home. Gage relies on a farmer, Mr. Stacey, for a ride from her home to Rodmell, and when she tries to travel alone and unassisted, it proves dangerous.

Mrs. Gage's disability is a subtle part of the story, as it is only mentioned twice, but it is also important in shaping the narrative and highlighting the networks of dependency at play in "The Widow and the Parrot"—the relationship alluded to in the very title. However, Woolf's depictions of disability elsewhere are also important to take into consideration. David Galef's 1991 essay on "Disfigured Figures" provides a helpful starting point for finding examples of physical disability throughout Woolf's oeuvre, but more recently critics have recognized a certain ambivalence in her work in the context of disability. Janet Lyon writes that it is an "uncontroversial proposition that modernist aesthetics, with its emphasis on disproportion, fracture, and incompleteness, shares with disability a foundational contestation of the category of 'the normal'" (552). Woolf, nevertheless, suggests in a now infamous 1915 journal entry that a "line of imbeciles" near Kingston "should certainly be killed" (qtd. in Lyon 551). For Lyon, though, such a statement is linked to Woolf's own anxieties about disability, including the institutionalization of her half-sister Laura Makepeace Stephen. Disability delivers a "sledge-hammer blow" for Woolf because she does not think she can "enter or dwell in its consciousness," yet Woolf herself had a deeply personal relationship to disability (Lyon 569).

Maren Linett and Michael Davidson have also written about the complex relationships between modernism and disability, focusing on Woolf in particular. In *Bodies of Modernism*, Linett writes that "there is a thin but durable strand of rhetoric about modernist art—from its own time and from ours—that uses deformity as a model for the reshaping modernists set out to perform on traditional art forms" (146). In a chapter on mobility and sexuality, Linett focuses on the figure of the dwarf in "Street Haunting" that has for so long been overlooked or problematically discussed by many Woolf scholars. Linett writes that the story frames disability and beauty as opposites (as well as sexuality and femininity), dehumanizing "disabled characters, none of whom returns the narrator's gaze" (20). The dwarf in the story/essay is transformed into a sexual being once her shoe is off and her "normal" foot is revealed, but otherwise her disability, as Linett shows, tends to eclipse any other facet of the dwarf's identity in Woolf's writing. Davidson, in *Invalid Modernism*, builds on Tobin Siebers's assertions that disability "enriches and complicates notions of the aesthetic" (3), especially when it comes to modernist writing and visual art. However, in the context of Woolf, Davidson writes that disability is often a problematic hurdle to be overcome: when Woolf asks in "Street Haunting," for instance, "What then is it like to be a dwarf?" the question "remains unanswered since it is less about what it feels like to be a dwarf but what it feels like not to be oneself" (Davidson 136-37).

In essays like "On Being Ill," however, as Linett points out, Woolf suggests that to be an invalid is to see from a unique and valuable perspective: "The body, then, is a key aspect of Woolf's work, both affecting her process [. . .] and serving as a subject she seeks new methods to express" (Linett 10).

What we see in "The Widow and the Parrot" is in some ways a "narrative prosthesis"—a term David Mitchell and Sharon Snyder use to refer to the tendency of disability to be used as a plot device without developing an extended disabled perspective. The narrative prosthesis is a "crutch upon which literary narratives lean for their representational power, disruptive potentiality, and analytical insight" (49). However, we can extend the ways that we might understand disability in "The Widow and the Parrot" beyond thinking of it as a mere narrative device by linking it to the animal ethics that are much more apparent throughout the children's story. Disability plays an important role in characterizing Mrs. Gage: she is dismissed by many in the society around her—such as the citizens of Rodmell, particularly the solicitor with whom she speaks—because of her age, poverty, and disability (three aspects of identity that are not mutually exclusive). At the start of the story, we learn that Mrs. Gage is poor, that she must mend her own clogs because she cannot afford new ones, which is a characterization that serves to further contextualize her disability. Mrs. Gage has difficulty moving and traveling, and, arguably, it is only with the help of James that she survives. Again, this is not to conflate disabled people with nonhuman animals; instead, it is to suggest that disability, old age, poverty, and interspecies ethics are deeply related in the ways bodies are coded and understood within various socio-economic and historical environments. The clear moral of Woolf's children's story is that one should be kind to animals; nevertheless, in advancing this claim she also touches on larger questions in bioethics. The "question of the animal," to borrow a phrase from Derrida, always lingers behind and alongside other questions about what it means to be human, to be happy, to suffer, and to be comforted.

Nonhuman Animals and the Children's Story

Early in the narrative, as Gage prepares for her journey to speak to the executor of her brother's will, it is made clear that she cares about animals. "The most important part [of her preparations]," the narrator observes, "was the care of her dog Shag during her absence, for in spite of her poverty she was devoted to animals, and often went short herself rather than stint her dog of his bone" (2). Here, we learn that Mrs. Gage prioritizes her relationship with domestic animals, even though she lives in poverty. And, at the end of the narrative, she lives with "her dog Shag in great comfort and happiness to a very great age" (24). The protagonist of Woolf's children's story has meaningful relationships with the animals around her, implying that it is because of these relationships that she acquires comfort and happiness. This characterization serves to support Woolf's ethics throughout the narrative, highlighting the interdependence of human and nonhuman animals.

Woolf's use of the name "Shag" in "The Widow and the Parrot" is a reference to one of her former pets, which she writes about in his obituary, titled "On a Faithful Friend." Published in 1905 in *The Guardian*, this essay represents one of the earliest examples of Woolf's more mature published writing, and—notably—it centers on the relationship between humans and their pets. In it she writes that "There is something, too, profane in the familiarity, half contemptuous, with which we treat our animals. We deliberately transplant a little bit of simple wild life, and make it grow up beside ours, which is neither simple nor wild" (12). Here, Woolf reveals for her readers the complexity of human-animal relations, such as the ways in which we project our own image onto animals, as well as the close relationships human beings may have with animals. In "On a Faithful Friend," we learn that the Stephen family had to send Shag away after he bit another dog, but that he returned to the family household, now blind and deaf, before he died. We see in this essay a slippage between the domestic and wild portraits of Shag, as, in similar stories such as *Flush*, the canine world is limited by human systems of classification and discipline. Woolf implies that Shag is sent away for breaking the rules of the human world—for biting another dog—yet that his behavior is part of his animal nature. She concludes by affirming that "dogs have few faults" (14), reevaluating her relationship with her pet and the inherent tension that exists for nonhuman animals in an anthropocentric world. "On a Faithful Friend," as the title implies, also illustrates Woolf's interest in the emotional ties that link human and nonhuman animals, celebrating Shag's friendship beyond his mere status as a dog.

The fictionalized version of Shag in "The Widow and the Parrot" allows Woolf to reflect on the emotional links between her and her pets, including the centrality of companionship in shaping her view of the animal kingdom. While the real Shag died when he was hit by a hansom cab while crossing the street, in "The Widow and the Parrot" he takes on a literary afterlife and is cared for to the end of his life by Mrs. Gage. Though Shag does not save Gage's life nor lead her to treasure, as James the parrot does, we learn that she nevertheless values him because of his companionship. Such a relationship reaffirms the interspecies interdependence that is developed throughout the narrative, revealing in plain terms the ways Woolf elevates certain forms of nonhuman life.

This interdependence is perhaps best evidenced by Mrs. Gage's relationship with James, the parrot left to her by her brother. Early in the story we learn that James was "a seaman's parrot and had learnt his language in the east," and that "Mr. Joseph [Gage's brother] was very fond of him" and "talked to him as if he were a rational being" (5). Not only does Mrs. Gage have meaningful relationships with animals, but it also appears that her brother, who is characterized as a rigid and miserly man, benefitted from this type of companionship. She feeds the parrot sugar upon meeting, and the two soon form a connection.

The parrot's eastern origins illustrate the problematic and pervasive colonial networks in the late nineteenth and early twentieth centuries, including Woolf's own ambivalence toward imperialism. As Rohman writes in a chapter on imperialism and animals in modernist writing, animality in high modernism represents the growing destabilization of the British Empire and subject, and nonhuman animals often come to represent the "lowly," the "vigorous reentrenchment of Western sovereignty through the primarily racialized displacement of animality" (*Stalking* 30). Thus, James's origins allude to the long history of Western imperialism and the association between animality and non-Western cultures. As the only "representative" of the colonized Other, James comes to stand in for the pervasive and often implicit assumptions about the non-Western world. While brief, this reference to James's origins represents a broader indirection in Woolf's writing, in which she seeks to recover a more ethical stance toward nonhuman animals, while at the same time relying on problematic representations of the so-called Orient. As Anna Snaith and Elleke Boehmer suggest, Woolf had a complex view of imperialism in her writing, including, but not limited to, her collaboration with Leonard to write *Empire and Commerce in Africa*. Virginia was "thinking about empire" in terms of anti-imperialism and economic exploitation in the 1920s. However, in "The Widow and the Parrot," Woolf maintains the link between non-Western cultures and animality, which is one way ideological forms of imperialism persisted in the modernist era.

Parrots have an important role in modernist literature beyond the latent imperialist assumptions associated with an "eastern" bird, which may have also inspired Woolf's writing. In particular, Flaubert's "Un Coeur Simple," or "A Simple Heart," a short story included in his *Three Tales* (1877), has several parallels with Woolf's story.[7] Flaubert, who composed the story with a stuffed parrot on his desk (Jehlen 87), writes about Félicité, who acquires a parrot named Loulou from a neighbor. As Félicité grows to old age, she treasures her relationship with the parrot. When it dies, she is so attached to it she has Loulou stuffed and displayed in her room. On her deathbed, Félicité sees an apparition of the parrot floating above her head, which, for Myra Jehlen, represents an ironic conflation between the Holy Spirit (commonly figured as a dove) and the bird Loulou. Religious readings aside, Flaubert's narrative parallels Woolf's "The Widow and the Parrot," including not only the relationship between an elderly widow and a parrot, but also the reference to a ghostly bird. At the very end of "The Widow and the Parrot," Woolf writes that, "if you visit [the widow's house] in the moonlight you may hear a parrot tapping with his beak upon a brick floor, while others have seen an old woman sitting there in a white apron" (26). Evoking the image of a spectral parrot, much like the one seen in Flaubert's story, Woolf suggests that Mrs. Gage and James continue their relationship in the afterlife. Woolf was well aware of Flaubert's story, as she references "Un Coeur Simple" in her essay "On Re-Reading Novels," writing, "we have reached our conception of *Un Coeur Simple* by working from the emotion outwards, and, the reading over there is nothing to be seen; there is everything to be felt" (130). Here, Woolf privileges the emotional relationship between the elderly Félicité and her parrot, emphasizing

---

[7] I must thank Debra Rae Cohen for drawing my attention to the parallel between Flaubert's story and Woolf's story.

the affective tone of Flaubert's writing and indicating Flaubert's potential influence on her children's story. While Flaubert's parrot may be said to take on a highly symbolic meaning—for instance, Julian Barnes's 1984 novel *Flaubert's Parrot* investigates the legacy of the literary avian—Woolf in many ways foregrounds the companionship between Félicité and Loulou ("everything to be felt") rather than any literary metaphor.

The scene that introduces Gage to James describes the parrot as though he is a "rational being," raising questions about sentience and intelligence—questions that are reaffirmed at the end of the narrative when James helps Mrs. Gage find the treasure Mr. Joseph had hidden away. Such questions of intelligence and sentience raise questions of ethical value in Woolf's work which are not unique to "The Widow and the Parrot." In *Flush*, for instance, Woolf's speculative biography of Elizabeth Barrett Browning's cocker spaniel, we learn about the complex experiences of a dog. As Jamie Johnson writes about nonhuman experience in *Flush*: "[J]ust as a human character might develop, transform, and manifest into a complex being, so too does Flush grow [. . .] Woolf remains ambitious in her attempt to create not a human character but a nonhuman character based on the specific details exclusive to canine being" (35). In focusing on nonhuman experience, Woolf therefore emphasizes the animal's intelligence and experience. Alternatively, for David Herman, "Woolf's textual designs enable interpreters of *Flush* to co-construct and imaginatively inhabit. Woolf's use of a nonhuman protagonist as an internal focalizer or reflector creates a hybrid discourse, in which narrative techniques conventionally associated both with fiction and with nonfiction cross-pollinate" (9-10). While such critics are aware of the ways in which Woolf is a human imagining a dog's experience in *Flush*, Johnson and Herman recognize that the textual design is itself much more complicated, creating a complex perspective of canine experience.

The narrative point of view in "The Widow and the Parrot" is clearly different than that of *Flush*, as the children's story does not provide readers with the parrot's perspective; nevertheless, Woolf does make us aware of the ways in which James's intelligence is either diminished by or illegible to those in the society around him. For instance, as the children's story draws to its apex, Joseph's house burns to the ground in what at first seems like an accident. The Rev. James Hawkesford tells Mrs. Gage not to "worry for the dumb creatures. I make no doubt the parrot was mercifully suffocated on his perch" (13). Gage, however, insists that she look for the bird, resisting the reverend's insistence that she not worry for "dumb creatures." And, when James returns to Mrs. Gage in the night to wake her, she asserts that "The creature has more meaning in its acts than we as humans know" (15). James leads Gage to the ruins of Joseph's house, and in his excitement taps the floor with his beak. He shouts, "Not at home!," which Gage "understood to mean that she was to move [the bricks on the floor]" (17). The wealth is discovered beneath the floor, and Gage claims that "it was only by extraordinary coincidence of the fire and the parrot's sagacity that old Joseph's craft was defeated" (19). In each of these examples, the narrator emphasizes that James is communicating with Gage, that he is "sagacious," or more intelligent than humans assume. The children's story in part reveals the ways in which animality is itself constructed, including the ways we categorize nonhuman animals as less rational or intelligent than humans. To suggest that James has "more meaning" than "we as humans know" is to imply that there is a complex social dynamic at play that projects assumptions about James onto his intelligence.

While the story might be said to privilege intelligence in such a manner, there are other ways in which Gage raises the ethical status of James by refusing to commodify him or reduce him to his functional use. For example, despite suggestions from a banker who handles Joseph's estate and others in the community, Mrs. Gage refuses to sell James despite her poverty. At one point, someone offers to buy the bird for half a crown out of pity, "but Mrs. Gage refused his offer with such indignation, saying that she would not sell the bird for all the wealth of the Indies . . . [the man] concluded that the old woman had been crazed by her troubles" (22). Gage refuses to see the parrot as mere material; not only does she develop relationships with animals, but she also resists the tendency of those around her to view animals as mere assets. James the parrot and Shag, her dog, cannot be reduced to soulless machines (in the Cartesian sense);[8] for Gage, humans benefit from their associations with nonhuman animals in a way that necessarily establishes ethical—as opposed to purely material or economic—relationships.

Woolf's ethics of dependency, in which the disabled Mrs. Gage relies on the animals around her, impels her readers to reconsider the divide between human and nonhuman animals. She questions the ways those around her reduce the intelligence of nonhuman animals like James, packaging a distinct critique of ideology within a children's story. The didactic tone of the story, in which Gage is rewarded for her "kindness to animals," illustrates that this type of animal ethics was important enough to Woolf to communicate it to her young readers. Considering the context of the modernist period, Woolf is responding to the tendency of humanistic approaches to privilege anthropocentrism and ableism.

Moreover, it is important not to overlook the relationship between disability and nonhuman animals in "The Widow and the Parrot." In challenging the ways others view nonhuman animals, including Shag and James, as functional assets, Gage necessarily raises questions about how they view her old age and lameness. If one should not rescue James, for instance, because he is viewed as a "dumb creature"—a phrase that carries with it the long shadow of ableism in Western society—then Gage implicitly asks why the citizens of Rodmell should care about a disabled individual such as herself. While not "dumb," Gage's mobility impairment is viewed as less "functional" than normative embodiment. Therefore, her defense of James is in many ways a defense of her own status; even if we maintain the important boundaries between nonhuman animals and disabled individuals, Gage's undermining of functionalist approaches to ethical value have far-reaching implications.

---

[8] Descartes knew animals produce calls, cries, songs, and various gestures that express their "passions"; however, he still maintained they never produce declarative speech in which they "use words, or put together other signs, as we do in order to declare our thoughts to others" (1637/1988, p. 45). Hence, they are, for Descartes, "automata" without thought.

Conclusion

While "The Widow and the Parrot" is a relatively obscure work, it helps us to understand Woolf's ethical perspectives more broadly. This short story supports Rohman's suggestion that "Nurse Lugton's Curtain" is a reflection of the role of nonhuman animals in shaping aesthetics, as well as the recent surge in writing on Woolf's longer fiction, such as *Flush*. For example, in *Flush*, the invalid Barrett Browning and the canine Flush share an intimate (and, as I would argue, inherently ethical) relationship (see Smith). For critics such as Karalyn Kendall-Morrick, Woolf develops "a model of literary character that reflects humans' entanglement in the more-than-human contexts of multispecies life" (508). Such an entanglement is also apparent in "The Widow and the Parrot"; Woolf creates complex arrangements and networks of life, emphasizing interdependency. Furthermore, the use of the children's story as a literary genre works to uncover the ways Woolf frequently relied on the common cultural repository of Victorian children's literature and fairytales to extend the ways such genres refigure animal ethics.

This is just one way we might think through the interspecies interdependence that is so prominent in Woolf's "The Widow and the Parrot." As Philip Armstrong suggests in *What Animals Mean in the Fiction of Modernity*, it is necessary to move beyond "reading animals as screens for the projection of human interests and meanings, which until recently was the predominant way of treating cultural representations of animals" (2). Literary critics in the twenty-first century have a responsibility to rethink the ways we talk about nonhuman animals in literature and culture, including their ethical value. We must, in other words, consider nonhuman animals as ends in themselves, not as tools or assets—an ethics laid bare by Oliver's interspecies interdependence. In this way it is also necessary to think about the complex links between animal studies and disability studies, including the networks of dependency at play in various relationships. Woolf's use of the children's story allows her to circumvent the limitations of so-called highbrow literary genres, and we see in her writing a challenge to the "functionalist" approach to both nonhuman animals and disabled individuals. Companionship and emotional engagement are just two of the many ways we might extend our understanding of ethical value within the moral community, which is precisely the reason it is necessary to note that James and Shag are valued by Gage, but also that Gage herself has an important role to play in her society. Much like disability and animality intersect in Woolf's other work, such as *Flush* (the invalid Barrett Browning and her canine companion), "The Widow and the Parrot" links disability and animality in a productive manner to undermine a wider, increasing cultural investment in anthropocentric ableism in the late nineteenth and early twentieth centuries.

"The Widow and the Parrot" is still often found in the children's section of many libraries, which is perhaps one reason the story has not received much critical attention. As evidenced by the surge in scholarship on *Flush* in the past two decades as well as more recent writing on "Nurse Lugton's Curtain," though, it seems clear there is much to be gained in researching Woolf's lesser-known writing. "The Widow and the Parrot" is a unique genre for Woolf, and her argument for kindness to animals is difficult to miss. Not only does this story help us to learn more about Woolf, but it also participates in a much wider reevaluation of bioethics in the modernist era, particularly the anthropocentric ableism that reduces individuals to functional use or utilitarian metrics.

Works Cited

Armstrong, Philip. *What Animals Mean in the Fiction of Modernity*. Routledge, 2008.
Attridge, Derek. *The Singularity of Literature*. Routledge, 2004.
Bell, Quentin. "Afterword." *The Widow and the Parrot*. Harcourt, 1988, p. 25.
Czarnecki, Kristin. "Virginia Woolf, Authorship, and Legacy: Unravelling Nurse Lugton's Curtain." Bloomsbury Heritage Series. Cecil Woolf Publishers, 2013.
Davidson, Michael. *Invalid Modernism: Disability and the Missing Body of the Aesthetic*. Oxford UP, 2019.
Derrida, Jacques. *The Animal That Therefore I Am*. 2002. Fordham UP, 2008.
Descartes, René. "Discourse on the Method." *Descartes: Selected Philosophical Writings*, edited and translated by Cottingham, Stoothoff, and Murdoch. 1637. Cambridge UP, 1988.
Duckworth Stephen, Julia. "The Black Cat or the Grey Parrot." *Julia Duckworth Stephen: Stories for Children, Essays for Adults*, edited by Diane F. Gillespie and Elizabeth Steele. Syracuse UP, 1987, pp. 115–37.
Galef, David. "Disfigured Figures: Virginia Woolf's Disabled List." *University of Mississippi Studies in English*, vol. 9, 1991, pp. 135–40.
Gubar, Marah. "On Not Defining Children's Literature." *PMLA*, vol. 126, no. 1, January 2011, pp. 209–16.
Henig, Suzanne. "Introduction." *Virginia Woolf: A Cockney's Farming Experiences*, edited by Suzanne Henig. San Diego State UP, 1972, pp. i–viii.
Herman, David. "Modernist Life Writing and Nonhuman Lives: Ecologies of Experience in Virginia Woolf's *Flush*." *Modern Fiction Studies*, vol. 59, no. 3, 2013, pp. 547–68.
Hodgkins, Hope. "High Modernism for the Lowest: Children's Books by Woolf, Joyce, and Greene." *Children's Literature Association Quarterly*, vol. 32, no. 4, 2007, pp. 354–67.
Hunt, Peter. *Criticism, Theory, and Children's Literature*. Blackwell, 1991.
Jehlen, Myra. "Félicité and the Holy Parrot." *Raritan: A Quarterly Review*, vol. 26, no. 4, 2007, pp. 86–95.

Johnson, Jamie. "Virginia Woolf's Flush: Decentering Human Subjectivity through the Nonhuman Animal Character." *Virginia Woolf Miscellany*, vol. 84, no. 1, 2013: pp. 34–36.

Jones, Clara. "Virginia Woolf's 1931 'Cook Sketch.'" *Woolf Studies Annual*, vol. 20, no. 1, 2014, pp. 1–23.

Kendall-Morwick, Karalyn. "Mongrel Fiction: Canine Bildung and the Feminist Critique of Anthropocentrism in Virginia Woolf's Flush." *Modern Fiction Studies*, vol. 60, no. 3, 2014, pp. 506–26.

Linett, Maren Tova. *Bodies of Modernism: Physical Disability in Transatlantic Modernist Literature*. U of Michigan P, 2017.

Lyon, Janet. "On the Asylum Road with Woolf and Mew." *Modernism/modernity* 18, no. 3, 2011, pp. 551–47.

Martin, Ann. "Modernist Transformations: Virginia Woolf, Cinderella, and the Legacy of Lady Ritchie." *Woolf Studies Annual*, vol. 11, 2005, pp. 33–53.

Mitchell, David and Sharon Snyder. *Narrative Prosthesis: Disability and the Dependencies of Discourse*. U of Michigan P, 2000.

Oliver, Kelly. "Service Dogs: Between Animal Studies and Disability Studies." *philoSOPHIA*, vol. 6 no. 2, 2016, pp. 241-58.

Paul, Lissa. "Enigma Variations: What Feminist Theory Knows about Children's Literature." *Signal*, vol. 53, no. 1, 1987, pp. 186–201.

Rohman, Carrie. *Choreographies of the Living: Bioaesthetics in Literature, Art, and Performance*. Oxford UP, 2018.

—. *Stalking the Subject: Modernism and the Animal*. Columbia UP, 2009.

Ryan, Derek. "Following Snakes and Moths: Modernist Ethics and Posthumanism." *Twentieth-Century Literature*, vol. 61, no. 3, pp. 287–304.

Siebers, Tobin. *Disability Theory*. U of Michigan P, 2008.

Smith, Craig. "Across the Widest Gulf: Nonhuman Subjectivity in Virginia Woolf's Flush." *Twentieth-Century Literature* vol. 48, no. 3, 2002, pp. 348–61.

Snaith, Anna, and Elleke Boehmer. "Leonard and Virginia Woolf: Writing against Empire." *The Journal of Commonwealth Literature*, vol. 50, no. 1, 2015, pp. 19–32.

Steele, Elizabeth. "Stories for Children." *Julia Duckworth Stephen: Stories for Children, Essays for Adults*, edited by Diane F. Gillespie and Elizabeth Steele. Syracuse UP, 1987, pp. 29–35

Taylor, Sunaura. *Beasts of Burden: Animal and Disability Liberation*. New Press, 2018.

Wolfe, Cary. *What is Posthumanism?* U of Minnesota P, 2009.

Woolf, Virginia. "A Cockney's Farming Experience." *Virginia Woolf: A Cockney's Farming Experience and The Experiences of a Pater-familias*, edited by Suzanne Henig. San Diego State UP, 1972, pp. 1–4.

—. *Flush: A Biography*. 1933. Oxford UP, 2009.

—. "On a Faithful Friend." *The Essays of Virginia Woolf: Volume I: 1904–1912*, edited by Andrew McNeillie. Harcourt, 1986, pp. 12–15.
—. "On Re-Reading Novels." *The Moment and Other Essays*. Hogarth, 1947, pp. 126–34.
—. "The Widow and the Parrot." 1982. Harcourt, 1988.

Guide to Library Special Collections

This list reflects updates or changes received by January 2020. Readers are advised to check an institution's website for the most current information. Suggestions for additions to this list are always welcome.

Name of Collection:	The Beinecke Rare Book and Manuscript Library
Contact:	Timothy Young, Curator of Modern Books and Manuscripts Nancy Kuhl, Curator of American Literature
Address:	Yale University Library P.O. Box 208240 New Haven, CT 06520-8240
URL:	http://beinecke.library.yale.edu/
Access Requirements:	Registration required at first visit.
Holdings Relevant To Woolf:	General Collection includes autograph manuscript of "Notes on Oliver Goldsmith." Comments on Edward Gibbon, William Beckford Collection. Letters from Virginia Woolf in the Bryher Papers, the Louise Morgan and Otto Theis Papers, the Rebecca West Papers, the James Lees-Milne Papers, and the Mary Smyth Hunter correspondence. Related material: 41 letters from Vita Sackville-West to Violet Trefusis; files relating to Robert Manson Myers's *From Beowulf to Virginia Woolf* in the Edmond Pauker Papers. Yale Collection of American Literature includes typewritten manuscripts of "The Art of Walter Sickert," "Augustine Birrell," "Aurora Leigh," "How Should One Read a Book?" "Letter to a Young Poet," "The Novels of Turgenev," "Street Haunting." Dial/Scofield Thayer Papers: manuscripts of "The Lives of the Obscure," "Miss Ormerod," and "Mrs. Dalloway in Bond Street." Letters from Virginia Woolf in the William Rose Benet Papers, the Benet Family Correspondence, Henry Seidel Canby Papers, the Seward Collins Papers, the Dial/Scofield Thayer Papers, and the *Yale Review* archive. Material relating to translations of Woolf in the Thornton Wilder papers. Related material:

Clive Bell, "Virginia Woolf" (Dial/Scofield Thayer Papers); 43 letters from Leonard Woolf to Helen McAfee (*Yale Review*); 11 letters from Leonard Woolf to Gertrude Stein.

Name of Collection: The Henry W. and Albert A. Berg Collection of English and American Literature

Contact: Carolyn Vega, Curator

Address: The New York Public Library
Stephen A. Schwarzman Building
476 Fifth Avenue, Room 320
New York, NY 10018

Telephone: 212-930-0815
Email: carolynvega@nypl.org; berg@nypl.org
URL: https://www.nypl.org/locations/divisions/berg-collection-english-and-american-literature

Hours: Tue.–Sat. 10 am–5:45 pm
Closed Sun., Mon. and legal holidays

Access Requirements: A New York Public Library card and current government-issued photo identification are required to complete registration. Please contact the division in advance to schedule your research visit.

Restictions: Virginia Woolf's bound manuscripts, because of their fragile condition, are made available on microfilm or through digital surrogates.

Holdings Relevant To Woolf: The Virginia Woolf collection of papers (Berg Coll MSS Woolf) includes the manuscripts and/or typescripts of all of Woolf's novels except *Orlando*, including: *Between the Acts, Flush, Jacob's Room, Mrs. Dalloway* (notes and fragments), *Night and Day, To the Lighthouse, The Voyage Out, The Waves, The Years*; 12 notebooks of articles, essays, fiction and reviews, 1924–1940; 36 volumes of diaries; 26 volumes of reading notes; and correspondence with Vanessa Bell, Violet Dickinson, Shuhua Ling, Ethel Smyth, Vita Sackville-West and others.

In 2019, the Berg Collection acquired the William Beekman Collection of Virginia Woolf and Her

Circle, which comprises extensive correspondence, remarkable examples of scarce printed books, and unique material such as photographs, original artwork by Vanessa Bell, and ephemera, including Woolf's 1923 passport. The Berg also holds related collections of Vita Sackville-West, Leslie Stephen, and others.

Finding aid for the Virginia Woolf collection of papers: http://archives.nypl.org/brg/19159
Finding aid for the William Beekman Collection of Virginia Woolf and Her Circle: http://archives.nypl.org/brg/25777
List of all finding aids in the Berg Collection: http://archives.nypl.org/brg

Name of Collection:	The British Library Manuscript Collections
Contact:	Manuscripts and Maps Reference Team
Address:	96 Euston Road London NW1 2DB England
Telephone:	0207-412-7513
Fax:	0207-412-7745
Email:	mss@bl.uk
Hours:	Mon. 10 am–5 pm; Tues.–Sat. 9:30 am–5 pm
Access Requirements:	British Library Reader Pass (signed I.D. required and usually proof of post-graduate academic status, or other demonstrable need to use the collections—see www.bl.uk). In addition, access to most literary autograph material only available with letter of recommendation.
Restictions:	Paper Copies, Microfilms, and Photography of selected items available upon receipt of written authorization for photo duplication from the copyright holder.
Holdings Relevant To Woolf:	Diaries 1930–1931 (microfilm); *Mrs. Dalloway* and other writings (1923–1925) three volumes (Add MS 51044-51046); letter from Leonard Woolf to H. G. Wells (1941) (Add MS 52553); two letters

from Virginia Woolf and three letters from Leonard Woolf to John Lehmann (1941) (Add MS 56234); letters from Virginia Woolf (1923-1927) and one written on behalf of Leonard Woolf to S. S. Koteliansky (1946) (Add MS 48974); notebook of Virginia Stephen (1906–1909) (Add MS 61837); Stephen family papers (Add MS 88954); travel and literary notebook of Virginia Woolf (Add MS 61837); A sketch of the past revised ts (1940) (Add MS 61973); letters from Virginia Woolf in the correspondence files of Lytton and James Strachey (Add MS 60655-60734); letter from Virginia Woolf to Mildred Massingberd (Add MS 61891); letter from Virginia Woolf to Harriet Shaw Weaver(1917) (Add MS 57353); (in the same volume as the letter on behalf of Leonard); letter from Virginia Woolf to Frances Cornford (1929) (Add MS 58422); letter from Virginia Woolf to Ernest Rhys (1930) (Egerton MS 3248); correspondence of Virginia Woolf in the Society of Authors archive (1934–1937) (Add MS 63206-63463); letter and postcard from Virginia Woolf to Bernard Shaw (1940) (Add MS 50522); three letters (suicide notes) from Virginia Woolf (1941) (Add MS 57947). "Hyde Park Gate News" 1891–1892, 1895 (Add. MSS 70725, 70726). Letters of Virginia and Leonard Woolf to Lady Aberconway, 1927–1941 (Add MS 70775). List related to a fund for Desmond MacCarthy, annotated by Virginia Woolf, 1927 (Add MS 70776). Letters from Virginia Woolf to Macmillan Co. 1903, 1908 (Add MS 54786-56035). Letters from Virginia Woolf to P. Strachey, 1935-1937 (Add MS 81956). Letter to Marie Stopes from Adeline Virginia Woolf, 1941 (Add MS 58495). Collection of RPs ("reserved photocopies"– copies of manuscripts exported, some subject to restrictions).

Name of Collection:	Harry Ransom Center
Contact:	Head, Research Services
Address:	Harry Ransom Center The University of Texas at Austin P.O. Box 7219 Austin, TX 78713-7219

Telephone:	512-471-9119
Fax:	512-471-2899
Email:	reference@hrc.utexas.edu
Hours:	See web site for most current information: www.hrc.utexas.edu
Access Requirements:	Completed online research application; current photo identification.
Holdings Relevant To Woolf:	The manuscript collection includes the typed manuscript with autograph revisions of *Kew Gardens*, and the typed manuscript and autograph revisions of "Thoughts on Peace in an Air Raid." The Center holds 571 of Woolf's letters, including correspondence to Elizabeth Bowen, Lady Ottoline Morrell, Mary Hutchinson, William Plomer, Hugh Walpole and others. Further mss. relating to Virginia Woolf include letters to her from T. S. Eliot and reviews of her work. A substantial collection of the first British and American editions of Woolf's published works, as well as 130 volumes from Leonard and Virginia Woolf's library and a collection of books published by the Hogarth Press, is also housed.
	An art collection holds a landscape painting of Virginia's garden and a series of Cockney cartoons in a sketch book, signed "V.W." The center also has extensive holdings of materials related to Leonard Woolf, Ottoline Morrell, Mary Hutchinson, Lytton Strachey, Dora Carrington, E. M. Forster, Clive Bell, Roger Fry, Vanessa Bell, Bertrand Russell, Elizabeth Bowen, William Plomer, Stephen Spender and Hugh Walpole.
Name of Collection:	Houghton Library (Monk's House Photograph Albums)
Contact:	Houghton Public Services
Address:	Harvard Yard Cambridge, MA 02138 United States
Telephone:	617-495-2440
Fax:	617-495-1376

Email:	houghton_library@harvard.edu
URL:	http://hcl.harvard.edu/libraries/houghton/
Hours:	Mon, Fri, Sat 9 am–5 pm; Tue–Thu 9 am–7 pm
Access Requirements:	http://hcl.harvard.edu/info/special_collections/index.cfm
Holdings Relevant To Woolf:	Virginia Woolf Monk's House photograph album, MH-1 Virginia Woolf Monk's House photograph album, MH-2 Virginia Woolf Monk's House photograph album, MH-3 Virginia Woolf Monk's House photograph album, MH-4 Virginia Woolf Monk's House photograph album, MH-5 Virginia Woolf Monk's House photograph album, MH-6 Virginia Woolf Monk's House photographs Users can also page through the albums by following the links on this website (http://press.pace.edu/woolf-studies-annual-wsa/)
Name of Collection:	The Lilly Library
Contact:	Joel Silver, Director and Curator of Early Books and Manuscripts Erika Dowell, Associate Director and Curator of Modern Books and Manuscripts
Please Note:	**The Lilly Library is preparing for a major renovation and is closed until at least March 2020.** By that date, it is expected that the Public Services operation will have moved to the main library at IU, the Wells Library. There will be a Reading Room at the Wells Library on the 10th floor. The address there is:
Address:	Herman B Wells Library 1320 E 10th St. Bloomington, IN 47405

Information during the move and renovation is available at:

https://libraries.indiana.edu/lilly-library/faq

Patrons wishing to use collections from March 2020 through approximately summer 2021 would be best served by contacting our Public Services Department email account at liblilly@indiana.edu to check on collection availability and access. Some collections will be inaccessible for the duration of the renovation but most will be available with advance notice.

Holdings Relevant To Woolf: Corrected page proofs for the American edition of *Mrs. Dalloway*; letters to Woolf from Desmond and Mary (Molly) MacCarthy; 77 letters (published in Letters) from Woolf to correspondents including Donald Clifford Brace, Robert Gathorne-Hardy, Barbara (Strachey) Halpern, Richard Arthur Warren Hughes, Desmond MacCarthy and Molly MacCarthy; "Preliminary Scheme for the formation of a Partnership between Mr Leonard Sidney Woolf and Mr John Lehmann to take over The Hogarth Press" (includes contract signed by Lehmann, Leonard Woolf, and Virginia Woolf and receipt for Lehmann's payment to Virginia Woolf to purchase Virginia Woolf's share in the Hogarth Press); photographs of Virginia Woolf, Leonard Woolf, Lytton Strachey, Strachey family, Roger Fry, and Vanessa Bell (Hannah Whitall Smith mss.); (Richard) Kennedy mss. (four hand-colored lithographs of Virginia Woolf: artist's proofs for RK's portfolio, VIRGINIA WOOLF: "AS I KNEW HER"; Sackville-West, V. mss. (10,529 items: includes the correspondence of Vita Sackville-West, and Harold Nicolson); MacCarthy mss. (ca. 10,000 items: papers of Desmond and Molly MacCarthy); correspondence between LW and Mary Gaither regarding publication of *A Checklist of the Hogarth Press* (1976, repr. 1986); Todd Avery, *Close and Affectionate Friends: Desmond and Molly MacCarthy and the Bloomsbury Group* (The Lilly Library/Indiana University Libraries, 1999).

Name of Collection:	Jane Marcus Collection
Contact:	Mount Holyoke College Archives and Special Collections
Address:	Mount Holyoke College 50 College Streeet 8 Dwight Hall South Hadley MA 01075
Telephone:	413-538-3079
Fax:	413-538-3029
Email:	archives@mtholyoke.edu
Hours:	Mon.–Fri. 9:30 am–12 pm and 1 pm–4:30 pm
Access Requirements:	Please contact the staff to make an appointment for your visit. Researchers complete a registration form upon arrival.
Restrictions:	The Jane Marcus Collection was received in December 2016 and is currently being reviewed. Please contact the Archives and Special Collections staff for updated access information.
Holdings Relevant To Woolf:	Jane Marcus, who died in May 2015, laid the groundwork for feminist studies to become a mode of inquiry within the academy and her work established Virginia Woolf as a major canonical writer. The collection includes several of Marcus's unpublished manuscripts, as well as her research files and correspondence.
Name of Collection:	Literature & Rare Books, Special Collections, University of Maryland Libraries
Contact:	Amber Kohl, Curator of Literature and Rare Books in Special Collections and University Archives
Address:	University of Maryland 2208 Hornbake Library College Park, MD 20742
Telephone:	310-405-9212
Email:	askhornbake@umd.edu
Hours:	Dates and hours of operation subject to change.

Regular hours are Mon.–Fri. 10 am–5 pm. Extended hours are available on select days during the academic school year. Email askhornbake@umd.edu before planning a research visit.

Access Requirements: Photo ID.

Holdings Relevant To Woolf: Papers of Hope Mirrlees contain five autograph letters and postcards (1919–1928) from Virginia Woolf to Mirrlees. Also in the collection are 113 letters from T. S. Eliot to Mirrlees, and three letters from Lady Ottoline Morrell to Mirrlees. A finding aid is available at http://hdl.handle.net/1903.1/1536.

Name of Collection: Monks House Papers/Leonard Woolf Papers/Charleston Papers/Nicolson Papers

Contact: University of Sussex, Special Collections

Address: The Keep
Woollards Way
Brighton & Hove
BN1 9PB

Telephone: 01273 482349
Email: library.specialcoll@sussex.ac.uk
URL: http://www.thekeep.info

Access Requirements: Seats in the reading room can be booked in advance. Identification is required to complete registration on your first visit to The Keep. Registration and material requests can be made through our website.

Restrictions: Access to some of the papers is by surrogate. Digital photography is allowed for private research, charges apply.

Holdings Relevant To Woolf: The University of Sussex holds two large archives relating to Leonard and Virginia Woolf: The Monks House Papers, primarily correspondence and MSS of Virginia Woolf, including the three scrapbooks relating to *Three Guineas*, and Virginia Woolf's engagement diaries from 1930 to her death in 1941; and The Leonard Woolf Papers, primarily correspondence and other papers of Leonard Woolf. (Monks House

Papers are available on microfilm in many research libraries.) The Charleston Papers consist in the main of letters written to or by Clive and Vanessa Bell and Duncan Grant which had accumulated in their home; the library houses Quentin Bell's photocopied set; letters from Roger Fry, Maynard Keynes, Lytton Strachey, Virginia Woolf, Vita Sackville-West, E. M. Forster, T. S. Eliot, Frances Partridge and others. The Maria Jackson letters comprise some 900 letters from Maria Jackson to Julia and Leslie Stephen. The Nicolson Papers complement these three Sussex archives relating to the Bloomsbury Group, and consist of Nigel Nicolson's correspondence relating to his editorial work as principal editor of the six-volume Letters of Virginia Woolf, published between 1975 and 1980.

The Bell Papers. A. O. Bell's correspondence relating to her editorial work on Virginia Woolf's diaries, a parallel collection to the Nicolson Papers. Collection level description may be accessed at www.archiveshub.ac.uk

Name of Collection:	The Morgan Library & Museum
Contact:	Reading Room
Address:	225 Madison Avenue New York, NY 10016
Telephone:	212-590-0315
Email:	readingroom@themorgan.org
URL:	www.themorgan.org
Access Requirements:	Admission to the Reading Room is by application and by appointment. See www.themorgan.org/research/reading.asp for application form.
Recent Acquisitions:	Letter from Virginia Woolf, Wells, to Clive Bell, 1908 August 3? : autograph manuscript initialed. 1 item (6 pages) MA 22718. Gift from the estate of Nancy N. Brooker, 2018 Letter from Virginia Woolf, London, to Clive Bell, 1909 July? : autograph manuscript initialed. 1 item (2 pages) MA 22719. Gift from the estate of Nancy N. Brooker, 2018

Letter from Virginia Woolf, Cornwall, to Clive Bell, 1909? December 26: autograph manuscript initialed. 1 item (7 pages) MA 22720. Gift from the estate of Nancy N. Brooker, 2018

Letter from Virginia Woolf, London, to Clive Bell, 1909 December 31?: autograph manuscript initialed. 1 item (4 pages) MA 22721. Gift from the estate of Nancy N. Brooker, 2018

Letter from Virginia Woolf, London, to Clive Bell, 1910?: autograph manuscript. 1 item (2 pages) MA 22722. Gift from the estate of Nancy N. Brooker, 2018

Letter from Virginia Woolf, Beddingham, to Clive Bell, 1917 December 22? : autograph manuscript initialed. 1 item (3 pages) MA 22723. Gift from the estate of Nancy N. Brooker, 2018

Letter from Virginia Woolf, London, to Clive Bell, 1922 March 20?: autograph manuscript initialed. 1 item (2 pages) MA 22724. Gift from the estate of Nancy N. Brooker, 2018

Letter from Virginia Woolf, London, to Clive Bell, 1922 November 7? : autograph manuscript initialed. 1 item (1 page) MA 22725. Gift from the estate of Nancy N. Brooker, 2018

Letter from Virginia Woolf, London, to Clive Bell, 1923 February? : autograph manuscript initialed. 1 item (2 pages) MA 22726. Gift from the estate of Nancy N. Brooker, 2018

Letter from Virginia Woolf, London, to Clive Bell, 1927 November? : autograph manuscript signed. 1 item (2 pages) MA 22727. Gift from the estate of Nancy N. Brooker, 2018

Postcard from Virginia Woolf, London, to Clive Bell, 1931 June 9: autograph manuscript initialed. 1 item (1 page) MA 22728. Gift from the estate of Nancy N. Brooker, 2018

Letter from Virginia Woolf, Rodmell, to Eric Duthie, 1927 October 2: typescript signed. 1 item (1 page). Saying that she is very interested in the series of biographies that he has described, but unfortunately she is too busy to write a volume for it. MA 22729. Gift from the estate of Nancy N. Brooker, 2018

Postcard from Virginia Woolf, London, to A.W. Brickett, 1937 February 17: autograph manuscript signed. 1 item (1 page). Thanking him for sending her a copy of the "Saturday review of literature."

MA 22730. Gift from the estate of Nancy N. Brooker, 2018

Virginia Woolf reclining in an armchair [photograph]. Rodmell, England, between 1919 and 1941. Gelatin silver print. 6 15/16 x 4 13/16 inches (17.6 x 12.3 cm) MA 22731. Gift from the estate of Nancy N. Brooker, 2018

Holdings Relevant To Woolf:

Virginia Woolf. Autograph manuscript notebook, 1931 Sept. 24. 1 item (52 p.) ; 265 x 208 mm. Contains drafts of "A Letter to a Young Poet," a brief letter to the press entitled "The Villa Jones" [ff. 3–5] and a monologue by a working-class woman [ff. 44–46]. MA 3333. Purchased on the Fellows Fund with the special assistance of Anne S. Dayton, Enid A. Haupt, Mrs. James H. Ripley, Mr. and Mrs. August H. Schilling, and John S. Thacher, 1979.

Virginia Woolf. Autograph letters signed (2) and typed letter signed, dated London [etc.], to E. McKnight Kauffer, 1931 Apr. 4 and 23, and undated. 3 items (4 p.). Concerning a drawing of her and a bibliography of her works. MA 1679. Purchased from Marion Dorn Kauffer in 1955.

Vanessa Bell. 84 autograph letters, 3 typed letters, 7 postcards, and 3 telegrams. Most, but not all, are written by Vanessa Bell to John Maynard Keynes. Concerning Duncan Grant, Roger Fry, Clive Bell, the Bell children, Leonard and Virginia Woolf, Lytton Strachey, John Maynard and Lydia Lopokova Keynes, David Garnett, Ottoline Morrell, and others. MA 3448. Items in this collection are described in 97 individual records (MA 3448.1-97). Purchased on the Fellows Fund, special gift of the Gramercy Park Foundation (Mrs. Michael Tucker), 1980.

Letter from Virginia Woolf, London to R. W. Chapman, 1930 November 13. 1 item (1 p.). Concerning revisions to the criticism section of a bibliography of Jane Austen. Accompanied by carbon copy of a letter from Chapman to Woolf dated 1930 November 11. MA 8893. Purchased on the Drue Heinz Fund, 2017.

GUIDE TO SPECIAL LIBRARY COLLECTIONS 133

Name of Collection:	1. Katherine Mansfield Papers 2. Arts Club of Chicago Papers
Contact:	Martha Briggs, Lloyd Lewis Curator of Modern Manuscripts Liesl Olson, Director, Scholl Center for American History and Culture
Address:	The Newberry Library 60 West Walton Street Chicago, IL, 60610
Telephone:	312-255-3554 (Briggs) 312-255-3665 (Olson)
Email:	briggsm@newberry.org olsonl@newberry.org
Hours:	Tues.–Fri. 9 am–5 pm; Sat. 9 am–1 pm
Access Requirements:	The Newberry's reading rooms are open to researchers who are at least 16 years old or juniors in high school. Before using the collections, all researchers must apply for and receive a reader's card. Issued in the Reference Center on the third floor, cards require a valid photo ID, proof of current home address, and a research interest that is supported by the Newberry's collections.
Holdings Relevant To Woolf:	The papers of the Arts Club of Chicago—since 1916, a private club and preeminent exhibitor of international art—contain material related to Bloomsbury artists and how they were received in Chicago. The papers of Katherine Mansfield contain manuscript copies of some of Mansfield's most important work, and outgoing correspondence—the bulk to artist Dorothy Brett and Lady Ottoline Morrell. There are a few incoming miscellaneous letters, printed works, photographs and memorabilia.
Name of Collection:	University of Reading Special Collections
Contact:	Special Collections Service
Address:	Special Collections Service University of Reading 6 Redlands Road Reading RG1 5EX

Telephone:	0118-378-8660
Email:	specialcollections@reading.ac.uk
URL:	http://www.reading.ac.uk/special-collections/
Access Requirements:	Prior appointment suggested to consult material. Permission required to consult or copy material in the Hogarth Press, Jonathan Cape, and Chatto & Windus collections from Random House:

Random House Group Archive & Library
1 Cole Street
Crown Park
Rushden
Northants. NN10 6RZ

Archive@penguinrandomhouse.co.uk

Holdings Relevant To Woolf: Hogarth Press (MS 2750): editorial and production correspondence relating to publications of the Press including Woolf's own titles. Production ledgers 1920s–1950s. Correspondence between Leonard Woolf and Stanley Unwin about progress with his collected edition of the works of Freud. Order books – e.g. lists of booksellers, book clubs and how many books they have ordered for a particular title. Newscuttings—press clippings of advertisements for Hogarth Press books including Virginia Woolf publications. Correspondence files regarding translation rights of Virginia Woolf's publications, 1924-1983, (MS 2750/C). Photographs of Leonard Woolf, Virginia Woolf, and other Bloomsbury figures (MS 2750/D).

Chatto & Windus (CW): small number of letters 1915–1925; 1929–1931.Various letters and notes by Leonard Woolf; outgoing letters to Leonard Woolf: 22 November 1927 (CW A/119); outgoing letters to Virginia Woolf: 29 January 1936 (CW A/172), 22 December 1931 (CW A/135), 31 December 1931 (CW A/135), 15 December 1920 (CW A/100), 20 December 1920 (CW A/100).
George Bell & Sons (MS 1640): 5 letters from Leonard Woolf 1930–1966.

Routledge (RKP): Reader's report by Leonard Woolf on George Padmore's "Britannia rules the blacks" (1935); "How Britain rules Africa." 1 letter from Leonard Woolf (June 1941) from Miscellaneous publishing correspondence 1941-1942 Wi-Wy RKP 174/15. Draft introduction by Leonard Woolf to *Letters on India* by Mulk Raj (1942) and 1 letter to Leonard Woolf from Mulk Raj Anand 1942-1943 RKP 178/3. Correspondence concerning the publication of The War for Peace by Leonard Woolf, 1939-1940 RKP 160/5. 1 letter from Virginia Woolf declining an invitation from Routledge to write a biography of Margaret Bondfield, 25 May 1940 RKP 160/5.

Megroz (MS 1979/68): 2 letters from Leonard Woolf, 1926.

Allen & Unwin (MS 3282): Correspondence with Leonard Woolf c.1914-1918 (re. his book *International Government*), 1923-1924; 1939-1940; 1943; 1946; 1950-1951; 1953; 1965 (concerning ill-founded rumors about the Hogarth Press); 1967 (concerning a reprint of *Empire and Commerce in Africa*).

Jonathan Cape (MS 2446): All correspondence from file JC A43. Correspondence between Jonathan Cape and Virginia Woolf and Cape and A. C. Gissing concerning Virginia Woolf's introduction to George Gissing's *Ionian Sea* to which A. C. Gissing objects. 1 postcard (1935), 1 letter (1933), 2 letters (1932) from Virginia Woolf. 1 letter (1932) from Virginia Woolf declining to write an introduction to Jane Austen's *Northanger Abbey*. 4 letters (1931) from Virginia Woolf declining to write an introduction to one of Miss Thackeray's books.

Letters from Vanessa Bell: 1 letter from Bell CW 152/2; 1 letter from Bell CW 171/10; 2 letters from Bell CW 578/1; 1 letter from Bell CW 59/9; 1 letter from Bell (1936) CW 61/10. Artwork by Vanessa Bell for various Virginia Woolf titles.

Artwork by Angelica Garnett, Philippa Bramson and others for various books in the Chatto & Windus archive.

Name of Collection:	Frances Hooper Collection of Virginia Woolf Books and Manuscripts. Elizabeth Power Richardson Bloomsbury Iconography Collection.
Contact:	Karen V. Kukil, Associate Curator of Special Collections.
Address:	Mortimer Rare Book Collection Young Library 4 Tyler Drive Northampton, MA 01063
Telephone:	413-585-2908
Email:	kkukil@smith.edu
URL:	https://libraries.smith.edu/special-collections
Access Requirements:	Appointment to be made with the Curator.
Holdings Relevant To Woolf:	The Hooper Collection emphasizes Woolf as an essayist but also includes many Hogarth Press first editions, limited editions of Woolf's works, and translations. The collection includes page proofs of *Orlando*, *To the Lighthouse*, and *The Common Reader*, corrected by Woolf for the first American editions, a proof copy of *The Waves* that Woolf inscribed to Hugh Walpole, and the proof copies of *The Years* and of *Flush*. The Collection also has one of the deluxe editions of *Orlando* that was printed on green paper. Other items include twenty-two pages of reading notes from 1926, three pages of notes on D. H. Lawrence's *Sons and Lovers*, thirty-three pages of notes for *Roger Fry*, a six-page ms. "As to criticism," a five-page ms. of "The Searchlight," and a fourteen-page ms. of "The Patron and The Crocus." The Hooper Collection also owns 140 letters between Woolf and Lytton Strachey as well as other correspondence, including a 13 February [1921] letter to Katherine Mansfield and ten letters to Mela and Robert Spira. The Richardson Collection is a working collection of books and materials used by Richardson in preparing her Bloomsbury Iconography. It includes Leslie Stephen's photograph album, ninety-eight original exhibition catalogs dating back to 1929,

clippings and photocopies of such items as reviews of early Woolf works, and Bloomsbury material from British *Vogue* of the 1920s. The Collection also has three preliminary pencil drawings by Vanessa Bell for Flush.

The Mortimer Rare Book Collection also owns Woolf's 1916 Italian ms. notebook and her corrected typescripts of "Reviewing" and "The Searchlight." In addition, there is a 1923 photograph of Woolf at Garsington. Original cover designs for Hogarth Press publications include *The Common Reader*, *On Being Ill*, and *Duncan Grant*. The Mortimer Rare Book Room also has a Sylvia Plath collection that includes eight of Woolf's books from Plath's library, several of which are underlined and annotated, as well as Plath's notes from her undergraduate English 211 class at Smith (1951–1952) in which she studied *To the Lighthouse*. The collection also includes Woolf's 26 February 1939 letter to Vita Sackville-West, a 1931 bronze bust of Virginia Woolf by Stephen Tomlin, a 1923 Hogarth Press edition of T. S. Eliot's *The Waste Land*, a 1919 Hogarth Press edition of *Paris* by Hope Mirrlees and first editions of Vita Sackville-West and Katherine Mansfield publications. Additional Bloomsbury items include *Original Woodcuts* (Omega Workshops, 1918), Vanessa Bell's original woodcut for the cover of *Monday or Tuesday* (1921), and exhibition catalogs for *Manet and the Post-Impressionists* (Grafton Galleries, 1911), *Friday Club Members* (Mansard Gallery, 1921) *Paintings and Drawings by Vanessa Bell* (Independent Gallery, 1922). Additional photographs include the Mary L. S. Bennett (née Fisher) Family Photographs. A recent gift of the Henrietta Worth Bingham Papers (1905-1968) includes her correspondence with Stephen Tomlin and John Houseman, photographs, ephemera, books and research files. Online exhibitions are available on the Mortimer Rare Book Room's website.

The Mortimer Rare Book Collection continues to acquire through gift and purchase first editions of Virginia Woolf titles in their original dust jackets of *To the Lighthouse* (Hogarth Press) and American editions of *The Voyage Out*, *Night and Day*, and *Mrs. Dalloway*.

Name of Collection: Woolf/Hogarth Press/Bloomsbury

Contact: Carmen Königsreuther Socknat

Address: Victoria University Library
71 Queens Park Crescent E.
Toronto M5S 1K7
Ontario Canada

Telephone:
Email: victoria.library@utoronto.ca
URL: http://library.vicu.utoronto.ca/special/bloomsbury.htm

Hours: Mon.–Fri. 9 am–5 pm

Access Requirements: Prior notification; identification

Restrictions: Limited photocopying.

Holdings Relevant To Woolf: This collection, the most comprehensive of its kind with nearly 5,700 items, contains all the work of Virginia and Leonard Woolf in various editions, issues, variants and translations; all the books hand-printed by Leonard and Virginia Woolf at the Hogarth Press, including many variant issues and bindings, association copies and page proofs; a nearly comprehensive collection of Hogarth Press machine printed books to 1946 (the year Leonard Woolf and the Press joined Chatto & Windus) including presentation copies, signed limited editions, page proofs, variants as well as substantial amounts of ephemera, such as the Catalogue of Publications to 1939 with annotations by Leonard Woolf. The collection is also very strong in Bloomsbury Art and Artists, especially the decorative arts, including important examples of Omega Workshops publications and exhibition catalogues. Materials include the catalogue of the second post-impressionist exhibition, 1912; catalogues relating to Vanessa Bell and Duncan Grant exhibitions; bronze medal of Virginia Woolf by Marta Firlet; oil on canvas portrait of Amaryllis Garnett by Vanessa Bell (c.1958); Portrait sketch of Leonard Woolf by Vanessa Bell; portrait of Leonard Woolf by Duncan Grant; portrait of Julia Duckworth by Henry Holiday (1839-1927); Duncan Grant and Vanessa Bell designed

Clarice Cliff dinner plates; original Vanessa Bell and Duncan Grant sketches and designs for dust jackets, novels, and other special projects; Duncan Grant charcoal portrait of Virginia Woolf (1968); Quentin Bell set of five pottery plates based on the novels of Virginia Woolf (ca. 1979); Quentin Bell pottery figurine in aid of Charleston (ca. 1980); a selection of other pottery by Quentin Bell; bronze busts of Lytton Strachey and Virginia Woolf by Stephen Tomlin (1901–1937); as well as the Marcel Gimond bust of Vanessa Bell and the Tomlin bust of Henrietta Bingham. Book hand bound by Virginia Woolf. Wooden plaque from the Hogarth Press at 24 Tavistock. Examples of programs, posters, and handbills relating to productions of plays, movies, and dance productions with content relating to Bloomsbury group members. Original correspondence and mss. material includes that by Vanessa Bell; Leonard Woolf; Ritchie family re: Anne Thackeray Ritchie/Stephen family; Duncan Grant; Quentin Bell; S. P. Rosenbaum mss. Letters from E. M. Forster, Bertrand Russell, James Strachey, Raymond Mortimer, David Garnett, Nigel Nicolson and others in the Bloomsbury Circle; as well as biographers, scholars and bibliographers such as Joanne Trautmann, Carolyn Heilbrun, J. Howard Woolmer, Leon Edel, Leila Luedeking, P. N. Furbank, Noel Annan and others. Large Ephemera Collection includes items revealing Virginia Woolf's effect on popular culture.

Name of Collection:	Library of Leonard and Virginia Woolf (Washington S U)
Contact:	Trevor James Bond Head, Manuscripts, Archives, and Special Collections
Address:	Washington State University Libraries Pullman, WA 99164-5610
Email:	tjbond@wsu.edu
URL:	www.wsulibs.wsu.edu/holland/masc/masc.htm
Hours:	Mon.–Fri. 8:30 am–4:30 pm
Access Requirements:	Letter stating nature of research preferred; student or other identification.

Restrictions:	Materials must be used in the MASC area under supervision. Photocopying or photographing is permitted only when it will not harm the materials and is permitted by copyright.
Recent Aquisitions:	Correspondence to Clive and Vanessa Bell (approximately 30 items), with most items addressed to Clive. Correspondents include Stephen Tallant, Eric MacLagan, John Pollock, H. J. Norton, Lyn Irvine (including one letter mentioning Mrs. Raven Hill), Sir George Grahame, Karen Costelloe, John Alford, Ivor Churchill, the Earl of Sandwich, George Lansbury, Clifford Sharp, F. H. S. Shepherd, Gilbert Seldes, Lord Evan Tredegar, C. E. Stuart, Max Eastman, E. Hilton Young, Col. Heward Bell.
Holdings Relevant To Woolf:	WSU has the Woolfs' basic working library including many works which belonged to Woolf's father, Sir Leslie Stephen, and other family members. Over 800 titles came from their Sussex home, Monks House, including some works bought at auction soon after Leonard Woolf died in 1969. Later additions include: 1,875 titles from his house in Victoria Square, London; 400 titles from his nephew Cecil Woolf; and over 60 titles from Quentin and Anne Olivier Bell. WSU has been actively collecting: all works in all editions by Virginia Woolf; all titles by Leonard Woolf; dust jackets; works published by the Woolfs at the Hogarth Press through 1946; books by their friends and associates, especially those by Bloomsbury authors and about Bloomsbury artists; relevant correspondence and original works of art. Original artwork by Vanessa Bell; scattered letters by Vanessa Bell, E. M. Forster, Roger Fry, Leslie Stephen, Lytton Strachey, and Leonard Woolf. Original artwork by Richard Kennedy for illustrations in his book *A Boy at the Hogarth Press*; scattered letters by Roger Fry, Leslie Stephen, Ethel Smyth, and Leonard Woolf. Virginia Woolf's initialed copy of *Cornishiana*; Leonard Woolf's annotated copy of *An Anatomy of Poetry* by A. Williams-Ellis; Leslie Stephen's copy of *Lapsus Calami and Other Verses*, inscribed by James Kenneth Stephen. Several letters from Virginia Woolf, including two written in 1939 to Ronald Heffer, and a letter to Edward McKnight Kauffer. New in

GUIDE TO SPECIAL LIBRARY COLLECTIONS   141

the Hogarth Press Collection are a copy of E. M. Forster's *Anonymity, an Enquiry*, bound in cream paper boards, and what Woolmer calls the third label state of Forster's *The Story of the Siren*. The Library of Leonard and Virginia Woolf is once again shelved separately so that scholars visiting Pullman may see the collection apart from the other rare book collections.

Name of Collection: Yale Center for British Art

Contact: Elisabeth Fairman, Chief Curator of Rare Books and Manuscripts

Address: 1080 Chapel Street
P.O. Box 208280
New Haven, CT 06520-8280

Telephone: 203-432-2814
Fax: 203-432-9613
Email: elisabeth.fairman@yale.edu

URL: https://britishart.yale.edu/collections

Hours: Tue.–Fri. 10 am–4:30 pm

Access Requirements: Patron registration required to visit Study Room. Can provide images upon request but cannot grant permissions.

Holdings Relevant To Woolf: Rare Books & Mss Department: 94 letters from Vanessa Bell and Duncan Grant to Sir Kenneth Clark; 6 letters from Lytton Strachey (to Clive Bell, Siegfried Sassoon, et al.).
Prints & Drawings Department: 7 drawings by Vanessa Bell; 6 drawings by Duncan Grant; 16 drawings by Wyndham Lewis; 1 drawing by Frederick Etchells; 2 photographs by Julia Margaret Cameron.
Paintings Department: 3 paintings by Vanessa Bell, 7 paintings by Duncan Grant (including 2 portraits of Vanessa Bell); 4 paintings by Roger Fry.

Reviews

Night and Day.
Michael H. Whitworth, ed. (Cambridge UP, 2018) ix-cxiii + 745pp.

Virginia Woolf's often neglected second novel, *Night and Day*, receives the comprehensive attention it deserves in the latest volume in the Cambridge Edition of the Works of Virginia Woolf. Michael H. Whitworth's introduction and notes are illuminating and exhaustive, granting new insights into the novel's composition and production history, and its cultural and intellectual contexts. Like the other works in the series, this edition will quickly become the definitive scholarly reference for the novel.

Night and Day has been marked by its in-between state since its publication. Like its characters, it hovers between Victorian and modernist sensibilities and styles, its length and often conventional plotting precluding it from much scholarly attention and many syllabi. As Whitworth's early critical history of the novel clarifies, its early reception—which was largely positive, though mixed—shifts once novels like *Jacob's Room* and *Mrs. Dalloway* appear. Few novels would stand comparison with such works, and Woolf herself came to view the novel as a useful if limited experiment in craft. The novel rewards careful study, though, and contemporary scholarship by Megan Quigley, Steve Ellis, Helen Wussow, Randy Malamud, and myself suggest the essential place of the novel within Woolf's larger accomplishments. This new edition should open new opportunities for further research.

The volume begins with a preface in which general editors Jane Goldman, Susan Sellers, and Bryony Randall lay out the editorial approach to the whole series. A central goal, they note, is transparency, with no changes made to the text without citation. For the whole series (with the exception of *Between the Acts*, edited by Mark Hussey), the copy text used is the first British edition, with variants noted in the textual apparatus and notes at the end of the volume. Another key aim—certainly met in this volume—is to balance the pleasures of reading a clean text without unnecessary distractions while still meeting the need for thorough annotation and explanatory notes. The editors clarify, too, that their goal is not interpretation; beyond the early critical reception histories, these are not editions that delve into the contemporary scholarship or that lay out new theories. Instead, they aim, essentially, to open up critical doors, offering a thorough mapping of both variants and context from which future scholars may draw.

Whitworth follows the preface with an exemplary Composition History of the novel, piecing together from Woolf's diaries, letters, essays, and manuscripts as complete a picture of her composition process that we have to date. He first notes the relative lack of manuscript material for *Night and Day*. For most of Woolf's novels, composition materials are more abundant, with surviving proofs, holograph copies, notes, diary entries, and the like. For *Night and Day*, however, we only have seven chapters in manuscript form (sections of chapters 11-17), and the diary entries are spotty and at times simply stop. Despite these limits, though, and in an impressive display of scholarly sleuthing, Whitworth details Woolf's progress on the novel alongside what she was reading, whom she was seeing, what she was writing, the progress of the war, her own health, and more. He sketches the environment within which the novel's composition unfolded in ways that are richly suggestive without being reductive or overly biographical. While necessarily mainly descriptive, the section also grants new insights, making the case, for example, for the possibility that Woolf started an early version of the novel in 1914, much earlier than Leonard Woolf's dating of 1916. Woolf's reading materials during this period are noticeably steeped in Victorian works alongside more modern literature like James Joyce's *Portrait of the Artist as a Young Man* and her own experiments in stories like "The Mark on the Wall"; her reading and writing suggest a fertile environment for the emerging novel whose characters are caught looking forward and back in literary history. The narrative composition section is augmented with a later Chronology of Composition, laying out in list form the timeline and including further details on Woolf's reading, opinions, and health as she composed the novel.

The Publication History that follows grants a detailed look at the various editions of the work and will likely be of interest mainly to advanced scholars. Whitworth outlines the five editions published in Woolf's lifetime that are represented in the volume, and the provenance of each. One notable detail from this section is the frustration Woolf feels in having her book published by her half-brother Gerald Duckworth. The experience helped fuel her turn to the Hogarth Press, which as many critics have observed, enabled her shift to more experimental novels.

The next two sections cover the early critical reception of the novel, encompassing both the private reactions shared with Woolf and the public reviews. The material illuminates the contradictory and shifting responses to the novel that continue to reverberate in the contemporary scholarship. Here again Whitworth offers new evidence, tracking down reactions and reviews that critics have previously missed, as well as new insights. For example, it has been widely assumed that Anne Thackeray Ritchie—the sister of Woolf's father's first wife on whom the character of Mrs. Hilbery is at least partially drawn—had read the manuscript and had been unsettled by the depiction. Piecing together the timeline and the way Woolf rarely shared her manuscripts, Whitworth makes the convincing case that Ritchie was unlikely to have seen it before her death in February 1919.

Whitworth tracks down seemingly every early review of the novel, noting the generally favorable reception as well as the criticism. Acknowledging Katherine Mansfield's well known criticism of the novel as a Victorian throwback that leaves out the war, Whitworth builds a much wider critical history that continues to inform the novel's reception today. Critics praised the novel's subtleties and descriptions, comparing Woolf favorably to Jane Austen and George Eliot, while other critics complained of the detached coldness of the characters, the novel's separation from the events of the day, and its length. While some felt the work was a throwback to the Victorians, others made the case that it was more modern, grouping Woolf with Joyce, Wyndham Lewis, Dorothy Richardson, and others. The section illuminates how the lens through which *Night and Day* was seen changes once Woolf's later novels appear; as Whitworth observes, the later reviews are necessarily tempered by an "awareness of what she went on to achieve" (lxxix).

The introduction's final sections cover the methods and criteria used for editing and annotations, of interest both for their specific uses in this volume and also for the way they reveal the myriad decisions editors face when selecting a copy text and deciding which elements of a text need explanatory notes. After carefully explaining the reasoning for selecting the first British edition for the copy text, Whitworth describes the five categories he used for deciding what details needed an explanatory note, from glosses on singular events, to notes that flag repeated patterns or allusions, to moments in the text that paralleled actual people and places. He observes the challenge of deciding on the years when the novel is set; he settles on 1911-1912—based on references to political bills and other details—but also notes how this timing is not always consistent. Hints of the war do creep in, especially in the references to darkness in the streets, a perhaps deliberate blurring of times woven into the novel's structure. The volume again stays focused on revealing context rather than offering interpretation; if a given moment or object might have multiple possible references, the strategy is not to pick among them but to keep the possibilities multiple, providing the evidence rather than fixing a particular meaning. This approach underscores the volume's utility for scholars, opening avenues for future research.

The Explanatory Notes at the end of the volume succeed in these aims, granting an invaluable and exhaustive map of the novel's many contexts. Whitworth weaves together histories, politics, diary entries, letters, and more in ways that position the novel within its many frames of reference. Character names are explored in their origins and possible meaning, neighborhoods and regions are mapped in their signification, and the often obscure contemporary cultural meaning of things—from side-whiskers to malacca canes, to Venetian mirrors, to light yellow gloves—are glossed. A history of suffragettes and women's rights threads its way through the notes, alongside political markers like the Insurance Bill and subtle references to the war. Models for characters—like Anne Thackeray Ritchie for Mrs. Hilbery and Vanessa Bell for Katharine—are noted without being reductive.

While the price of the volume places it out of reach for most readers, this Cambridge Edition should make its way to libraries, where it will quickly become the standard reference volume for scholars.

—Elizabeth Outka, *University of Richmond*

Modernist Lives: Biography and Autobiography at Leonard and Virginia Woolf's Hogarth Press.
Claire Battershill (London: Bloomsbury Academic, 2018). xiii + 231 pp.

Virginia Woolf and the World of Books.
Nicola Wilson and Claire Battershill, eds.
(Clemson, SC: Clemson UP, 2018) x + 302 pp.

Scholarship on the Hogarth Press emerged in the 1980s, at the time when the field of modernism was starting to pay more attention to the material format in which the new literature appeared. This first wave of scholarship led to Donna E. Rhein's study of the handprinted books published by the Woolfs (1985) and J. Howard Woolmer's *A Checklist of the Hogarth Press* (1986), followed by J. H. Willis's *Leonard and Virginia Woolf as Publishers* (1992). The methodology was deeply anchored in history and bibliography: first editions were examined, letters and diaries were read, testimonies from Hogarth Press veterans were gathered. But it was not until the 2000s that the archival turn in modernist studies led to a greater emphasis on the Hogarth Press archive at the University of Reading (UK). The narrative of the press as an elite institution targeting a coterie of readers has been challenged by a new generation of scholars, including Claire Battershill and Nicola Wilson, who are leading the Modernist Archives Publishing Project (MAPP) with Helen Southworth, Alice Staveley and Elizabeth Willson Gordon.[1] Battershill's *Modernist Lives* and the edited collection *Virginia Woolf and the World of Books* contribute to a new story on the Hogarth Press, a story that emphasizes the diversity and commercial appeal of its publications. The same story is at the core of the chapter on the Hogarth Press that Battershill wrote for my edited collection *Modernist Fiction and Poetry* (Edinburgh UP, 2019).

In *Modernist Lives*, Claire Battershill adopts a historical and chronological approach to document the publication of biography and autobiography at the Hogarth Press. Virginia Woolf's interest in this genre is well known. In "How Should One Read a Book?" she wrote that biographies and memoirs satisfy our curiosity: "they show us people going about their daily affairs, toiling, failing, succeeding, eating, hating, loving, until they die" (Battershill 1). Woolf engaged with the genre as a reader, as a writer (with *Orlando*, *Flush*, and *Roger Fry*), and as a publisher. The Hogarth Press's "Books on Tolstoi," published from 1920 to 1924, exemplify Woolf's fascination for Russian writers and the lives they led.

Battershill's focus on biography and autobiography contributes to a more diverse understanding of the Hogarth Press list. Until about ten years ago, scholarly research had "focused on a relatively small group of publications written by prominent figures of modernism" (3). Following Helen Southworth and others,

---

[1] https://www.modernistarchives.com/ (accessed 19 Sept. 2019)

Battershill points out that the Hogarth Press published all kinds of books, including a series of biographies for children, an etiquette book and even a manual on diet and high blood pressure (7). The press became a successful commercial enterprise without losing its ability to convey taste and distinction. From its origins in 1917, the Hogarth Press was associated with cultural prestige. As Battershill notes, "early subscribers to the Press were subscribing as much to a cultural identity and an affiliation with the Woolfs as tastemakers as they were to a purchasing scheme" (10). By the 1930s, the small press had become a mid-sized firm that kept strong ties with individual authors, while developing sophisticated marketing strategies and distribution practices (11).

The commercial aspect of the press is well documented in the Hogarth Press archive at Reading and other collections. In addition to this archival work, Battershill has done extensive research at the E. J. Pratt Library at Victoria College in the University of Toronto. The Pratt collection finds its origins in a personal library, and includes Hogarth Press books with their original dustjackets (unlike the copies at the British Library or the Bodleian, which have been stripped from their jackets). The cover for *The Development of English Biography* (1927) displayed a description of the Hogarth Lectures series, which targeted students and teachers but also ordinary readers.

The Press marketed its books to a general audience, and the structure of *Modernist Lives* reflects this broad focus. Chapter One gives an overview of the Hogarth Press's publications from its origins to the immediate aftermath of the Second World War. Drawing on a large amount of bibliographical data, this chapter classifies the Hogarth Press titles to discover which genre dominated the list. Poetry came first, followed by Novels; Politics/ International Relations; Literary Criticism; and Biography/ Autobiography (which accounted for approximately ten percent of the Press's total output). Battershill's attempt to quantify the publisher's list is welcome. As James English has argued, literary studies remain largely hostile to numbers and "counting" disciplines, despite the rise of interdisciplinarity (xii).

However, Battershill's quantitative approach is not perfect. She recognizes that "quantitative analyses in studies of categorization or grouping can give an appearance of authority that may be misleading when representing subjective categories" (29). The overlap of genres means that some of the books appear in more than one category, which results in a total number of titles higher than the number that the Press actually published. Another problem is that the Biography/ Autobiography genre represented only a small minority of titles published by the Press. Why focus on this category rather than, say, Psycho-Analysis or Short Fiction? This issue could have been addressed in more detail in the introduction.

The next two chapters look at the 1920s, a decade of rapid expansion for the press. Chapter Two examines the perspectives on the life of Leo Tolstoy that the Hogarth Press published in the early 1920s. These four biographies were written by different authors, offering contradictory views on Tolstoy's life. Battershill argues that the "Books on Tolstoi" can be viewed as "an act of modernist cultural intervention."

Instead of the traditional single-authored biographies published in two volumes, the four books "could present character in a more nuanced, if also more complex, fashion" (38). Chapter Three considers the debates about biography and autobiography in the late 1920s, at a time when life writing was becoming increasingly popular. Despite its importance in the literary culture of modernism, the genre remains neglected in modernist studies and book history. Yet, these non-canonical works have something to tell us about "cultural hierarchy, the labeling of works in the period and the relationships that might be traced between and within genres," argues Battershill (62).

In the 1930s, the press continued to sell its books to a wide audience. Chapter Four focuses on the marketing of Woolf's own biographical/autobiographical works. For Battershill, the popularity of *Orlando* and *Flush* is probably related to their genre since life writing reached a large market in the interwar period. In contrast, "Woolf's other late novels, such as *Between the Acts* and *The Years* did not achieve similarly high sales in the UK" (106). In the mid-1930s, the Woolfs launched the Hogarth Press Biography Series, which is the topic of Chapter Five. The series aimed to make an intervention in contemporary debates on literature and culture—a grand ambition that was supported by energic marketing strategies. Battershill rightly notes that publishers' series are often "marketing ploys," a way to encourage readers to buy all the books issued in the same collection (119).

Moving to the late 1940s, Chapter Six examines the works of Henry Green and Christopher Isherwood, focusing particularly on the fears of libels associated with controversial life writing. *Modernist Lives* ends on "a note of excitement about future work to be done in the emerging scholarly area of modernist publishing studies" (176). Digital resources make publishers' archives more accessible to users, and facilitate international collaborations—as the Modernist Archives Publishing Project shows.

Modernist Lives is a model for a new kind of scholarship, deeply anchored in print culture but moving towards the digital. Battershill frequently uses the first person to talk about her own experience as a researcher, which makes her book pleasant to read. For a first monograph that finds its origins in doctoral work, *Modernist Lives* is an impressive achievement. One limitation is that it is quite narrow in focus. It would have been interesting to study the links between the Hogarth Press and other international publishers. For example, the American publisher Harcourt Brace presented *Orlando: A Biography* as a hybrid between fiction and biography ("a work of fiction that presents an enlargement of human life as a classic must"). Moreover, Battershill's focus on neglected works is not always convincing. We continue to pay attention to the Hogarth Press because of its association with Virginia Woolf, not because of the non-canonical works it published. Instead of grouping *Orlando*, *Flush*, and *Roger Fry* into one chapter, it might have been a good idea to dedicate more space to each of these texts, and to reduce the discussion on lesser works.

With Nicola Wilson, Battershill also edited *Virginia Woolf and the World of Books*, a collection of papers presented at the Annual Conference on Virginia Woolf held in 2017 at the University of Reading. To celebrate the centenary of the founding of the Hogarth Press, the conference organizers curated an exhibition at the Museum of English Rural Life in Reading, in the same building as the Special Collections. Materials on display included "original Hogarth artwork and advertisements, Order Books, correspondence, woodblocks by Vanessa Bell and Roger Fry, as well as the Woolfs' travelling bags (loaned from the Penguin Random House archives in Rushden)" (viii). The organizers also scheduled other impactful activities such as a printing workshop in partnership with Oxford's Centre for the Study of the Book, and a talk on BBC Radio 4's "Open Book" program.

The selected conference papers illustrate several big trends in Woolf studies, and more generally modernist studies. Wilson and Battershill have grouped the papers in eleven sub-sections, starting with "In the Archives" and ending with "Lives in Writing." A common theme in these essays is the search for a physical connection with the dead writer through archival documents. The keynote speaker Ted Bishop reminded the audience that when he was a young Woolf scholar working in the British Museum, he found himself reading a handwritten letter he had read in print several times before. He felt physical shock as he realized he was holding Woolf's suicide note. "The episode taught me about the impact of the material text," Bishop said, "but what I hadn't considered was that I was responding to ink. Ink testifies to the presence of a body in a particular place at a particular time" (3). The same emphasis on the physicality of the writer can be found in Alice Staveley's essay on voice in the archives. She focuses on her search for a lost tape that would complement the only known surviving recording of Virginia Woolf, part of a 1937 BBC radio broadcast. The excitement of the quest reminds us of the materiality of the archive, and the deep-seated need for an emotional connection with the past.

Like many edited collections, *Virginia Woolf and the World of Books* is of uneven quality. Instead of selecting thirty-six papers grouped in eleven sections, the editors could have chosen fewer essays that reflect current scholarship on Woolf. Three big trends seem to emerge: Material Culture and the Archive; Global Woolf; and Sexuality/Queer Studies. On the whole, it is encouraging to see so many new approaches to study a writer who has already attracted entire shelves of critical commentary. Publishers' archives include largely-neglected documents–from financial records to marketing materials–that can shed new light on canonical writers. *Modernist Lives* and *Virginia Woolf and the World of Books* will be valuable not only to Woolf specialists, but also to the growing number of modernist scholars who study publishing enterprises and material culture.

—Lise Jaillant, *Loughborough University*

Work Cited

English, James F. "Everywhere and Nowhere: The Sociology of Literature After 'The Sociology of Literature.'" *New Literary History*, vol. 41, no. 2, 2010, pp. v–xxiii.

Modernism à la Mode: Fashion and the Ends of Literature.
Elizabeth M. Sheehan (Ithaca: Cornell UP, 2018). xiii + 256pp.

In its survey of literary history, *A Room of One's Own* reminds readers that books are often evaluated in light of the implied gender of their subject matter. Woolf observes, "it is the masculine values that prevail. Speaking crudely, football and sport are 'important'; the worship of fashion, the buying of clothes 'trivial.' And these values are inevitably transferred from life to fiction. This is an important book, the critic assumes, because it deals with war. This is an insignificant book because it deals with the feelings of women in a drawing-room" (*AROO* 73-74). Although Woolf's argument focuses on the novel, one is tempted to think that it equally accounts for the reception of scholarship: this is an important book because it deals with conflict or global inequality; this is an insignificant book because it deals with fashion. And yet, recent studies by Jessica Burstein, Caroline Evans, and others have demonstrated how much we have to learn about and through the purportedly insignificant—the "little black dress," the mannequin parade—even though those excellent books have not received recognition via the prizes the profession awards to important work. Scholars in the field have noticed: at the 2019 Modernist Studies Association conference in Toronto, Burstein called *Modernism à la Mode* her personal pick for a first book prize, an assessment many will share after reading this sweeping study of fashion as a way of reading and knowing modernism. There can be no doubt that this is an important book, one that teaches readers a great deal about Woolf and her contemporaries as it reflects on the relationships among fashion, politics writ large and small, and how we do business in contemporary literary criticism.

Sheehan's larger argument traces how "fashion underpins a central way that . . . texts [by British and American authors] seek to matter" (3). The matter at hand may be an engagement with everyday life, with national or international politics, or with history, and fashion also offers a mode of thinking about possibilities for change (17). Chapters focus on Woolf, D. H. Lawrence, W. E. B. DuBois, and F. Scott Fitzgerald, but these writers are examined in light of contemporary fashion and beauty icons like Paul Poiret, Madame C. J. Walker, and A'Lelia Walker, and Sheehan constellates her treatment of major figures with shorter forays into the fiction of other authors, such as Jessie Fauset and Nella Larsen. The result is a dazzling and utterly compelling account of fashion's centrality to modernism's ways of being and knowing.

Sheehan's chapter on Woolf, for instance, deploys theories of affect and mood to argue that Woolf "foregrounds how seemingly personal feelings are formed with and through objects, bodies, thoughts, experiences, beliefs, and historical conditions" (27). This argument positions fashion as a profoundly influential form of mediation, as "representations of feeling and fashion make clearer how accounts of everyday life can provide tools for understanding broader political and historical forces. In addition to making things legible, the connection between mood and *la mode* helps Woolf to grapple with what and how things are sensed and known in the first place" (29). Sheehan weaves her argument through readings of "Modern Fiction," "The

New Dress," *Mrs. Dalloway*, the dressmaking of the Omega Workshops, *Three Guineas*, and *The Years*, demonstrating, for example, that in *Dalloway*, "many of the characters experience their intimacy with and disaffection from other characters and social worlds via frock consciousness—that is, a mutual focus on clothing that generates and delimits collective thoughts and feelings" (49). Sheehan makes clear that individuals cannot change the mood or mode alone—think Mabel Waring—but fashion can reveal the work of those in power and also offer moments of a "mutual and mutually reparative process" (49). Her example of such repair is Septimus and Rezia's collaboration in hat-making, a scene in which frock consciousness creates a brief moment of intimacy and connection.

Other chapters address D. H. Lawrence's persistent association of garments with utopian futures in *The White Peacock, Women in Love*, and *Lady Chatterley's Lover*; F. Scott Fitzgerald's writing of a "romantic historicism" that employs fashion to limn "the contours of a given era" (158) in his essays, *The Great Gatsby*, and *Tender Is the Night*; and a chapter that explores how African Americans used beauty and fashion to think through possibilities for Pan-African and -Asian political movements. This chapter is the crown jewel of the book, ranging across work by DuBois, Larsen, the Walkers, and Fauset to address the relationship between aesthetics and politics for African-American thinkers and writers (115). It illuminates DuBois's novel *Dark Princess*, which casts natural beauty as power and brings Pan-Africa and -Asia into contact (120); Madame C. J. Walker's conflation of "beauty work and political work" (129), a vision of beauty as a means of countering white supremacy (131); and Fauset's and Larsen's representations of Orientalist imaginaries that might "cultivate modes of internationalist subjectivity and belonging" (139). This dazzling and original chapter will encourage those interested in fashion to turn their attention to the Harlem Renaissance with fresh eyes. While alert to the possibilities and futures that fashion allowed African-American men and women to imagine, Sheehan also traces the limits of the projects she explores. She admits, for example, that beauty doesn't create possibilities for "immediate or legible political action" (151) and offers moving and persuasive readings of *There is Confusion* and *Quicksand*. Her argument should encourage readers to teach the former and change how we teach the latter.

Throughout *Modernism à la Mode*, those who work on Woolf will be delighted to discover juicy readings of her texts interleaved with analysis of other authors. Sheehan's argument about Fitzgerald, for instance, is sharpened through a brief, crucial tour of *Orlando*, a novel in which "fashion history [is] exaggerated to the point of absurdity" (166). In contrast to Fitzgerald's romantic historicism, "*Orlando* parodies the enormous historical and biographical weight carried by garments" (168), a reading that economically highlights the difference between the two authors. This excursus into the mock biography has more substance to it than many an article, so Woolf scholars will be rewarded for reading Sheehan's work cover to cover.

There is little to find fault with—the first duty of a reviewer!—in this clear, beautifully written, and engaging study. Occasionally Sheehan's linkage of fashion's modes and moods with the operations of the contemporary academy appear a bit single-minded, as when she outlines parallels between fashion and scholarly journals: "literary studies is itself circulated largely through periodicals that are organized according to a given period and that promise to deliver new material in each issue" (191). While this will chime with readers suspicious of "the merely fashionable" in the humanities, it is a bit of a shock to find a scholarly book of such excellence making rather light of its own form. More important, the scholarly journal significantly predates the fashion paper (and even fashion proper for most people): the first academic journal was published in the seventeenth century while fashion magazines emerged two centuries later. Nevertheless, this is a minor quibble with a local point; Sheehan's argument otherwise carries one persuasively along.

Toward the end of *Room*, Woolf encourages her audience to "write books of travel and adventure, and research and scholarship, and history and biography, and criticism and philosophy and science" (109). In 1929, the point was that the world needed more books written by women, full stop. In 2019, we might now think that books of and about fashion belong in that list. Sheehan concludes *Modernism à la Mode* by tracing parallels between modernist writers and the work of contemporary artist Mariam Ghani, and she closes with the observation that the writers taken up in her study "all turn to fashion to evoke temporalities and ways of knowing through which to sense out the force and fragility of existing institutions and their relation to those institutions" (202). At a time when many of us worry about institutions we have long taken for granted—the college/university, the Supreme Court—it is heartening to read this important book, which reminds us that the texture of fashion can be a way of knowing the world we live in and, equally important, of imagining what might be.
—Celia Marshik, *Stony Brook University*

The Politics of 1930s British Literature: Education, Class, Gender. Natasha Periyan (London: Bloomsbury Academic, 2018). xi + 278pp.

The title of this work suggests that it is to be a far more wide-ranging study than is in fact provided, that it will be an all-encompassing study of the wide range of what was written in Britain during the 1930s with special attention to the three categories cited in the subtitle. Some attention in the text is paid to class and gender, but this study is actually almost exclusively about education, as is stated explicitly in the introduction. Within those far more limited but legitimate intentions this is an interesting and insightful study, in effect in its five chapters a study of the writings of mostly prominent 1930s British writers, almost exclusively devoted to what they thought about education, primarily at the secondary and private (i.e., public school) level. The book does suffer, in my view, from some of the hallmarks of being a revised dissertation. There is too much citation of what others have said on the subject rather than the author sufficiently trusting her own voice and views. In the dissertation version, authors feel the need to demonstrate their mastery of the "literature." Most of that scaffolding should be discarded in the published version. Such authors also seem to feel the need to demonstrate that they can use the currently modish terms of literary criticism. Their elimination would have made for a better written work.

Virtually all of the writers considered here went to English public schools and quite a few of them in the 1930s had experience as teachers. Periyan suggests that in some cases that was a deliberate choice, but I suspect it was frequently more the default decision for would be writers as a way of earning some income, as was famously true in *Decline and Fall* (1928) by Evelyn Waugh, a writer not considered here. Edward Upward who had a successful and distinguished career as a secondary school teacher continually bemoaned the necessity of doing so for financial reasons and how it kept him from writing. The first chapter here considers W.H. Auden and the importance for his shaping as a poet of his experiences as a teacher, being something of a subversive figure in the classroom. She also discusses his concern with pedagogic purposes in the anthologies he did of poetry, particularly *The Poet's Tongue* (1935) which was co-edited with John Garrett, the headmaster of the Raynes Park School. The next chapter considers Vera Brittain and Winifred Holtby with greater emphasis on the latter as she was more concerned with educational questions, particularly in her most famous work, *South Riding*. The continual theme of this study is the belief of the writers it considers of the importance of secondary education and the implication that it needs to be reformed. This is perhaps most vivid in the third and most interesting chapter. It deals with Graham Greene and the publication he edited, *The Old School* (1934). He was the son of the headmaster of the school he attended. The collection mostly consists of chapters by various public school old boys dwelling on the horrors of their experiences. Yet the paradox of the situation is that in many ways the education was excellent and in effect it gave these rebellious students the tools with which to try to change the schools and the society that had trained them: it made them writers. As Antonia White remarked: "In the matter of writing I owe a great deal to that education and I may as well admit it. I have not used my pen for purposes of which the Lippington authorities would approve but, were it not for them, I should probably never have used it at all" (Periyan 136). In this chapter there are also intelligent discussions of Stephen Spender's *The Backward Son* and Walter Greenwood's *Love on the Dole*, but they don't particularly advance the argument of the book.

The most important chapter for the readers of this journal is the fourth: "'Altering the Structure of Society': Virginia Woolf's Class-Critique of Educational Institutions in the 1930s." Again, it has intelligent observations based mostly on *The Years* and "The Leaning Tower," the talk that she gave for the Workers' Educational Association, almost the last thing she wrote. She depicts herself as the uneducated daughter of "educated men" as well as an outsider as a woman, but both conceptions were in my view something of an exaggeration. She was hardly in the same position as those likely to be her audience. To a degree, the talk had elements that might be taken to argue for better secondary education for all. But I believe that the main thrust of that fascinating piece is the contrast between those writers who were on the upright towers of pre-First World War England and those, particularly the Auden group, who had similar education to those of their class before 1914 but were instead on a leaning tower that adversely affected their work. To me, the fascination of the essay is the degree to which it deals with her ambivalent relationship to the dominant poets of the 1930s. The Hogarth Press was their publisher, but she had doubts about their skills. Three of the four responders to her essay in a subsequent issue of *New Writing* were public school old boys: Edward Upward (Repton), Louis MacNeice (Marlborough) and John Lehmann (Eton). Their education had enhanced their skills as writers. I don't think she attacked education as practiced in England at the time to any great degree in her essay, although she is fully aware of how important a role it played in individuals' class position. She does express the hope that class might disappear in education, that a school might combine the quality of Winchester with the egalitarianism of a village school.

The last chapter deals with three Etonians, George Orwell, Cyril Connolly, and Henry Green. It seems rather tangential to the rest of the book although it discusses some of their writings relevant to education. Orwell hated his prep school, St. Cyprian's, where Cyril Connolly was a contemporary of his, as he was also at Eton. Connolly got more from his Eton education than Orwell but he recognized how it could be emotionally stifling, as in his "Theory of Permanent Adolescence." Their schools trained them as writers. But in all of this text, interesting as it might be to read, there is certainly little in a general way about the politics of British 1930s literature or how influential these writings were in shaping educational policy. We are told aspects of the educational thinking of a significant group of writers. There is not a conclusion to the story but rather a two page Coda mentioning the improvements in education, particularly at the secondary level, made by the Labour government of 1945. The author makes the point that "fourteen members of the Labour government, including the chancellor of the exchequer, had some involvement with the Workers' Educational Association" (224). She does not mention that the Chancellor was Hugh Dalton. Or indeed that the Prime Minister, Clement Attlee, was a public school old boy. Dalton's prep school was the progressive Summer Fields School but he was also an old Etonian and his father, a Canon at Windsor, was the tutor to the royal princes. As John Strachey once remarked, if there were ever a Communist government in Britain, half the Cabinet would be old Etonians. The writings discussed here may have helped make English education more democratic, but the public schools, though somewhat less powerful than they once were, still play an important and perhaps restrictive role in English life. English institutions are clever in changing in many ways in order to stay as much as possible the same. What would Virginia Woolf have thought about the present state of English education?

—Peter Stansky, *Stanford University*

Virginia Woolf: Music, Sound, Language.
Elicia Clements (Toronto: U of Toronto P, 2019). xi + 288pp.

"Freedom of listening," observed Barthes in 1976, "is as necessary as freedom of speech" (89). In our own historical moment, when political discourse is so frequently characterized by assertion, dissembling and the stifling of dissenting voices, the need to listen carefully, respectfully, and empathetically to others is increasingly necessary and increasingly difficult. As Elicia Clements's timely and accomplished book demonstrates, listening—and not listening—are crucial topics of Woolf's fiction and essays. From Mrs. Ramsay's divided attention to the sounds of family life, to Septimus Warren Smith's anguished, intense scrutiny of street noise, to the bells, songs and vocal animals that permeate her fictional environments, Woolf's writing is acutely alert to the production and reception of sound. Woolf invites her readers to be similarly alert. Listening, Clements proposes, is an "ethically crucial" (90) mode of social interaction and an activity central to Woolf's feminism, her critiques of materialism and Fascism, and her envisaging of utopian chora which are often (like the working-class children's choir at the end of *The Years*) composed of the disenfranchised. Clements's book explores Woolf's sustained attention to the production and reception of sound, gathering together arguments about sonic events, art music, and language in Woolf's work. Through her bold scope, astute close readings, and careful theoretical expositions, she provides a sophisticated account of the vital importance of sound production and reception to Woolf's ethics and experimentation.

Clements's work builds on recent critical attention to the "historical and political" connotations of Woolf's intermediality with music but foregrounds instead the "conceptual and aesthetic implications of this intermedial pairing" (6). Clements approaches music and sound primarily as processes and networks rather than as art works or texts and it is this which produces many of her most original insights. To explore Woolf's intermediality, Clements casts her critical net wide: scholarship on Woolf and sound studies shapes her arguments (Melba Cuddy-Keane's and Pamela Caughie's work provides fruitful concepts and terminology) and she also extends musicologically-informed scholarship on Woolf by Emilie Crapoulet, Joyce E. Kelley, Adriana Varga, and others that has documented and explored the implications of Woolf's immersion in classical repertoire (my own monograph is generously acknowledged). But Clements also turns directly and with assurance to a wide range of theorists: particularly Michel Chion and R. Murray Schafer within sound studies, and Mladen Dolar, Latour, Barthes, and Bahktin for insights drawn from Lacanian psychoanalysis, network theory and semiotics. If there is the occasional slightly abrupt shift of gear between the theory and her close readings, it is offset by the scrupulous rigor of her exegeses: they are likely to stimulate further work. Her study provides detailed discussions of all the long fictions (*Orlando* and the short fictions get less attention) and these are enriched by judicious readings of less-discussed works, such as the essays "Why?" (1934) and "Three Pictures" (1929). The book is suffused with thoughtful comparisons among Woolf's works and also draws rewardingly on Leonard Woolf's music criticism. It offers many astute close readings and some valuable pieces of new information: she establishes, for instance, that Woolf commissioned the popular book on musical "appreciation" from Basil de Selincourt for the Hogarth Essays, Second Series (12). Additionally, in her introduction and her coda on the term "rhythm," *Roger Fry* gets welcome, overdue attention as the work to which Woolf was most immediately referring when she famously remarked, "I always think of my books as music before I write them" (4).

Her tripartite study begins by examining the role of songs and cries in Woolf's writing, focusing on the relationship between sound and space. The central trope of this section is the "earcon," a sonic event of special symbolic meaning, such as a cry or Woolf's numerous street songs. Woolf uses such events, Clements argues, to expose the politicization not only of public spaces but also of seemingly benign private domestic sites so that the "aural architecture" of her narratives reveals social inclusion or its opposite (27-28). A series of wonderful close readings explores sound in sites that are ambivalently rural and urban—public parks, and new suburban spaces such as Hampstead Garden Suburb in *Jacob's Room*, where the disruptive song of a thrush critiques Fanny's unquestioning admiration for the heteronormative scene of nannies with prams (40-41). Proposing that Woolf frequently associates earcons with female-centered communities in exterior spaces, Clements explores the way in which the earcon often "dislodge[s] assumptions about knowledge acquisition" by reconfiguring gendered relationships between meaning and language (20). Many have discussed Woolf's singers, but Clements successfully anchors them in a broader argument about Woolf's use of language to resist fixed signification and unsettle hierarchies—a strategy crucial to Woolf's politics and formal innovations.

The second part turns to listening, discussing—for example—the freedoms and risks that come of not listening or from the unwelcome omnipresence of sound. These sections include incisive readings of Woolf's ambivalence towards the BBC (building on Todd Avery's work) and new types of listening community enabled by sound technologies. Clements reads the ubiquitous communication in *Jacob's Room*, for instance, in relation to Woolf's experimental narrative technique: the ominously all-hearing narrator prompts the reader to listen profoundly to apparently insignificant details (such as aural evocations of war) and thus to cultivate social responsibility. Her comparison of Evans's disembodied voice in *Mrs. Dalloway* to that of Pythagoras, which originated from behind a curtain, leads to a thoughtful discussion of "national" discourse and "obedience to a master's voice" (113), revealing the affinity between Woolf's concerns in the '20s and '30s and those of fellow modernists such as Forster.

The third section turns to art music, focusing firstly on female performers: discussion of Rachel's performances in *The Voyage Out* is followed by an attentive reading of Clara's (self-)effacement as a pianist in *Jacob's Room* (at times, Woolf even leaves us uncertain whether Clara has played or only turned the pages of the score for another) and of the importance of improvisation to Sara in *The Years*, a practice Clements reads as Woolf's ethical and aesthetic response to political crisis.

The section ends with *The Waves*: Clements's syllabic analysis explores similarities between Woolf's "phrasal compositional technique" (197), the "rhythm" of her prose and formal conventions in classical repertoire by Bach, Mozart and Beethoven. Then, building on her razor-sharp 2005 essay, she compellingly argues that *The Waves'* structure and its representation of six subjectivities are indebted to the six movements of Beethoven's late string quartet Op.130.

There were a very few moments when I felt the book's scope came at a cost: there are some works on literary modernism and music (such as Eric Prieto's *Listening In: Music, Mind and the Modernist Narrative* [2002] or Josh Epstein's *Sublime Noise: Musical Culture and the Modernist Writer* [2014]) that Clements might usefully have drawn on. Epstein's example, which discusses colonial and racial politics in many modernists' allusions to sound, might have prompted Clements to reflect further on the racial politics of music and sound in some of the passages she discusses (as might my own essay on the "cries" of the Amerindian village women in *The Voyage Out*). A phrase such as "the swarm of sound" in the 1910 section of *The Years* (68), the importance of "rhythm" (which had highly racialized connotations in early twentieth-century musicology) to Woolf's creative practice and criticism, and the comparison of Terence Hewet's improvised movements to an "Indian maiden dancing before her Rajah" (163-4) invite attention in terms of primitivism and ethnicity. Equally, despite a valuable discussion of parallels to Greek theatre, it was a pity that the analysis of *Between the Acts* didn't offer detailed exploration of the significance of the pageant *as a genre*: pageants' collaborative, community-based, outdoor, intermedial aesthetics would have been a fascinating topic for Clements's readings. We still, notwithstanding Jed Esty's work, lack extended close textual study of pageants' extensive intersections with modernism and Bloomsbury, despite the involvement of Eliot, Forster, Walpole, and Woolf's own plan to write a pageant for the local Women's Institute.

A book of such conceptual breadth is at risk of omissions or simplification, flattening out differences—even resistance—between its subjects. But Clements pulls off her argument with panache. Whilst keen to draw language, sound and music into conversation, she rightly reminds us that Woolf "gravitated" towards music's "distinctiveness" from the verbal and literary as well as the parallels among them (16). Clements's own ease in discussing musical forms, genre conventions and music history compellingly demonstrates the insights that come from musically-informed readings of Woolf as well as those which explore Woolf's wider interest in sound and language. Indeed, as she proposes at the outset, "what constitutes music," sound and language is at stake in Woolf's writing (7). Clements invokes the musical trope of theme and variations as her structural model but the trope might equally well describe our readings of this book: it is an impressively rich study to revisit with pleasure.

—Emma Sutton, *University of St. Andrews*

Religion Around Virginia Woolf.
Stephanie Paulsell (University Park, PA: Pennsylvania State UP, 2019). ix + 237pp.

Stephanie Paulsell's *Religion Around Virginia Woolf* refuses "aggressive agnosticism" as the "only lens" through which we might legitimately read the life and writing of Virginia Woolf. Paulsell recognizes the important scholarship of Pericles Lewis, Vincent Pecora, Jane Marcus, and especially Jane De Gay, in clarifying Woolf's "complicated engagements" with religion, but she intends to go deeper. As she writes in the "Introduction," the "something more" she is after includes, among other things, Woolf's study of the history of religion, her reading of letters and diaries of Christian ministers, her response to the debate on women's ordination, and her study of religious art. Indeed Paulsell casts a remarkably wide net, drawing together seemingly incongruous materials, everything from the mysticism of Teresa of Avila to the process theology of Alfred North Whitehead, to prove her thesis that, despite her disbelief in God, Virginia Woolf created literature that does remarkably various "religious work."

Chapter One, "Family Resemblances," traces the lineage of Woolf's religious imagination back several generations to the Evangelical Clapham Sect. Paulsell digs deep into this history, noting how Woolf's grandfather, James Stephen's, *Essays on Ecclesiastical Biography*, which she read at age 15, bears fruit later in her own biographical and stream-of-consciousness methods. While researching the lives of the Clapham Sect, Woolf's grandfather would "dip down into the lives of its members, one by one, letting their interior convictions and habits illuminate their public accomplishments" (17). In one passage, Stephen notes how human beings construct their lives from fragments. Even the Lord God creates by "searching out affinities in the elements of man's moral and social nature; by separating such as are incongruous, and by combining the rest into organic forms, animated by a common life" (18-19). Paulsell finds an echo of this idea throughout Woolf's writing, especially in *To the Lighthouse*. According to Lily Briscoe, the vocation of the artist is "to choose out the elements of things and place them together and so, giving them a wholeness not theirs in life, make of some scene, or meeting of people (all now gone and separate), one of those globed compacted things over which thought lingers, and love plays" (19).

Inspired perhaps by Woolf's contention that women writers "think back" through their mothers, Paulsell devotes fourteen pages in this chapter to the legacy of Woolf's Quaker aunt, Caroline Emelia Stephen. It is a well-known fact that Stephen's legacy in 1909 provided Woolf the income needed to purchase a "room of her own" and the economic freedom to write. Paulsell contends for a spiritual legacy as well: "The space [Woolf] occupied as an artist and as a human being seems closer to her aunt's fluid, undogmatic view of religion than to the more settled, convinced positions of her agnostic father and Christian grandfather" (43). Woolf's experience of an incommunicable "presence" in the universe resonates with descriptions found in her aunt's writings of encounters with Divine Radiance and Inner Light. Citing Stephen's book *Light Arising*, Paulsell writes that "some people experience the Inner

Light as a dim glimmer, others as glory, and others as 'flashes of revelation, which have changed for them the whole aspect of life as the blaze of lightning reveals the midnight landscape'" (45). Although Woolf did not share her aunt's Quaker convictions, this kind of mystical language, "rapture, ecstasy, revelation" (46), appears regularly in her novels and essays until her death in 1941.

Chapter Two, "Fresh Chapels," offers a wide-ranging discussion of Woolf's reading, her travels and friendships, and her marriage. The term "fresh chapel" comes from an entry in Woolf's diary dated Sunday, August 1906. On that day, while out walking, she and her friends passed a church just as "6 Methodists" and "2 ½ Anabaptists" were leaving. For Woolf, children counted as one half because "when they grow up they may think for themselves," "swell the number of the hostile sect" or "build a fresh chapel for themselves" (51). Paulsell uses this incident to launch a lively discussion of Bloomsbury, where the "grown up," 22-year-old Virginia Stephen thought for herself, imagining "distinctive forms of marriage, friendship, and art making"(51). At the same time, she was harassed by her cousin Dorothea Stephen, whose religiosity was "bent on the conversion of others" (53). Paulsell cites another diary entry to illustrate Woolf's lifelong aversion to such meddling: "I find a letter from Dorothea Stephen—that cumbersome, square footed cousin—to say, as one might say it was hot weather—that 'Christianity rests on a fact—the Resurrection. Believe this or be damned. Goodbye'" (54). Dorothea is the model for the character Doris Kilman, whom Clarissa despises for similar reasons in *Mrs. Dalloway*. Other "fresh chapels" that Paulsell discusses in this chapter include Woolf's friendship with anthropologist Jane Ellen Harrison; her own study of religious art, in particular the work of the Russian Orthodox painter Wassily Kandinsky; and her reading of G. E. Moore, whose *Principia Ethica* is often described as the "sacred text" of Bloomsbury intellectuals.

Chapter Three, "Religious Reading," considers self-transcendence through reading and reading to discover "common ground" as recurring themes in Woolf's letters, diaries, essays, and novels. What stands out in this chapter is the author's skillful literary analysis, itself a "religious reading," of *Mrs. Dalloway*. As most readers know, the original title of *Mrs. Dalloway* was *The Hours*. This fact prompts Paulsell to historicize the novel within the framework of medieval monasticism. Clarissa's day is structured by Big Ben, but the hours tolled are the hours of the Divine Office: Lauds, Terce, Nones, Vespers, Compline, Matins. As Clarissa meditates on the suicide of Septimus Smith, she observes an old woman staring at her from across the way. "Who is she?" my students ask every time I teach this novel. "[A]nother nun at home, just finishing her night vigil" (115), answers Paulsell. Equally compelling is her explication of the "diamond" imagery that represents Clarissa's "hidden treasure," her private self, or soul, and the historical gloss connecting that image with another nun, the sixteenth century mystic Teresa of Avila, whose book on mystical theology, *Interior Castle* (1577), depicts the soul as a diamond-shaped castle with seven chambers representing the journey of the soul towards union with God. Finally, for Paulsell, the way Clarissa and Septimus meditate on a "sacred text" throughout the day—"Fear no more the heat o' the sun"—reflects the contemplative practice of *lectio divina*.

The question of Woolf's atheism comes up in Chapter Four, "Still Denser Depths of Darkness: Virginia Woolf and God." While Paulsell does not shy away from Woolf's proclamation, "there is no Beethoven, there is no Shakespeare; certainly and emphatically there is no God," neither does she allow this oft-quoted passage to obscure the complexity of Woolf's thinking about God over her lifetime. In some of her early journals, Woolf imagines God in positive terms as a "creative force undergirding her own creativity" (132). Later, that image darkens, perhaps reflecting her outrage at religious zealots like Dorothea Stephen. For whatever reason, in her later fiction and essays, God appears as a "brutal old bully," "Milton's bogey," "a malignant torturer" (133). In the end, Paulsell puts an "agnostic" spin on Woolf's atheism. "There may be no Beethoven, no Shakespeare, and no God, but human beings have the capacity to create like them" by means of an "elusive creative power" that surges through the universe. "Is that power divine? Woolf and her characters cannot say" (158-59).

The final chapter, "Overflowing Boundaries: Sacred Community and the Common Life," examines Woolf's social and political writings as imaginative rebuttals to the "idea of Christian society" offered by T. S. Eliot, among others, in the years leading up to World War II. Instead of Eliot's "Church within the Church," Woolf imagines a "Society of Outsiders," who would "reimagine and remake the university, the professions, and the church." Such efforts would prepare the way for Shakespeare's sister "by cultivating communities within which women could thrive and create" (175). Whether such communities can satisfy the longings of those seeking a transformative encounter with the divine is uncertain, but they may conceivably do the "religious work" of feminism and pacifism. Close readings of *Three Guineas*, *A Room of One's Own*, *To the Lighthouse*, and *Between the Acts* support Paulsell's overarching argument that Woolf intentionally placed herself within "overlapping communities: women, artists, pacifists, common readers," and used her creative gifts to help us "see connections that would otherwise remain invisible" (171). Stephanie Paulsell has used her creative gifts similarly in *Religion Around Virginia Woolf*. Placing her scholarship at the intersection of overlapping disciplines—literature, art history, women's studies, biblical studies, church history, theology—she helps us see "otherwise invisible connections" between religion and Woolf. From this well-researched book, readers will take away a new understanding of how religion works in and "around" literature and a deeper appreciation of Virginia Woolf's religious contribution, despite her professed atheism, to secular modernity and literary modernism.

—Emily Griesinger, *Azusa Pacific University*

Leonard Woolf: Bloomsbury Socialist.
Fred Leventhal and Peter Stansky (Oxford, UK: Oxford UP, 2019). xviii + 213 pp.

This compact biographical study distinguishes itself from the literary biography by Victoria Glendinning, *Leonard Woolf: A Life* (2006), and the more politically oriented one by Duncan Wilson, *Leonard Woolf: A Political Biography* (1978), to the extent that it is able to abridge the one and update the other. Success is somewhat bound in a thesis that evolves in the course of the book and made to fit the prescriptions of the Spiritual Lives series, new from Oxford Religion. Besides Woolf, the series so far features lives of W. T. Stead, John Stuart Mill, Christina Rossetti, and Woodrow Wilson, "leading politicians" and writers who "have engaged deeply with religion in significant and resonant ways that have often been overlooked or underexplored," some of them being, like Woolf, "lifelong unbelievers" who "navigated and resisted religious questions, assumptions, and settings" (ii). Thus, in both parts of *Leonard Woolf: Bloomsbury Socialist*—"The Personal Journey," mostly by Stansky, and "The Political Journey," largely by Leventhal—the aim is to recast Woolf "in fresh and thought-provoking ways" (ii). Paradoxically, this book's thesis depends on the Jewish background about which Woolf had little to say in his autobiographical writings and on the means that collaborating social historians share with Woolf's own strong interest in history, psychology, and politics. The method of these two historians differs from the treatment of constructs by political scientist Peter Wilson, in *The International Theory of Leonard Woolf: A Study in Twentieth-Century Idealism* (2003), though sometimes in Leventhal's critique of "communal psychology" in *After the Deluge* (1931, 1939) and *Principia Politica* (1953), biographical narrative also seems subordinated to the assessment of political ideas.

As an avowed atheist, Woolf is said to embody the synthesis of Arnoldian Hebrew and Hellene, due to influences at home as well as formative years at Cambridge under the influence of G. E. Moore. In the end, while nothing mattered on a universal scale, his "Hellenist ideals endured without effacing his Hebraic code of conduct" (199). The case for this embodiment is laid out in Part I, in the first two chapters ("Youth" and "Cambridge"), and, most persuasively, in the last chapters of Part II ("Socialism and Civilized Society" and "Journey's End"). Between those two points, the biographical incidents of an entire life are outlined with impressive succinctness, allowing that the authors are not attempting a full-length biography and acknowledging that the more familiar facts of Woolf's life with his more famous wife would inevitably prove difficult to coordinate in Parts I and II. To some extent, the problem can be seen as incumbent to thesis-driven, shaped biographical writing. Hence, Stansky follows an account of Woolf's service in Ceylon with a chapter on "Virginia and After," not just because marriage to Virginia Stephen marked the end of that service chronologically but also because her anti-Semitic attitude about marrying a "penniless Jew" (55) is apparently relevant to a thesis. Indeed, his "fatalism" (74) and "tough-mindedness" (77) are identified as traits of Jewishness that bolstered his ability to cope during the bouts of mental illness she suffered in the early years of their marriage; and, in the end, these traits helped him to manage the devastating grief he felt after her suicide in 1941. Oddly, the compression of their shared life in barely 24 pages seems puzzling for a transitional movement anticipating that the book's narrative is to resume, in Part II, with Professor Leventhal's singular account of Leonard's distinguished career as a public intellectual. Beginning redundantly at Leonard's return from Ceylon, the authors take for granted one's familiarity with scholarship that has emphasized common interests and activities of the Woolfs as a writing couple, editors, and partners in publishing for more than two decades. Natania Rosenfeld's *Outsiders Together: Virginia and Leonard Woolf* (2000) comes to mind in light of this deficit, with the order of names in the title indicative of the difference in emphasis. One might have expected, too, some acknowledgment of the airing of the topic of "Virginia Woolf and Jews" in a special themed volume of recent date, *Woolf Studies Annual* 19 (2013).

For most readers, though, Part II, "The Political Journey," has most to offer as a cogent outline of Leonard Woolf's development in a body of work so extensive that there is merit in having his ideas systematically abstracted now that the surviving canon has been inventoried in the bibliographies of Luedeking and Edmonds (1992) and Manson and Chapman (2005, 2017). Most of Woolf's numerous books and pamphlets, including those to which he contributed, are reduced to thirty-four and seven, respectively, and most of those are cited in the 119 agile pages of Part II. Although *The Village in the Jungle* (1913) and *The Wise Virgins* (1914) had been discussed thirty pages earlier, they also serve as starting-posts in the resumed race through major works, marking the extent of his career as a novelist (save for several later short stories) at the threshold of paid journalistic work as a prolific contributing editor and journalist. A third novel—called "The British Empire" by Stansky (45) but cited as "The Empire Builder" by Leventhal (84)—was abandoned after an opening scene. Volunteer work for the Charity Organisation Society and the Women's Co-operative Guild "broadened his topical scope and periodical audience" (86) by 1914. Association with the Webbs, Bernard Shaw, and newspaper mogul Joseph Rowntree gave further impetus to important studies on behalf of the Fabian Research Department, the Labour Party, and the cause of peace during and after the war. In short, Leonard Woolf became a recognized authority as the author of *International Government* (1916), wrote the introduction to *The Framework of a Lasting Peace* (1917), and began long service as secretary of Labour's Advisory Committee on International Questions, until retiring in 1946, and as the head of the International Section of the New Fabian Research Bureau.

Leventhal's next three chapters—"Anti-Imperialist," "The Wars for Peace," and "Socialism and Civilized Society"—necessarily involve a certain amount of backtracking to pick up threads introduced previously in relation to multiple causes and affiliations. That said, the chronology is largely (One) Woolf's interwar effort to promote development of a *supernational* government in the League of Nations,

(Two) opposition to fascism during World War Two, and (Three) appraisal of Woolf's magnum opus, *After the Deluge* I and II and *Principia Politica*. Of Woolf's stint as literary editor of *The Nation and The Athenaeum* in the 1920s and his co-editorship of *Political Quarterly* from 1930 to 1958, the latter proves more useful here. On balance, Leventhal avers that *Empire and Commerce in Africa* and condensations such as *Mandates and Empire*, and *Economic Imperialism* (each of 1920) might have been more persuasive had he served in Africa rather than Ceylon. Woolf's support of the second war effort was, like his pro-British sympathy as a committee secretary, tinged with British exceptionalism. He favored self-government in India and Ceylon and believed that British colonial rule had done a better job preparing for that eventuality than had other European states, generally. As a socialist with a difference, his later opinion was decidedly to the left of Sidney Webb on imperial questions, and he participated in "vitriolic quarrels" with the pro-Soviet Kingsley Martin, from 1949 through the Korean War and after, on the Anglo-American alliance. While the chapter "Socialism and Civilized Society" still carries the torch for Leonard in the fight against the quackery of despots, "The Wars for Peace" stands out as perhaps Leventhal's most complimentary section of the book, giving opportunity to quote and paraphrase extensively Leonard's "defense of the Jew in a Christian world" (141) while denouncing Nazism in *Quack, Quack!* (1935) and *Barbarians at the Gate* (1939) and going on to draft international policies for the Labour Party in anticipation of the UN (154-56). Rather, "Socialism and Civilized Society" is memorable as a critique of Woolf's treatment of history in *After the Deluge* (derided for digressive style), in the self-proclaimed political autobiography *Principia Politica* (toxically titled in Latin), and in *The Modern State* (1933; summarized by Leventhal at surprising length). Criticism is warranted for work that "suffers from ... protracted composition, [having been] written in fits and starts over a decade" (174).

Yet, the final impression of this book is made in tribute to its subject—a "Bloomsbury Socialist," to be sure, but at heart a complex person of great courage and principle. In the last chapter, "Journey's End," the authors correct Woolf's verdict that he had "achieved practically nothing" in a long career by grinding through "between 150,000 and 200,000 hours of perfectly useless work," because, in "personal life, ... certain things are of immense importance: human relations, happiness, truth, beauty or art, justice and mercy" (199). Thus, to confirm a thesis: tension between the Hebraism and Hellenism that Leonard seemingly embodied "provided the dynamic for his moral and spiritual evolution" (188).

—Wayne K. Chapman, *Clemson University*

*Threshold Modernism: New Public Women and
the Literary Spaces of Imperial London.*
Elizabeth Evans (New York: Cambridge UP, 2019). vii + 261 pp.

Virginia Woolf's Rooms and the Spaces of Modernity.
Suzana Zink (New York: Palgrave, 2018). xiii + 223 pp.

Modernist spatial studies is going strong and the "spatial turn" appears increasingly frequently in this decade's book titles, course descriptions, and conference themes, indexing scholarly interest in how space functions as a trope in fiction and marking a shared critical desire to theorize modernist space. Just under a century after Woolf published a novel that explicitly references a room as its titular framing device, a few interesting shifts have emerged in the ways that critics understand Woolfian space and modernist geographies more generally. First, there has been a distinct veering away from the midcentury association of space primarily with psychology. For literary scholars now, depictions of city streets and rooms certainly indicate something about individual psychology, but recent work by Christopher Reed, Victoria Rosner, Anna Snaith, and Andrew Thacker, among others, has assimilated the Joseph Frankian interest in interiority to broaden the conversation with readings that draw on disciplines as varied as biology, anthropology, and political science. Second, relatedly, while some critical readings heavily privilege philosophical treatments of space—David Spurr's excellent *Architecture and Modern Literature* comes to mind here—there is a distinct move within the subfield to view concepts like Hegelian dwelling and Lefebvrean space through historical lenses to better understand the topos of modern, and modernist, space and place.

Elizabeth F. Evans's *Threshold Modernism: New Public Women and the Literary Spaces of Imperial London* and Suzana Zink's *Virginia Woolf's Rooms and the Spaces of Modernity* are two timely interventions in this busy field. Thoroughly researched and historically grounded, Evans and Zink offer ways to understand how modernist writers used public and private spaces as writerly motifs to probe social and political questions about the role of women in the interwar era. Evans's point of entry is the middle class woman in the 1880s-1940s, whom she names the "new public woman." This figure exercises a modern material and social independence in public, distinct from those women who have always been forced onto the streets by circumstance. Evans argues that the new public woman was actively involved in manipulating the intrusive male gaze, using stereotypical responses to her presence in ambivalent threshold locations for her own ends. The difficulty of categorizing such a figure—she is dangerous to the established social order and simultaneously in danger herself from intrusive male attentions—made her an unlikely but popular character in fiction from the early years of the twentieth century, allowing both English and colonial authors to view her as a sympathetic figure. Evans moves between a breathtaking range of authors: Woolf, James Joyce, and H. G. Wells speak to Dorothy Richardson, Una Marson, and the Egyptian Duse Mohamed Ali, among others. Evans's interest is not only in how the new public woman is depicted, but also where she moves. Using historical maps and archival materials, Evans suggests that modernists used this opaque figure as a tacit representation of socio-economic and cultural mobility that was itself viewed with suspicion. Modernist spatiality has as much to do with disrupting barriers of class and nationality, Evans suggests, as it does with establishing feminine interiority in a stereotypically masculine urban space.

It is fruitful to read Zink in tandem with Evans because of their shared interest in difficult social transitions. Focusing closely on real and fictional rooms in Woolf's writing and her life, Zink presents Woolfian space as a trope that always operates relationally, moving between "individual consciousness and history as embedded in specific—albeit unstable—cultural, ideological and discursive spatial formations" (215). For example, Zink reads the Cambridge sections of *Jacob's Room* as a way for Woolf to fictionally mediate the real university and an extremely contentious debate from 1920 to 1921 about granting women degrees and full membership to it. Jacob's Cambridge years are presented prismatically in the novel as a source of both ironic teasing and real anger. Woolf's published draft emphasizes that for Jacob, Cambridge is a cloistered, masculine intellectual home. Zink argues that Woolf expressly excised all references to women students, the two women's colleges, Girton and Newnham, and women professors (except Miss Umphelby) from earlier drafts of the novel to heighten the gender divide that Jacob experiences at Cambridge. Zink reads Woolf's fictional Cambridge in light of Jane Ellen Harrison's exasperated battles in 1920 with university dons to allow full student rights to women attendees, and notes the depressing fact that Cambridge would remain a bastion of male privilege until after World War II. Woolf herself is later explicitly critical of women's education in *Three Guineas*. However, Zink finds that although Woolf remains silent in her diaries and letters about the struggle of women students at Cambridge in the early 1920s, her novel responds to these issues tacitly and directly, through figures like the angry and uncomfortable Julia Hedge who glares at Jacob in the British Library.". Zink clarifies that Woolf's spatial politics often operate through absences in her writing, as in the erased women in Jacob's version of university life. The silent diary entries form the obverse of such fictional removals. Zink thus presents erased feminine spaces as crucial to Woolf's fictional landscapes, and suggests that these early instances of resistant erasure—an ironic and unstable literary device, to be sure—anticipate the masterful takedown of masculinist fears and phobias in *Three Guineas*.

Taking different approaches, both Evans and Zink advance the boundaries of modernist spatial studies, rethinking gendered modern urban spaces. Reading both critics together, it seems to me that modernist writers are themselves the best guides in developing theories of literary spatiality. Despite Woolf's tendency to avoid totalizing schemes, her writings on interior and exterior spaces as sociocultural indices are rich enough that one agrees with Zink that "Woolf's modernist writing of rooms may be said to anticipate Lefebvre's multilayered model of space," and ultimately resonates with much newer work by feminist geographers like Doreen Massey, for whom spaces are always already gendered and carry out critical political functions (32). Similarly, treatises by philosophical heavyweights like Deleuze and Foucault certainly clarify and strengthen implicit literary arguments, and Evans and Zink engage with them to a limited extent. However, these connections add interest to the extant conversation without greatly affecting its terms. Even Benjamin, whose formulation of the modernist *flaneur* encouraged the critical interest in spatiality, proves to be only limited help on a granular level when theorizing Woolfian space. Evans notes that Benjamin was often contradictory about the status of a *flaneur* and *flanerie* as a resistant mode of mapping the city, and in any case, Woolf's depictions of women walking through urban streets have starkly different implications than those he offers, as Evans shows by reading the "new public woman" as a locus of revisionary feminist impulses. Evans finds a more useful interlocutor in H. G. Wells's *Ann Veronica* (1909), contrasting Wells's emphasis on the danger to women walkers posed by men to Woolf's authorial excisions of similar passages from *The Years*. In a striking reading that echoes Zink's conclusions about purposely erased feminine spaces and experiences, Evans argues that Woolf chose to restrict the role of "street love" (which refers to unwanted lechery, not romance in public) when depicting women walkers on late-night or lonely routes (125). Her omissions are "a refusal to replicate the lessons implicitly offered by Wells and others. By excising most references to . . . harassment, and sexual danger, the novel avoids contributing to the closeting of women and girls" (126). Woolf purposely reimagines the nature of early twentieth century streets, replacing the emphasis on sexuality (as commodity or as danger to women) with her preferred focus on feminine agency and intellectual production. Modernism's streets are thus incorporated into its interest in social change. Woolfian spaces offer increased freedom for women in personal and public life, at least in literature if not in reality.

Spaces never exist in isolation, and Evans and Zink both focus on English locations without losing critical interest in transnational spatiality, especially important for an Imperial nation whose hold upon the colonies appeared to be stronger than ever after World War I before it crumbled after World War II. Evans argues that in the 1910s, marginalized colonial subjects from India and Africa saw themselves allied with white British women who were agitating for suffrage and full citizenship rights—and, as Zink adds, for a full Cambridge education. Evans finds this connection dissipating in the 1930s, when British women gained a number of political privileges and the "sense of shared struggle [between them and colonial subjects]… diminished or disappeared" (227). However, for a brief period, English cultural life accommodated an unlikely political bond between these two groups of outsiders. Zink also discusses national loyalties, primarily using diary entries from Woolf's 1906 trip to Greece with her siblings that reveal many attempts to understand England better through unlikely comparisons between European and English landscapes. Zink is careful to note the complexity of Woolf's thoughts about national spaces and identifications, writing that Woolf's method of better understanding the familiar through the unfamiliar leads sometimes to startling formulations. For example, when she visited Ireland in 1934 with Leonard, the depressing sights inspired her to record that "if I were Irish, I should wish to belong to the Empire" (52). Such acquiescence to colonial rule is uncomfortable, even if readers grant that her private diaries cannot be held to absolute political or ethical standards. Evans's and Zink's comparativist approaches create moments like these, that challenge critical understandings of modernism's overall liberal and experimental literary spaces.

—Ria Banerjee, *Guttman Community College, CUNY*

Virginia Woolf's Portraits of Russian Writers: Creating the Literary Other. Darya Protopopova (Cambridge: Cambridge Scholars Publishing, 2019). xv + 228.

Explorations of Woolf's lifelong fascination with Russian literature frequently take as their starting point her 1925 essay "The Russian Point of View," reading it as part of a fascinating trilogy of writing on foreign languages and literatures also comprised of "On Not Knowing Greek" and "On Not Knowing French." Roberta Rubenstein's landmark study of Woolf's Russian writings as an œuvre, *Virginia Woolf and the Russian Point of View* (2009), set the tone, and lastingly defined the field. The same inflection reverberates in the title of the latest contribution to "Russian Woolf Studies": Darya Protopopova's *Virginia Woolf's Portraits of Russian Writers: Creating the Literary Other*, but the viewpoint and the cognitive challenge of alterity are framed rather differently. It is a work that those of us familiar with Protopopova's rich, doubly inflected Anglo-Russian, Russo-English writings have long been awaiting, and the volume proves that it was worth the wait.

While in many ways a graceful continuation of the growing body of criticism focusing on Anglophone modernists' complex, extended engagement with Russian literature in the context of a far broader Russophilia in the early twentieth century, Protopopova's work also shifts in focus slightly. Her objective is indeed only tangentially literary; her concern is less to trace the Russian themes and patterns in Woolf's novels than to revisit the representations of the Russian literary figureheads in biographies, essays, and translators' prefaces, and to reconstruct the context in which Russian literature was rediscovered by the modernists. She thereby invites a number of revisions of the era and of Woolf's Russian readings, which greatly enrich both our larger view of the scene and our intimate insights into the complexity of the Russians' reception in Great Britain, over the course of more than half a century's tumultuous history and cultural renaissance. The volume thus provides both a richly documented and generous contribution to ongoing scholarship, and a splendid panorama for advanced level students and young researchers first venturing into the field of how British modernists grappled with "Russianness" (a term, we learn, that was only lexicalised in 1937). In so doing, it also steps deftly aside from the more linguistic and cognitive inflections of "not knowing Russian" to show quite how rich and ambivalent the "Russian point of view" could be.

In perhaps a very Woolfian way, neither the title nor the cover illustration does full justice to the work within, at least at face value. The four sober cover photographs, reproducing perhaps the most famous portraits of Chekhov, Dostoevsky, Turgenev, and Tolstoy, appear quite conventional, and the spurious lure of image and representation conjured up by the "literary other" is never tackled head on—there is no philosophical, political, critical or aesthetic frame pinning alterity down. In fact, when the issue is really taken up, it is to concur that "one begins to wonder whether, at times, Woolf stopped seeing the Russian writers as representatives of 'the Other' and began noticing in their novels elements congenial to her own self, thus beginning to feel, perhaps, akin to an aesthetic foreigner in her native literary tradition" (97). Returning to the title and cover page when finally closing the volume, however, one perceives them differently. The poised portraits underline the gap between the writers' aura and image in their own time, and their almost remarked image in Britain in the first two decades of the twentieth century. For this is the paradox at the heart of Anglophone modernists' Russian fever, and indeed at the heart of Protopopova's work. How did these four eminently nineteenth-century male, often patriarchal writers, all of whom owed their literary apprenticeship more to the great classics of British and French realism than to a markedly "Russian" literary canon, come to play such a fundamental part in the great shift of scale that we conceptualize as modernist? The question is complex: what had these Russians 'seen' in one foreign literary heritage which could then, by ricocheting back, have so lasting and transformative an impact on the Modernist point of view? How do foreign literary traditions and codes of representation resonate on, yet on a slightly different wavelength, when read and re-read in translation, in a different context, by scholars and common readers schooled in quite different times and texts? This constitutionally alternative point of view, this doubly border-crossing, contradictory, literary otherness, shimmers even between the four portraits themselves: Chekhov looks wisely at us; Dostoevsky and Turgenev's gaze falls to one side, out of the picture; Tolstoy too looks askance but in a different direction, standing slightly ill at ease in his peasant's robe—in a picture by Repin which we know—because Goldenveizer recorded it and Woolf co-translated it—inspired his skepticism.[1] Here, in other words, is a first idea of the beguiling complexity of Woolf's literary portraits and her Russian point of view. In exactly the same way as her essay progressively complicates our vision and distances itself from the conventional viewpoint (that "alarming way" in which, when looking through Tolstoy's telescope we realize that he has actually fixed his gaze on us [*E4* 188-9]), so Protopopova is going to remind us how much more meets the eye if we look from a slightly different angle.

Take, for example, some of the more memorable, quotable observations that recur throughout Woolf's oeuvre, especially the diary and her essays (the volume's main focus). Protopopova's superbly panoramic coverage of the extended passion for Russian literature from the 1870s until the 1930s shows the extent to which so

---

[1] Virginia Woolf and S. S. Koteliansky, *Translations from the Russian*, ed. Stuart N. Clarke, Virginia Woolf Society of Great Britain, 2006, 222.

many of the images, metaphors and hyperbole we attribute to Woolf are actually gleaned from her prolific and sometimes unexpected readings—such as Dostoevsky's novels, pithily depicted as "seething whirlpools, gyrating sandstorms, waterspouts" (*E4* 186), to quote but one of many examples. Protopopova's wide-angled approach foregrounds the resonant echo within Woolf's image which harks back to Baring's *Landmarks of Russian Literature*: "There were perilous depths in his personality; black pools of passion; a seething whirlpool that sent up every now and then great eddies of boiling surge" (73). Woolf's point of view, in other words, is oftentimes decidedly anything other than hers, the distancing effects of irony, skepticism, reverence, and hypothesis getting neutralized by time and print. The same is true of reading notes and diary jottings—so often a phrase overheard or read in passing, is conserved on the page and yet not altogether hers.

Another welcome contribution to the field, thanks to Protopopova's panoramic approach, is her coverage of a vast number of writers, reviewers, essayists and media, thereby shifting the focus from Woolf's own portraits of "the Russians" (*L2* 529) to a whole era's representations, dialogues, misconceptions and insights. Amongst the host of Anglophone commentators she includes, we find Arnold Bennett, John Carruthers, John Middleton Murry, Vita Sackville-West, William Gerhardi, George Bernard Shaw, Maurice Baring, Edward Garnett, Lytton Strachey, E. M. Forster, T. S. Eliot, Katherine Mansfield, and John Maynard Keynes. Keynes's praise of a scene in *The Years* which he thought "beat Tchehov's Cherry Orchard" (*D5* 77) is "the only comparison between her work and Russian literature that Woolf ever recorded in her diary," Protopopova tells us (151). Insights like these are precious indeed. Another feature of the panoramic approach is the coverage of *all* Woolf's sources on Russia and Russian literature, and not just the quartet of the great four: D. S. Mirsky, Maxim Gorky, and Pyotr Kropotkin, Sergey Aksakov, Elizaveta Militsina, and Ely Halpérine-Kaminsky, Sophie and Tatiana Tolstoy, and Aimee Dostoevsky for example. Nor is her scope limited to literature; on the contrary, Protopopova shows the cultural breadth of Woolf's immersion in affairs Russian: above all biography and life writings, but also social history, cultural critique, the theater, the Ballets Russes and the visual arts. In this respect, the parallels between the visual dynamics and conceptual shifts of post-impressionism as perceived by Roger Fry and the embodied dynamics and sound/color spectacle of the Russian ballet are insightful indeed, inviting us to revisit both Fry's essays and the Russian music and stage/costume designs that most caught the eye.

Revisions and revisiting thus become the dominant mode of Protopopova's "Russian point of view," seen on a scale that is spatially and temporally vast (for we will look back not just to the Tartars, but to the Elizabethans and how they first forged the portrait of the Russian "Other"). In true Tolstoyan fashion, meanwhile, the panoramic vision includes telescopic close-ups—intimate glimpses and glances at Turgenev's giant thumbs, Sophie Tolstoy's suicide note, and Chekhov's medical observations, for instance. So rich is the coverage that the publisher is to be faulted for not having insisted on an index that would have made future readers' lives so much easier. But let this detail not put potential readers off: Protopopova's book will become as requisite a contribution to critical scholarship devoted to the Anglophone modernists' reception of Russian culture as Woolf's "interpretations of Chekhov, Dostoevsky, Tolstoy, and Turgenev have become, like the four writers themselves, an indispensable part of the literary canon" (194).

—Claire Davison, *Université Sorbonne Nouvelle*

Notes on Contributors

Catriona Livingstone was awarded her PhD from King's College London in 2018 for a thesis on Virginia Woolf, identity, and popular science. Her work has been published in the *Journal of Literature and Science* and *The Year's Work in English Studies*.

Josh Phillips is a PhD candidate at the University of Glasgow. He is researching Virginia Woolf's late manuscript drafts and the futures they imagine in the face of rising fascism and war. He is a contributor to *The Year's Work in English Studies*.

Sebastian Williams is a PhD candidate and instructor in the Department of English at Purdue University. His dissertation research focuses on pests, parasites, and contagion in modernist literature, and he has published or has forthcoming work on disability, animality, or related topics in *Mosaic*, the *Journal of Literary and Cultural Disability Studies*, the *Journal of Popular Culture*, *South Asian Review*, and the *Journal of Stevenson Studies*. Sebastian is also an editorial assistant for the Purdue University Press.

Submission Guidelines

*W*oolf *S*tudies *A*nnual invites articles on the work and life of Virginia Woolf and her milieu. The *Annual* intends to represent the breadth and eclecticism of critical approaches to Woolf and particularly welcomes new perspectives and contexts of inquiry. Articles discussing relations between Woolf and other writers and artists are also welcome.

Articles are sent for review anonymously to a member of the Editorial Board and at least one other reader. Manuscripts should not be under consideration elsewhere or have been previously published. It is strongly advised that those submitting work to *WSA* be familiar with the journal's content. Among criteria on which evaluation of submissions depends are whether an article demonstrates familiarity with scholarship already published in the field, whether the article is written clearly and effectively, and whether it makes a genuine contribution to Woolf studies.

Preparation of Copy

1. Articles are typically between 25 and 30 pages, and do not exceed 8,000 words. This is a guide rather than a stipulation, and inquiries about significantly shorter or longer submissions should be sent to the Editor at woolfstudiesannual@gmail.com.

2. A separate file should include the article's title, author's name, address, phone number, and email address. The author's name and any other identifying references should not appear on the manuscript to preserve anonymity for our readers.

3. All submissions must include an abstract of no more than 250 words.

4. Manuscripts should conform to the most recent MLA style.

5. Submissions should be sent as Word files by email to woolfstudiesannual@gmail.com.

6. Authors of accepted manuscripts are responsible for any necessary permissions fees and for securing any necessary permissions.

All editorial inquiries should be addressed to woolfstudiesannual@gmail.com.

Inquiries concerning orders, advertising, reviews, etc. should be addressed to PaceUP@pace.edu.

The Editors of *The Burney Journal* welcome manuscripts addressing any subject relating to the lives, contemporaries, and times of the Burney family, including Frances Burney d'Arblay, Charles Burney, James Burney, and Charles Burney Jr.

Submissions may vary in length from 5,000 to 7,500 words. Please use MLA format. For further information, please go to https://www.mcgill.ca/burneycentre/burney-society/burney-journal.

Please send electronic submissions in Microsoft Word to Marilyn.Francus@mail.wvu.edu.

The Burney Journal is catalogued by EBSCO Host.

Twentieth-Century Literature

Focusing on literary-cultural production emerging from or responding to the twentieth century, *Twentieth-Century Literature* offers essays, grounded in a variety of approaches, that interrogate and enrich the ways we understand the literary cultures of the times. This includes work considering how those cultures are bound up with the crucial intellectual, social, aesthetic, political, economic, and environmental developments that have shaped the early twenty-first century as well.

Lee Zimmerman, editor

Sign up for new issue alerts at **dukeu.press/alerts**.

Subscribe today.
Quarterly
Online access is included with a print subscription.

Individuals $40
Students $28
Single issues $12

dukeupress.edu/twentieth-century-literature

LEGACY
A Journal of
American Women Writers

Edited by Susan Tomlinson,
Jennifer Putzi, and Jennifer S. Tuttle

The only journal to focus exclusively on American women's writing from the seventeenth through the early twentieth centuries.

The official journal of the
Society for the Study of American Women Writers

Legacy is available online through Project MUSE and JSTOR.

Both offer free access via library subscriptions.

Read it at
bit.ly/LEG_MUSE
or *bit.ly/LEG_JSTOR*

There are additional resources and information about publishing in *Legacy* at **legacywomenwriters.org**

Follow *Legacy* on Twitter:
@LegacyWmenWrite

For information on membership in the Society for the Study of American Women Writers, visit *ssawwnew.wordpress.com*.

For subscriptions or back issues:
Visit nebraskapress.unl.edu
or call 402-472-8536

TSWL
Tulsa Studies in Women's Literature

Exploring new terrains in women's literature since 1982

tswl.utulsa.edu

The twenty-sixth volume of *Woolf Studies Annual*
was published in Spring 2020
by Pace University Press

Cover and Interior Layout by Delaney Anderson and Francesca Leparik
The journal was typeset in Times New Roman and Arial
and printed by Lightning Source in La Vergne, Tennessee

Pace University Press

Director: Manuela Soares
Associate Director: Sephanie Hsu

Graduate Assistants: Delaney Anderson and Francesca Leparik
Graduate Student Aide: Shani Starinsky

www.ingramcontent.com/pod-product-compliance
Lightning Source LLC
Chambersburg PA
CBHW061449300426
44114CB00014B/1896